Sullivan County
Tennessee

Deed Books 3 & 4

1795–1807

WPA RECORDS

Heritage Books
2024

HERITAGE BOOKS
AN IMPRINT OF HERITAGE BOOKS, INC.

Books, CDs, and more—Worldwide

For our listing of thousands of titles see our website
at
www.HeritageBooks.com

A Facsimile Reprint
Published 2024 by
HERITAGE BOOKS, INC.
Publishing Division
5810 Ruatan Street
Berwyn Heights, MD 20740

Originally published 1936

International Standard Book Number
Paperbound: 978-0-7884-8918-1

RECORDS OF SULLIVAN COUNTY

TENNESSEE

DEED BOOK RECORD VOL. 3

1795 - 1802

COPYING HISTORICAL RECORDS PROJECT

WORKS PROGRESS ADMINISTRATION

Official Project No. 65 - 44 - 1498

MRS. JOHN TROTWOOD MOORE

STATE LIBRARIAN & ARCHIVIST, SPONSOR

MRS. ELIZABETH D. COPPEDGE

STATE DIRECTOR OF WOMEN'S & PROFESSIONAL PROJECTS

MRS. PENELOPE JOHNSON ALLEN

STATE SUPERVISOR

MRS. MARGARET HELMS RICHARDSON

SUPERVISOR FIRST DISTRICT

WORKERS:

MRS. BESSIE BRADSHAW

MISS HELEN CARTER

WORK COMPLETED AUGUST 25, 1936.

INDEX

DEED BOOKS VOLS. 3 & 4.

(NOTE: Page numbers in this index refer to those of the original volume from which this copy is made. These numbers are carried in the left hand margin of this copy).

GRANTEE	GRANTOR
Borden, Henry 373	Bradley, Jonathan 503
Billingsley, Jesse 376, 377	Brooks, John 514
Birdwell, James 378	Besler, George 531
Birdwell, Benj. 406	Frances, Larry 555
Booker, John 411	Blevins, [illegible] 664
Beard, Thomas 423	Bolan, Lucy 668
Bragg, Thomas 442	Bridwell, Sandford 695
Buchong, Henry 454	Brackbill, Peter 705
Bird, Francis 501	Baughman, Saml. 720, 722, 725, 731
Bradley, Jonathan 503	Baughman, Jonathan 737
~~Brook, 496, 510, 524~~	Billingsby, Saml. 782
Bucher, Jacob 501, 603, 803	Blevins, William R. 792
Bocher, Mervin, 704	Blevins, Walter, 795
Burch, Richard 547	Bressing, Roger, 798
Baughman, Jonathan 557, 657, 720	Bright, Thomas 811
Bronstotter, Frederick 597	
Benham, Robert 636	
Blevins, John 664, 792	
Blevins, William R. 668, 708	
Berger, Nicholas 670	
Baer, Jacob 697, 693	
Barnett, John 722	
Bacon, Aron 727	
Baughman, Nathan 731	
Beard, John 750	
Brackbill, Peter 756	
Bonhamer, Phillemon 762	
Baker, Charles 783	
Baker, Endymion 789	

GRANTEE	GRANTOR
CLARKE, JAMES 5	Commissioners of Blountville, 5, 6, 17, 30, 90, 103, 109, 201, 235, 236, 417, 418, 743, 744.
Cole, Joseph 52, 370	
Cox, Jeremiah 25	
Carr, Alexander, 26	
Cafry, John 28	Childress, Wm. 41
Crumley, George 30, 227, 540	Gage, Wm. 42
Cox, Edward 97, 270, 298, 356, 357,	Cole, Joseph 53, 128
Carmack, John 99	Glover, John 59
Click, Mathias 101, 135, 617	Chrisman, John 62, 127
Cowan, Robert 111, 112	Cummings, Hugh 64
Chester, John 115, 594	Cox, Samuel 69
Crockett, Samuel 142	Choate, Chris 81
Casebolt, John 145	Cross, Wm. 97
Creddington, Geo. 154	Carmack, John Sr. 100
Christy, Hugh 171, 542, 668	Chester, John 119
Cox, Joseph 188	Cavitt, Moses 180
Cross, Elijah & Moses Looney 212	Copeland, Wm. 193
Crockett, Andrew 237, 541	Carrithers, Saml. 211
Cooke, James 270, 271	Casebolt, John 257
Cole, Sampson 281	Cooke, William
Cole, Samuel 292	Cooke, Joseph
Click, Henry 289, 616	Cooke, James 270, 283, 621
Carithers, Samuel 362	Greely, Patrick 302
Childress, William 379, 802	Cole, Joseph Jun. 305
	Craft, Michal 310

GRANTEE

GRANTOR

GRANTEE	GRANTOR
Holland, James 179	Holloway, John 199, 208.
Huffman, Daniel 200	Harris, James 111, 273
Harkleroad, Henry 203	Hughes, Wm. 114
Hughes, David 207	Hedrick, William 165, 234.
Hickman, John 239	Hughes, James, Exor. 171
Hall, John 248, 476	Huffman, Daniel 199
Harbour, Elisha 232	Hawk, John 244
Holt, Simon 256	Hughes, Thomas 258
Hummell, Peter 259. 968	Hix, Shadrack 298
Harkleroad, Martin 293	Holt, Simon 342
Hawke, Jacob 302	Hale, Alexander 377
Harden, Alexr. 303	Hicks, Isaac, 393, 409
Hobagh, Phillip 305	Hawkins, Nicholas 394
Hawk, John 324	Holloway, John Jr. 396
Hicks, Jemima 393	Hensley, Robert 437, 524, 781
Hutson, Abel 409	Hagan, Arthur 441
Hatcher, William 432	Harris, Jeremiah
Michael Hickman 437	Hickman, John 495
Hosley, Robert 453	Hartman, John 495
Hambleton, John 463	Headerick, John 560
Hartman, Jacob 543, 582, [illegible]	Houser, John 565, 569, 582, 583
Hicks. Thomas 593, 645, 661	Hicks, Jemima 566
Hunter, John 606	Holland, William 574
Harrington, Peter 614	Harris, Elizabeth 604
Hickman, Peter 623, 669	Hunter, John 617
Howard, John 639	Hamilton, Abraham 627
Howard, Baldwin 655	Holt, Simon 668
Hazelrig, Richard 671	Hudson, Abraham 627
Hicks, Stephen 696	Hart, Leonard 697, 810
Headerick, Abraham 702	Hollis, James 775
Huffman, Benjamin 725	Hughes, Henry 776
Hughes, Henry 752	
Hollis, James, 755	
Helton, Charles 771	
Hale, Alexander 795	
Harr, John 818.	
JOHNSON, THOMAS 14, 607	Jolley, Dudley 79
Jones, John 84, 340, 582, 603.	Johnston, Walter 166
Jones, Charles 93, 583	Jones, Henry 188, 189
Jones, Solomon 105	Isley, Philip 365
Jones, Henry 131	Job, Jacob 383, 384, 550, 753, 796.
Johnson, Michael 145	Jones, John 405
Jones, John, Jr. 149	Isley, Conrad, 505
Johnston, James 161	Johnston, James 588
Isley, Phillip 178	James, Walker 583, 666, 687.
Jolley, William 179	Jones, Ezekiel 603
James, Bennett 182, 184	Johnston, Michel 647, 648, 649.
Johnson, Mary 264	
Isley, Conrad 296	
Jobe, Samuel 383	
Jackson, William 384	
James, Walker 395, 763, 769	
Jones, Ezekiel 405	

GRANTEE	GRANTOR
Leonard, Frederick 524	
Lee, Benjamin 591	
Lowe, George 621	
Lowe, David 803, 811.	
Laughlin, James 815.	
MOOR, Alrxr. 15	McDonald, John 4
Mawk, Henery 18, 545, 642, 711	McCormack, Wm. 8, 66.
McElhery, John, 19, 20.	Myers, Martin 10, 400, 480.
Morrell, Edm. 26, 793.	Morrell, John 26
Miller, Joshua 28	Mercer, Edward 70
Molton, Wm. 42	Mercer, Forester 82, 85, 90, 107.
Musgrave, Moses 59, 138.	Morrell, Richd. 83.
Morrowson, James 68	Morrell, Jonathan, 108.
Mosely, William 79	Musgrave, John 138, 580.
Milliner, Wm. 80	Moore, Joseph 192, 211 .
Mercer, Forester 81	Mawk, Henry 252, 389, 392, 526, 529, 576,
Mercer, Edward, 82	625, 655, 755.
Moore, Samuel 92, 96, 692, 809.	Musgrave, Moses 260, 264, 265.
Morrell, Thomas 108, 116	Myers, Jacob 262, 263, 264, 375.
Malone, Michaek 123	McClelland, Andrew 299
Moyers, Jacob 155, 261.	Moiers, John 300
Myers, Martin 191	McNair, James.
McIntosh, Peter 198, 199.	Mash, John 337.
McCland, Andrew 218	Malone, Michael 364, 371.
McCulley, ~~Andrew~~ Robert, 228	McEldery, John 382.
Musgrave, John 234	Mullinix, Lin 404
McCrabb, Alexr. 235, 330, 331.	Morgan, Able 409.
Myers, Gasper 264	Morrison, Peter 426, 617
McCormick, Wm. &	Morras, John 458.
M. Montgomery 339	McKinley, Leonard 506
McChesney, Thomas 367, 368	McIntosh, Peter 547
Morrison, Thomas 392	Moore, Alexander 558, 575.
Mitick, James397	Morgan, Peter 572.
McCorkle, Samuel 398	McCorkle, Saml. 578, 599.
Martin, Hugh 404	Majors, Stephen 579, 739.
Moss, James 412, 413	Montgomery, Michael 580.
Morrison, George 426	Miller, John (CC) 600
Mullinix, William 441	Mark, John 639
Millard, George 460	Martin, David, 651
Miller, Conrad 473	Matheny, James 657
Montgomery, Michael 482, 779.	Maggers, Henry 671, 809, 822.
McKinley, Isaac 506	McConkey, Mary 684.
Matheny, James 418	Moodey's Excors. 727.
Mawk, John 562, 625.	McCrabb, Alexr. 747.
Miller, Adam 537	McDonald, Saml. 819.
Morgan, Peter 560, 574.	
Morgan, Gabriel 572	
Majors, 579, 739.	
Munsey, Nathaniel 590	
Miller, Jacob 604	
McDaniel, Sam'l. 619	
Martin, David & 660	

GRANTEE	GRANTOR
Majors, Stephen 662	North Carolina: 7, 8, 9, 11, 12, 13, 14, 15, 16, 25, 27, 28, 29, 30, 31, 32, 33, 47, 48, 49, 50, 51, 52, 55, 56, 67, 67, 68, 74, 74, 87, 98. 98, 104, 104, 105, 106, 126, 117, 118, 121, 122, 123, 124, 124, 125, 126, 186, 129, 130, 130, 133, 133, 139, 139, 140, 141, 141, 155, 155, 159, 160, 161, 162, 162, 163, 164, 167, 168, 168, 169, 170, 170, 171, 172, 173, 175, 176, 176, 177, 178, 179, 185, 185, 191,200, 201, 216, 217, 218, 219, 219. 220, 221, 222, 222, 223, 227, 237, 238, 240, 240, 242 253, 281, 282, 307, 308, 344, 345, 346, 347, 450, 532, 533, 577, 623, 646, 752, 753, 767, 792, 825.
Morrell, William 663	
Myers, Henry 690	
Malone, George697, 742.	
Morelock, George723	
McAlley, Thomas 799	
Nidiver, George 25	
Nicely, Michael 175	
Nidever, Jacob 176.	
Nash, William 201, 539, 827.	
Newton, Charles 363	
Nicely, George 468	
Nicely, Martin 513	
Nichodemus 531	
Newland, Joseph536, 637, 638,667	
Newland, John 647, 648, 649,	
	Neadeverm Jacob 233,
	Nash, WilliamJ372, 527.
	Nash, Willaim, Senr. 539
	Newland, John 636, 637, 638.
OWEN, Joseph 53	Owen, Willaim 53, 592
Owen, William 119	Offield, James 174
Offield, James 122	Osborn, Mack 198
Owen, Nathan 224, 225	Owen, Joseph 174
Owen, Jonathan 238	Owen, Nathan 368 368.
Olar, John 262, 263	
Chilmore, Fred 496	
Outlaw, Alexander 646, 711	
Odle, William 781	
PARKER, William 8	PALLET, William 37
Pickens, James 32, 693	Peoples, Nathan 71
Pemberton, William 48	Pendleton, E. & J. Taylor 96, 628, 765,
Peoples, John 71	Purdue, Jeseca 212
Parker, John 130, 738, 801.	Pear, Peter 258
Prutzman, John 233	Patterson, James 283, 284, 381
Peer, Matthias 258	Parker, Hannah 316
Patterson, James 281	Phillipps, Jonathan 349, 802.
Patterson, Able 282	Phillipps, Jonathan 349.
Pope, Felty 322	Pendleton, Edward, By Agts. 391
Potter, Abraham 338, 520	Perry, David 399
Phillipps, John349, 349.	Pallett, Abraham 423, 787.
Phillipps, Charles 369, 370, 371	Priggmore, Theodorus 433
Perry, Rowland, 399	Porterfield, Seth 456
Porterfield, Leth 457	Pruit, Isaac 464
Phillip, George 464.	Pope, Mary 508, 570, 605.
Pallett, Robert 467, 567.	Pallett, Robert 520

GRANTEE	GRANTOR
SPURGINm, John 163, 211, 211, 321, 385, 474, 621.	SIRKLE, Lewis. 72
Shelby, Isaac 65, 2 32, 640, 651, 652,	Smith, Ephraim 73
Sirkle, George 72	Sharp, William 76
Snodgrass, Wm. 75, 158, 160, 191,	Smith, Joseph 115, 118, 479
Shoemaker, John 83	Shoemaker, John 120, 334
Smith, William 113, 114, 348.	Sirkle, George 131
Shoemaker, Dan 120, 334.	Shultz, Jacob 134
Sheneker, Elias 163	Stephens, Ross Mae 137
Stone, John 195.	Stevenson, Nicholas 153, 154
Snapp, Phillip 202	Sulliwan, Henry 164
Shelby, Isaac Exor. 204	Sharp, John 181, 685
Smith, David206.	Snodgrass, William 183, 296
Sherets, Conrad 209, 312,535, 536.	Snapp, Laurence 202, 402.
Shelby, Peter 213, 296.	Shelby, IsaacExor. 203
Smalling, Solomon 219.	Shelby, John Junr. 209, 235, 356
Stammer, Henry 244, 430.	Smith, George 317
Susong, Jacob 248.	Sulliwan, Henry 319
Senter, John 249.	Snapp, Phillip 343
Snapp, Phillip 256.	Susong, Jacob 351
Smith, Richard 272	Shrite, Henry 395
Shipley, John 281, 508.	Strout, John 401
Sevair, John Junr. 327	Sevair, John Junr. 402
Susong, Andrew 351	Shrite, John 415, 421
Shelby, John Senr. 356	Shoun, Sarah 432, 448
Strout, John 406	Snider, Michael 443
Sigler, Henry 408, 448, 745.	Shopley, Richard 402, 533, 548
Sturm, Jacob 410, 666	Spurgin, John 433
Stoffle, Henry 415.	Shipley, John 455
Schroyer, Lewis 434	Smith, John 473, 475, 571, 557
Shelby, Catherine 495, 706.	Swiney, Terrance 496
Shipley, Benjamin 462	Smith, Joseph 512
Shipley, Richard 465	Sell, John 513
Stur, Michael 489, 492	Snapp, Jacob 554
Shipley, Eli 510	Shelby, Isaac 610, 706.
Sever, Jacob 527	Sink, Jacob 652
Sink, Jacob 542	Snodgrass, William 669
Stickley, Samuel 571	Sharp, Anthony 681
Stur, John 598	Stacy, William 699
Stewart, John 654.	Shipley, Samuel & other heirs 702, 770
Shell, John 683	Sharp, John Exor. 704
Sinclair, John 686	Stone, John 725
Shaver, David 786	Segler, Henry 745
Smith, John 810	Shroyer, Lewis 786
Scott, William 813	Smith, Richard 797.
Shrite, John , Certificate of survey 822	
Shultz, Christian, Copy Grant from Wash. 827	
Troxell, Adam 121	
Towson, William 144	
Torbett, John 151, 613	

GRANTEE	GRANTOR
Top, Roger 173	Torbett, John 149, 294, 596, 606.
Tyrwell, Wm. 283, 284	Torbott, Alexr. 151
Thompson, John 300	Taylor, John 152, 570.
Titsworth, Thos. Junr. 318, 585, 639.	Top, John 197, 241
	Tipton, John 256, 343, 410. 552, 553, 635, 774
Taylor, Archibald 347, 498, 551, 640.	Tyreell, Wm. 283, 287, 239
	Thompson, John 434
Tallis, David 388	Taylor, Jeremiah 467, 567, 608, 769.
Tipton, John 402, 677	Taylor, Joshua 472.
Taylor, Stephen 427	Tredway, William 501, 502.
Thompson, John 435	Thomas, Torrey 530, 620 — TOVERA
Taylor, Jacob 451, 746	Towson, William 543
Taylor, Joshua 455	Taylor, Stephen 607
Thomas, Terry 532 — TONEY	Torry, John 620
Taylor, John 558, 575	Tuller, David 653
Torbett, Joseph 596	Titsworth, Thomas 691
Torry, John 620	Tally, John 750
Thomas, John 757	Thompson, Susannah 760
Thomas, William 821	
VINCENT, Thomas 12	Vance, John 206
Varner, Henry 353	Vance, Samuel 554, 634, 780
Vance, John 265	Vance, David 569
Vance, Samuel 477	Vance, John & Sarah 693
Vanvacker, Benj. 514	Vincent, George 730
Vincent, John 730	Virginia, State of 803, 830
WORLEY, David 443, 480	Willson, Augusta 22,
White, Isaac 22,	Webb, Moses 60
Waddell, Martin 41, 245, 366	Walling, Stephen 63
Wirick, William 54, 250	Waddle, John 135
Wallin, Stephen 63, 402	Waldrup, John 187
Wiley, William 75	Waggoner, Barnabas 213, 542
Wasson, ~~Phbs~~ 84	Whitnal, Robert 271.)
Wallace, Joseph 98	Willoughby, Wallace 312, 313, 528, 533, 534, 536
Work, Robert 102, 103	Willoughby, William 312) 660, 676, 739, 756, 757, 804
Wadlow, William 128	Willoughby, An & Eli 314
Waggoner, Henry 134	Warren, Edwd. 330, 460, 483
Whitlock, Alexr. 137	Wirick, William 336, 337
Wheeler, Stephen 139, 140, 170, 171	Work, Jacob 363
Waggoner, Barnabas 183, 472	Wallace, Thomas 386
Work, Jacob 221	Wagner, Henry 406
Wicks, Zachariah 307	Wirick, Martin 408
Wicks, John 308	Wilson, Robert, Sr. 431, 506
Willoughby, Wallace 314, 318	Wertmiller, John 461
Woolford, George 401	Wadlow, John 589
Waller, John 422	Waddle, Martin 601
Weaver, John 422	Whiteman, Frederick 609
Wilson, William 431, 506, 784	Weaver, Christian 610
White, Benjamin 443	Whitnal, Jonah 656
Williams, John 445	Wadlow, William 673
Wornham, John 483	Wadlow, Thomas 673
Willard, George 529, 755	Wicks, Zachariah 694
Woolrick, Buler heir 660	Work, Jacob & Joseph 708
Welch, Roda 665	Weaver, Jacob 779, 746

GRANTEE	GRANTOR
Wedleow, Thomas 673	Wilson, Joseph 784
Wentling, Abraham 695	Wheeler, James 806
Whitesides, Jenkins, 736	Wolfe, Nicholas 821
Wright, Patrick 748	
Waddle, John 765	
Wheelor, John 792	
Whiteman, Frederick 495	
YANCEY? ROBERT 135	Young, Jas. & Jos. 142, 341, 402.
Yancey, John 364, 473, 747, 753.	Young, James 351
Young, James & Joseph 402	Yancey, John 364, 473
Yaest, Jacob 478	Young, Joseph 424, 512, 807
	Yancey, Robert [illegible].
	Yancey, John [illegible]

(Page)

(1) HENRY HUGHS :
TO : DEED OF WARRANTY
PHILIP FOUST :

Both of Sullivan T S R O (Tenn. South of the River Ohio)
Date: Aughst 25th, 1795.
Consideration: 12 £.
Amt. of land: 16 acres.
Location: Sullivan County, North Carolina.
Dezcription: A certain tract or parcel of land containing 16 acres be the same more or less lying and being on the waters of Reedy Creek and on the North side of Eaton's ridge.
Witnesses: John Anderson, David Brigham.
Certificate of Registration: Sullivan County, August Session, 1795 the within deed was proven by the oath of John Anderson, a witness thereto, to let it be registered.
Test: Matthew Rhea, C. S. C. September 15th, 1795, then regst.

****

HENERY KALBOUGH :
TO : DEED OF WARRANTY
HERMAN ARRANTS :

Date: June 11th, 1795.
Consideration: 200 £ Virginia currency.
Amt. of land :Not stated.
Location: Sullivan County, Western Territory.
Description: A certain piece or parcel of land lying and being in the County of Sullivan and Western territory bounded as followeth on both sides of the lower west fork of Indian Creek the waters of Holston including Blevins bottoms and his own survey.
Witnesses: John Scott, Isaac Miller.
Acknowledged: By Henry Kalbough August Sessionm 1795. Test: James Rhea, D. C. S. C., September 15thm 1795, thnn regst.

****

HENRY HARKLERODE :
(3) TO : DEED OF WARRANTY
DAVID WORLEY :

Date: March 10th, 1792.
Consideration: 25 £ Current money of North Carolina.
Amt. of land: 22 acres more or less.
Location: Sullivan County.
Description: A certain tract or parcel of land containing 22 acres more or less lying and being in the County of Sullivan in the Western territory.
Witnesses: Benj, Sharp, Joseph Gray, Ephraim Smith.
Acknowledged: Deed of conveyance proved by the oath of Ephraim Smith September 16th, 1795, then regst.
Test: James Rhea, D. C. S. C.

****

(4) JOHN MCDONALD :
TO : DEED OF WARRANTY.
MARTIN ROLLER, SR. :

Date: August 19th, 1795.

Consideration: 100 £ Virginia currency.

(Page)

Amt. of land: 144 acres.
Location: Sullivan County, Western Territory South of the Ohio.
Description: All that tract or parcel of land situate lying and being in Sullivan County on the waters of faul creek the plantation where said McDonald lives containing 144 acres of land.
Witnesses: Philip Snapp, George Roller.
Acknowledged: Sullivan County, August Sessions, 1795, by John McDonald.
Test: James Rhea, D. C. S. C. Sept. 16th. 1795; then regst.

---

(5) ROBERT HAMBLETON, SENR. : TO : DEED OF WARRANTY JAMES CLARK :

Date: April 24th, 1794.
Consideration: 133 L, 6s. current money.
Amt. of land: 195 acres.
Location: Sullivan County in the Territory South of the Ohio.
Description: A certain tract orparcel of land containing 195 acres be the samr more or less situate lying and being in the said county of Sullivan on the waters of Horse Creek including the plantation where the said clark now lives.
Witnesses: George Vincent, Isaac White.
Proven: By the oath of George Vincent Sept. Sessions, 1795.
Test: Mattw. Rhea, C. S. C., Sept. 17th, 1795, then regst.

---

(6) RICHARD GAMMON, JAS. GAINES, GEORGE RUTLEDGE, JOHN SHELBY, JUN. COMMISSIONERS, to COL. JAMES KING : COMMISSIONERS DEED

Date: August 25th, 1795.
Consideration: Purchaser to pay all state and other taxes.
Amt. of land: A certain Lott of Ground in the said town of Blountville, being one of the publick lotts.
Location: Town of Blountville.
Description: A certain lott of ground in the said town of Blountville being one of the publick lotts and heretofore sold by the Commissioners to John Shelby, Junr. and by him sold to the said James King.
Affadavit: Sullivan County, August Sessions, 1795, the within deed of conveyance was acknowledged in open court by thecommissioners subscribed their names a party thereto.
Test: James Rhea, D. C. S. C., Sept, 24th, 1795, then Regst.

JNO. ANDERSON, RICHARD GAMMON, GEORGE RUTLEDGE, JOHN ANDERSON, JUNR. COMM. to JOHN SHELBY : COMMISSIONERS DEED.

Date: August 25th, 1795.

Consideration: John Shelby to pay all state and other taxes.
Amt. of land: A lott of ground in said town of Blountville, being lott No. 19.
Location: In town of Blountville, County of Sullivan.
Witnesses: Written, sealed and executed by above mentioned commissioners.
Acknowledged: Sullivan County, August Sessions, 1795, by the within commissioners, who have assigned their names.
Test: James Rhea, D. C. S. C., Sept. 24, 1795, then Regst.

---

(6) STATE OF NORTH CAROLINA :
RICHD. DOBBS SPAIGHT, GOV. : LAND GRANT
to : NO. 659
WILLIAM PARKER :

Date: December 4th, 1794.
Consideration: 50 shillings for every 100 acres of land.
Amt. of land: 55 acres.
Location: Sullivan County, North Carolina.
Description: A tract of land containing 55 acres lying and being in our county of Sullivan South of the River Ohio.
Witness: Richard Dobbs Spaight, Gov. By his Excellys Comd.
J. Glasgow, Sec.
Registered: September 25th, 1795.

---

(7) STATE OF NORTH CAROLINA :
RICHARD DOBBS SPAIGHT, GOV. : LAND GRANT
to : NO. 647.
JOSEPH COLE :

Date: December 5th, 1794.
Consideration: 50 shillings for every 100 acres of land.
Amt. of land: 200 acres.
Location: Sullivan County, North Carolina.
Description: A tract of land containing 200 acres lying and being in our county of Sullivan, as by the plat hereunto annexed doth appear.
Witness: Richard Dobbs Spaight, Gov. By his Excellys. Comd.
J. Glasgow, Secretary.
Registered: September 24th, 1795.

---

(8) WILLIAM MCCORMACK :
to : DEED OF WARRANTY
JOHN RUCKLES :

Date: May 25th, 1795.
Consideration: 110 L.
Amt. of land: By estimation, 100 acres.
Location: Sullivan County, Territory aforesaid.
Description: A certain tract or parcel of land lying and being in our county of Sullivan and territory south of the Ohio on the South side of the Holston River containing by estimation 100 acres more or less.
Acknowledged: Sullivan County, August Sessions, 1795, by William McCormack. Test: Mattw. Rhea, C. S. C. November 17, 1795, then Reg.

(9) STATE OF NORTH CAROLINA :
ALEXANDER MARTIN, GOV. :
to : LAND GRANT
BENJAMIN BROWN : NO. 567

Date: December 10th, 1795.
Consideration: 50 shillings for every 100 acres of land.
Amt. of land : 200 acres.
Location: Sullivan County, North Carolina.
Description: A tract of land containing 200 acres lying and being in our county of Sullivan on the beaver dam fork of the Laurel Fork of Holston River.
Witness: Alexander Martin, Gov. By his Excellys. Comd. J. Glasgow, Sec
Registered: November 27th, 1792.

---

(10) MARTIN MYERS :
to : DEED OF WARRANTY
MICHAEL LINDAWOOD :

Date: August 22d, 1795.
Consideration: 60 L Virginia money.
Amt. of land: 163 acres.
Location: Sullivan County, Western territory.
Description: A certain tract or parcel of land containing 163 acres of land more of less lying and being in the county of Sullivan on a Dry Branch of Sinking Creek a branch of Holston River including the plantation formerly occupied by George Poster.
Witness: Proven by the oath of John Vance in Sullivan County November Sessions, 1795. Test: Mattw. Rhea, C. S. C.
Registered: December 10th, 1795.

---

(11) STATE OF NORTH CAROLINA :
RICHARD DOBBS SPAIGHT, GOV. : LAND GRANT
to : NO. 600
STEWART ANDERSON :

Date: June 27th, 1793.
Consideration: 50 shillings for every 100 acres of land.
Amt. of land: 50 acres.
Location: Sullivan County, North Carolina.
Description: A tract of land containing 50 acres lying andbeing in our county of Sullivan on the North Fork of Reedy Creek.
Witness: Richard Dobbs Spaight, Gov. By his Excellys. Comd. J. Glasgow, Sec.
Registered: December 10th, 1795.

---

(12) STATE OF NORTH CAROLINA :
RICHARD DOBBS SPAIGHT, GOV. : LAND GRANT
to : NO. 657.
THOMAS VINCENT :

Date: December 5th, 1794.
Consideration: 50 shillings for every 100 acres of land.
Amt. of land: 150 acres.
Location: Sullivan County, North Carolina.

(Page)

Description: A tract of land containing 150 acres lying and being in our County of Sullivan including the plantation where Thomas Buckner now lives.
Witness: Richard Dobbs Spaight, Gov. By his Excellys. Comd.
J. Glasgow, Sec.
Registered: December 14th, 1795.

(13) STATE OF NORTH CAROLINA :
RICHARD DOBBS SPAIGHT, GOV. : LAND GRANT
to : NO. 667
JEREMIAH COX. :

Date: December 5th, 1794.
Consideration: 50 shillings for every 100 acres of land.
Amt. of land: 84 acres.
Location: Sullivan County, North Carolina.
Description: A tract of land containing 84 acres lying and being in our County of Sullivan.
Witness: Richard Dobbs Spaight, Gov. By his Excellys. Comd.
J. Glasgow, Sec.
Registered: December 14th, 1795.

---

(14) STATE OF NORTH CAROLINA :
RICHARD DOBBS SPAIGHT, GOV. : LAND GRANT
to : NO. 655
THOMAS JOHNSTON :

Date: December 5th, 1794.
Consideration: 50 shillings foe every 100 acres of land.
Amt. of land: 50 acres.
Location: Sullivan County, North Carolina.
Description: A tract of land containing 50 acres lying and being in our county of Sullivan on Walkers fork of Horse Creek that runs through Horse Creek Mountain.
Witness: Richard Dobbs Spaight, Gov. By his Excellys Comd.
J. Glasgow, Sec.
Registered: December 14th, 1795.

---

(15) STATE OF NORTH CAROLINA :
RICHARD DOBBS SPAIGHT, GOV. : LAND GRANT
to : NO. 664
ALEXANDER MOOR :

Date: December 4th, 1794.
Consideration: 50 shillings for every 100 acres of land.
Amt. of land: 81 acres.
Location: Sullivan County, North Carolina.
Description: A tract of land containing 81 acres lying andbeing in our County of Sullivan.
Witness: Richard Dobbs Spaight, Gov. By his Excellys.Comd.
J. Glasgow, Sec.
Registered: December 14th, 1795.

(Page)
(16) STATE OF NORTH CAROLINA : LAND GRANT NO. 663
RICHARD DOBBS SPAIGHT, GOV.
to
DANIEL ALLEN

Date: December 4th, 1794.
Consideration: 50 shillings for every 100 acres of land.
Amt. of land: 64 acres.
Location: Sullivan County, North Carolina.
Description: A tract of land containing 64 acres lying and being in our countyof Sullivan.
Witness: Richard Dobbs Spaight, Gov. By his Excellys Comd. J. Glasgow, Sec.
Registered: December 15th, 1795.

---

(17) CHRISTIAN SHULTS : DEED OF WARRANTY
to
WILLIAM HODGES

Date: October 10th, 1795.
Consideration: 190 £.Virginia currency.
Amt. of land: 73 acres.
Location: Sullivan County, North Carolina.
Description: A certain tract or parcel of land lying and being in the County of Sullivan on the North side of Wataugah river.
Witnesses: Julius Conner, John Hodge.
Proven: By the oath of John Hodges Sullivan November Sessions 1795.
Test: Mattw. Rhea, C. S. C.
Registered: December 15th, 1795.

---

(18) JOB KEY : DEED OF WARRANTY
to
SAMUEL HAMPTON

Date: November 24th, 1795.
Consideration: 50 £.
Amt. of land: 90 acres.
Location: Sullivan County, Territory South of the Ohio river.
Description: A certain tract of land containing 90 acres more or less lying and being in the County aforesaid.
Witnesses: John Anderson, John Fegan.
Acknowledged: Sullivan County, November Sessions, 1795, by Job Key a party thereto.
Test: Mattw. Rhea, C. S. C.
Registered: December 15th, 1795.

---

(19) GEORGE HUNT : DEED OF WARRANTY
to
JOHN MCELDERY

Date: Feb. 28th, 1795.
Consideration: 55 £.
Amt. of land: 125 acres.
Location: Sullivan County, Territory South of the Ohio.

(Page)

Description: A certain tract of land containing 125 acres be the same more or less lying and being in the County aforesaid on the waters of Fall Creek.
Witnesses: John Anderson, William Melton.
Proven: By the oath of John Anderson, Sullivan May Session, 1795.
Test: Matthew Rhea, C. S. C. Dec. 15th, 1795, then Regst.

---

(20) CARR BAILEY : to : DEED OF WARRANTY JOHN MCELDERY :

Date: April 7thm, 1795.
Consideration: 75 L.
Amt. of land: 93 acres.
Location: Sullivan County, Territory South of Ohio.
Description: A certain tract of land containing 93 acres be the same more or less lying and being in the county aforesaid and on the waters of fall creek.
Witnesses: Henery Mauk, William Cody.
Proven: By the oath of Henery Mauk, May Session, 1795.
Test: Mattw. Rhea, C. S. C.
Registered: December 15th, 1795.

---

(21) PHILIP HORN : to : DEED OF WARRANTY JOHN FOUST :

Date: Nov. 25th, 1795.
Consideration: $150.00.
Amt. of land: 85 acres.
Location: Sullivan County, Territory of the U. S. South of the River Ohio.
Description: A certain tract or parcel of land containing 85 acres by estimation be the same more or less, lying and being in the County and Twrritory afowesaid on the North side of Eaton's Ridge.
Witnesses: Peter Drocke, James Gaines.
Proven: By the oath of Peter Troak Sullivan November Sessions, 1795.
Test: M. Rhea, C. S. C. December 16th, 1795, then Regst.

---

(22) AUGUSTIN WILSON : to : DEED OF WARRANTY ISAAC WHITE :
Date: June 11th, 1793.
Consideration: 50 L.
Amt. of land: 200 acres.
Location: Sullivan County, Territory South of Ohio.
Description: A certain tract or parcel of land containin2 00 acres be the same more or less lying and being in sd. County of Sullivan on the middle fork of Horse Creek.
Witnesses: Samuel McBee, Samuel Crawford,
Proven, By the oath of Samuel McBee Sullivan County, September Sessions, 1793. Test: Matw. Rhea, C. S. C.
Registered: December 16th, 1795.

(Page)
(23) HENRY HUGHES : to : DEED OF WARRANTY
ELENDER CARR :

Date: June 26th, 1795.
Consideration: 10 ₤.
Amt. of land: 10 acres.
Location & description: A certain tract or parcel of land containing 10 acres be the same more or less lying and being in the county of Sullivan.
Witnesses: James Anderson, William Molton.
Registered: November Sessions, Sullivan County, 1795.
Proven by the oath of James Anderson. Test: Mattw. Rhea, C. S. C.
December 16th, 1795, then regst.

---

(24) JACOB EMERT, ATTY. FOR WILLIAM DYER : to : WARRANTY DEED
JOHN KING : BY POWER OF ATTORNEY.

Date: August 15th, 1795.
Consideration: 100 ₤/
Amt. of land: 100 acres.
Location: County of Sullivan and territory.
Description: A certain tract or parcel of land situate lying and being in the County of Sullivan and Territory aforesaid on the North side of Watawgah joining John Torbet, Wm. Fain and George Emert.
Witnesses: John Scott, Thomas King.
Acknowledged: By Jacob Emert Sullivan Coutny, August Sessions, 1795. Test; James Rhea, D. C. S. C.
Registered: December 18th, 1795.

---

(25) STATE OF NORTH CAROLINA :
RICHARD DOBBS SPAIGHT, GOV. : LAND GRANT
to : NO. tore out.
GEORGE NEDEVER

Date: June 27th, 1793.
Consideration: 50 shillings for every 100 acres of land.
Amt. of land: 50 acres.
Location: Sullivan County, North Carolina.
Description: A tract of land containing 50 acres lying and being in our county of Sullivan on the waters of Indian Creek in Ashers cove.
Witness: Richard Dobbs Spaight, Gov. By his Excellys. Comd.
J. Glasgow, Sec.
Registered: February 8th, 1796.

---

(26) JOHN NORVELL :
to :
EDMOND MORRELL & : DEED OF WARRANTY
DANIEL MORRELL :

Date: October 20th, 1795.
Consideration: 40 ₤ Virginia money.

Amt. of land: 87 acres.
Location: Sullivan County, Territory South of the River Ohio.
Description: A certain tract or parcel of land containing 87 acres be the same more or less, lying and being in the County of Sullivan on the South side of the Holston River.
Witnesses: William McBride, Stephen Walling.
Proven: By the oath of Stephen Walling, Sullivan November Sessions, 1795.
Test: Mattw. Rhea, C. S. C., Feb. 8th, 1796, then regst.

---

(27) STATE OF NORTH CAROLINA, : SAMUEL ASHE, GOV. : LAND GRANT to : NO. 683. SHOCKLEY DONELSON :

Date: December 8th, 1795.
Consideration: 50 shillings for every 100 acres.
Amt. of land: 300 acres.
Location: Sullivan County, North Carolina.
Description: A tract of land containing 300 acres lying and being in the County of Sullivan on both sides of Beaver Creek adjoining the line of Julius Hacker and Henery Harkelrode.
Witnesses: Samuel Ashe, Esqr. By His Excellys. Comd. J. Glasgow, Sec.
Regst. Feb.18th, 1796.

---

(28) STATE OF NORTH CAROLINA : SAMUEL ASHE, GOV. : LAND GRANT to : NO. 687. ROBERT STEWART :

Date: December 2d, 1795.
Consideration: 50 shillings for ever 100 acres.
Amt. of land: 72 acres.
Location: Sullivan County, North Carolina.
Description: A tract of land containing 72 acres lying and being in our County of Sullivan on the South side of Holston River.
Witness: Samuel Ashe, Gov. By his Excellys. Comd. J. Glasgow, Sec.
Regst. Feb. 25th, 1796.

---

(29) STATE OF NORTH CAROLINA : RICHARD DOBBS SPAIGHT, GOV. : LAND GRANT to : NO. 642. SARAH SHOWN :

Date: January 6th, 1795.
Consideration: 50 shillings for every 100 acres.
Amt. of land: 150 acres.
Location: Sullivan County, North Carolina.
Description: A tract of land containing 150 acres lying and being in our County of Sullivan on the South side of Holston River.
Witness: Richard Dobbs Spaight, Gov. By his Excellys. Comd. J. Glasgow, Sec.
Registered: March 1, 1796.

(Page)

(30) STATE OF NORTH CAROLINA :
RICHARD DOBBS SPAIGHT, GOV. : LAND GRANT
to : NO. 676
GEORGE CRUMLEY :

Date: Nov. 12th, 1795.
Consideration: 50 shillings for every 100 acres of land.
Amt. of land: 110 acres.
Location: Sullivan County, North Carolina.
Description: A tract of land containing 110 acres lying and being in the County of Sullivan on both sides of Weavers Creek a branch of Holston River.
Registered: March 1, 1796, By his Excellys. Comd. J. Glasgow, Sec.

---

(31) STATE OF NORTH CAROLINA :
RICHARD DOBBS SPAIGHT, GOV. : LAND GRANT
to : NO. 665.
JAMES ARNOLD :

Date: Dec. 4th, 1794.
Consideration: 50 shillings for every 100 acres of land.
Amt. of land: 100 acres.
Location: Sullivan County, North Carolina.
Description: A tract of land containing 100 acres lying and being in our County of Sullivan South of the Ohio River.
Witness: Richard Dobbs Spaight, Gov. By his Excellys Comd.
J. Glasgow, Secretary.
Registered: March 1, 1795.

---

(32) STATE OF NORTH CAROLINA :
RICHARD DOBBS SPAIGHT, GOV. : LAND GRANT
to : NO. 649.
JAMES PICKINGS :

Date: December 5th, 1794.
Consideration: 50 shillings for every 100 acres of land.
Amt. of land: 100 acres.
Location: Sullivan County, North Carolina.
Description: A tract of land containing 100 acres lying and being in our County of Sullivan as by the plat hereunto annexed doth appear.
Witness: Richard Dobbs Spaight, Gov. By his Excellys. Comd.
J. Glasgow, Sec.
Registered: March 12th, 1796.

---

(33) STATE OF NORTH CAROLINA :
SAMUEL ASHE, GOV. : LAND GRANT
to : NO. 692.
NATHAN LEWIS :

Date: Feb. 27th, 1796.
Consideration: 50 shillings for every 100 acres of land.
Amt. of land: 200 acres.
Location: Sullivan County, North Carolina.

Description: A tract of land containing 200 acres lying and being in our County of Sullivan.
Witness: Samuel Ashe, Gov. By his Excellys Comd. J. Glasgow, Sec.

---

(34) HENERY HARKLEROD :
to : DEED OF WARRANTY
JAMES KING & COMPANY :

Place: Territory South of Ohio.
Consideration: $1000.00.
Amt. of land: 200 acres.
Location: Sullivan County, territory aforesaid.
Description: A tract of land containing 200 acres situate lying and being on Beaver Creek in Sullivan County being a part of a tract of land containing 295 acres granted to him, the sd. Harklerod by Govenor Johnston of North Carolina the 27th of November, 1798.
Witnesses: John Goodson, Lewis Tylor, John Punch.
Receipt: A receipt signed by Henery Harklerod for full amt. of consideration is attached to the deed.
Acknowledged: By Henery Harklerod Sullivan County February Sessions, 1796.
Test: James Rhea, D. C. S. C.
Registered: March 12th, 1796.

---

(35) JULIUS HACKER :
to : DEED OF WARRANTY
JAMES KING AND COMPANY :

Date: January 10th, 1796.
State: Territory South of the Ohio.
Consideration: $100.00.
Amt. of land: 190 acres.
Location: Sullivan County, Territory aforesaid.
Description: A certain tract or parcel of land on both sides of Beaver Creek containing 190 acres be the same more or less being part of a tract of 640 acres granted to the sd. Julius Hacker by Governor Martin of the State of North Carolina.
Witnesses: John Goodson, John Cooper, Lewis Tiver.
Receipt: A receipt signed by Julius Harklerod for full amt. of consideration is added to the deed.
Acknowledged: By Julius Hacker, Sullivan County, February Session, 1796.
Test: James Rhea, D. C. S. C.
Registered: April 9, 1796.

---

(37) JOHN SCOTT, SHERIFF :
to :: SHERIFF'S DEED.
DAVID BRIGHAM AND BENJAMIN DOWNS :

Date: November 25th, 1795.
State: Territory South of the Ohio.
Consideration: 25 £.
Amt. of land: 113 acres.
Location: Sullivan County, Territory aforesaid.

Description: A tract of land containing 113 acres be the same more or less said land lying and being in county aforesaid.
Signed, John Scott, Sheriff.
Acknowledged: In open Court Sullivan County, August Sessions, 1795, by John Scott, a party thereto.
Test: Mattw. Rhea, C. S. C.
Registered: April 9th, 1796.

---

(37) WILLIAM PALLETT : to :DEED OF WARRANTY SAMUEL DUNMAN :

Date: February 23d, 1796.
Consideration: 500 L current mmoney of Virginia.
Amt. of land: 304 acres.
Description: A certain piece or parcel of land situate lying & the drains of back creek (boundaries) containing 304 acres moreor less and which said tract of land was granted to the said Abraham Pallat now deceased by grant from the Registers office of Virginia bearing date the 13th day of July, 1789.
Witness: Isaac Shelby.
Acknowledged: In Sullivan County, February Sessions, 1796, by William Pallat.
Test: Matthew Rhea, C. S. C.
Registered: April 9th, 1796.

---

(39) PETER SHELLY : to : DEED OF WARRANTY MICHAEL DEVALT :

Date: February 22d, 1796.
Consideration: 50 L.
Amt. of land: 50 acres.
Location: Sullivan County, Territory South of the Ohio.
Description: A certain piece or parcel of land containing 50 acres lying and being in the County aforesaid.
Witness: John Anderson.
Acknowledged: Sullivan County, Feb. Sessions, 1796, by Peter Shelly.
Test: Matthew Rhea, C. S. C.
Registered: April 20th, 1796.

---

(40) JAMES BRIGHAM, SENR., : to :DEED OF WARRANTY BENJAMIN DOWNS & WILLIAM DOWNS :

Date: November 20th, 1795.
Consideration: 100 L.
Amt. of land: 470 acres.
Location: Sullivan County, Western Territory.
Description: A certain piece or parcel of land lying and being in Sullivan County aforesaid (bounds) and containing 470 acres be the same more or less.
Acknowledged: In open court Sullivan County November Sessions, 1795.
Test: Mattw. Rhea, C. S. C.
Registered: April 20th, 1796.

(41) WILLIAM CHILDRESS : to : DEED OF WARRANTY
MARTIN WADDLE :

Date: February 22, 1796.
Consideration: 200 L.
Amt, of land: 135 acres.
Location: Sullivan County, Tennessee.
Description: A certain tract or parcel of land situate lying and being in Sullivan County aforesaid (bounds) containing 135 acres more or less.
Acknowledged: In Sullivan County, February Sessions, 1796 by William Childress.
Test: Matthew Rhea , C. S. C.
Registered: April 20th, 1796.

---

(42) GEORGE HUNT : to : DEED OF WARRANTY
WILLIAM MOLTON :

Date: February 28th, 1795.
Consideration: 50 L Virginia money.
Amt. of land: 125 acres.
Location: Sullivan County, Territory South of the Ohio.
Description: A certain tract of land lying and being in Sullivan County, and Territory South of the Ohio, containing 125 acres be the same more or less.
Witnesses: John Anderson, John McEldery.
Proven: By oath of John Anderson, Sullivan County, May Sessions, 1795.
Registered: April 20th, 1796.

JOHN SHARP AND ALEXANDER LAUGHLIN : to : DEED OF WARRANTY
WILLIAM KING :

Date: February 21, 1795.
Consideration: 500 Spanish milled dollars.
Amt. of land: 265 acres.
Location: Sullivan County, Western Territory.
Description: A certain plantation or tract of land situate, lying and being in Sullivan County Western Territory (bounds) containing 265 acres be the same more or less.
Witnesses: William Oweh, John Williams.
Acknowledgement: Sullivan County, February Sessions, 1795, acknowledged in open court.
Test: Mattw. Rhea, C. S. C.
Registered: April 20th, 1796.

---

(44) BRYCE RUSSELL : to : DEED OF WARRANTY
JOHN SHIPLEY :

Date: February 22d, 1796.
Consideration: 55 L.
Amt. of land: 71 acres.
Location: Sullivan County, Tennessee.
Description: A certain tract of land containing 71 acres more or

less lying in County of Sullivan on the waters of Fall Creek.
Proven: Sullivan County, February Sessions, 1796, by Alexander Ford, a witness therto.
Witnesses: Alexander Ford, George Roller.
Test: Mattw. Rhea, C. S. C.
Registered: April 21, 1796.

---

(44) WILLIAM CAGE : to : DEED OF WARRANTY MARTIN ROLLER :

Date: Feb. 22, 1796.
Consideration: $230.00.
Amt. of land: 200 acres.
Location: Knox County, Tennessee.
Description: A certain tract or parcel of land lying and being in the County of Knox on the South side of Clinch River near the mouth of the second Creek below the papaw ford containing 200 acres.
Witnesses: William Nash, John Jennings.
Executed: In Sullivan County, February Sessions, 1796, by Thomas King, Attorney for William Cage.
Test: Mattw. Rhea, C. S. C.
Registered: April 22, 1796.

---

(46) JOHN ARONWINE : to : DEED OF WARRANTY JOHN SHELBY, JUNR. :

Date: Feb. 23d, 1796.
Consideration: $3000.00.
Amt. of land: 500 acres.
Location: Sullivan County, Western Territory.
Description: A tract or parcel of land containing 500 acres be the same more or less lying and being in the County of Sullivan, and Territory South of the Ohio.
Acknowledged: In Sullivan County, February Sessions, 1796, by John Aronwine,
Test: Mattw. Rhea, C. S. C.
Registered: April 25th, 1796.

---

(47) STATE OF NORTH CAROLINA : RICHARD DOBBS SPAIGHT, GOV. : LAND GRANT to : NO. 578. JAMES HOGARD :

Date: July 29th, 1793.
Consideration: 50 shillings for every 100 acres of land.
Amt. of land: 150 acres.
Location: Sullivan County, North Carolina.
Description: A tract of land containing 150 acres lying and being in our County of Sullivan on the North side of Reedy Creek including the plantation whereon sd. Hogard lives.
Witness: Richard Dobbs Spaight, Gov. By his Excellys. Comd. J. Glasgow, Sec.
Registered: May 4th, 1796.

(47) STATE OF NORTH CAROLINA : SAMUEL ASHE, GOV. : LAND GRANT to : NO. (omitted) JAMES KING AND COMPANY :

Date: May 5th, 1796.
Consideration: Granted under and Act of the General Assembly to encourage the Building of Iron Works in the State.
Amt. of land: 3000 acres.
Location: Sullivan County, North Carolina.
Description: 3000 acres of land situate lying and being in the County of Sullivan as by the plat hereto annexed doth appear.
Witness: Samuel Ashe, Gov. By his Excellys. Comd. J. Glasgow, Sec.
Registered: May 5th, 1796.

----

(48) STATE OF NORTH CAROLINA : SAMUEL ASHE, GOV. : LAND GRANT to : NO. 685. WILLIAM PEMBERTON :

Date: December 9th, 1795.
Consideration: 50 shillings for every 100 acres of land.
Amt. of land: 150 acres.
Location: Sullivan County, North Carolina.
Description: A tract of land containing 150 acres lying and being in our County of Sullivan on a small branch the waters of Holston River.
Witness: Samuel Ashe, Gov. By his Excellys. Comd. J. Glasgow, Sec.
Registered: May 10th, 1796.

----

(49) STATE OF NORTH CAROLINA : RICHARD DOBBS SPAIGHT, GOV. : LAND GRANT to : NO. 670. JOHN SHARP :

Date: December 5th, 1794.
Consideration: 10 £ for every 100 acres of land.
Amt. of land: 300 acres,
Location: Sullivan County, North Carolina.
Description: A tract of land containing 300 acres lying and being in our County of Sullivan on Sinking Creek, the North side of Holston River.
Witness: By his Excellys Comd.
Registered: May 30th, 1796.

STATE OF NORTH CAROLINA : SAMUEL ASHE, GOV. : LAND GRANT to : NO. 688. JOSEPH KINKEAD :

Date: December 5th, 1795.
Consideration: 50 shillings for every 100 acres of land.
Amt. of land: 700 acres.
Location: Sullivan County, South of the Ohio.
Description: A tract of land containing 700 acres lying and being in our County of Sullivan South of the River Ohio.

(50) Witness: Samuel Ashe, Gov. By his Excellys. Comd. J. Glasgow, Sec.
Registered: December 2d, 1795.

STATE OF NORTH CAROLINA :
(51) SAMUEL ASHE, GOV. : LAND GRANT
to : NO. 677
HENRY ROBERTSO :

Date: December 9th, 1795.
Consideration: 50 shillings for every 100 acres of land.
Amt. of land: 150 acres.
Location: Sullivan County, North Carolina.
Description: A tract of land containing 150 acres lying and being in our County of Sullivan on the wato4s of Reedy Creek.
Witness: Samuel Ashe, Gov. By his Excellys. Comd. J. Glasgow, Sec.
Registered: May 30th, 1796.

---

(52) STATE OF NORTH CAROLINA :
ALEXANDER MARTIN, GOV. : LAND GRANT
to : NO. 130.
JOSEPH COLE :

Date: October 23d, 1782.
Consideration: 50 shillings for every 100 acres of land.
Amt. of land: 50 acres.
Location: Sullivan County, North Carolina.
Description: A tract of land containing 50 acres lying and being in our County of Sullivan as by the plat hereunto annexed doth appear.
Witness: Alex. Martin, Gov. By his Excellys. Comd. J. Glasgow, Sec.
Registered: May 30th, 1796.

---

(53) WILLIAM OWEN :
to : DEED OF WARRANTY
JOSEPH OWEN :

Date: January 24th, 1796.
Consideration: £1330.30.
Amt. of land: One tract containing 110 acres,
" " " 220 acres.
Location: Sullivan County, Tennessee.
Description: (A) A certain plantation or tract of land situate lying and being in Sullivan County aforesaid.
(B) One other tract or parcel of land in Sullivan County aforesaid adjoining the sd. last mentioned tract.
Witnesses: Nathan Bachman, John Williams,
Acknowledged: In open court by William Owen Sullivan County May Sessions, 1796.
Test: Mattw. Rhea, C. S. C.
Registered: May 31m 1796.

---

(54) ARNOLD SHELL :
to : DEED OF WARRANTY
WILLIAM WIRICK :

Date: May 23d, 1796.
Consideration: 40 L.
Amt. of land: 67 acres.

(Page)

(54) Location: Sullivan County, Tennessee.
Description: A certain tract of land containing 67 acres be the same more or less lying and being in the County Aforesaid on the South side of Holston River.
Acknowlddged: In open Court Sullivan County May Sessions, 1796, by Arnold Shalll
Test: Mattw. Rhea, C. S. C.
Registered: June 1, 1796.

---

(55) STATE OF NORTH CAROLINA : LAND GRANT
RICHARD DOBBS SPAIGHT, GOV. : NO. 674.
to
JOHN RHEA

Date: May 1 1, 1795.
Consideration: 50 shillings for every 100 acres of land.
Amt. of land: 640 acres.
Location: Sullivan County, North Carolina.
Description: A tract of land containing 640 acres lying and being in our County of Sullivan on the North side of Holston River, on the waters of Beaver Creek.
Witnesses: Richard Dobbs Speight, Gov. By his Excellys. Comd. J. Glasgow, Sec.
Registered: June 2, 1796.

STATE OF NORTH CAROLINA : LAND GRANT
SAMUEL ASHE, GOV. : NO. 679
to
JOHN RHEA

Date: December 8th, 1795.
Consideration: 50 shillings for every 100 acres of land.
Amt. of land: 50 acres.
Location: Sullivan County, North Carolina.
Description: A tract of land containing 50 acres lying and being in the County of Sullivan on the South side of Holston River.
Witness: Samuel Ashe, Gov. By his Excellys. Comd. J. Glasgow, Sec.
Registered: June 2d, 1796.

---

(57) JAS. GAINES, RICHARD GAMMON, : COMMISSIONERS DEED.
GEO. RUTLEDGE, JOHN SHELBY,
COMMISSIONERS,
to
JOHN BURK

Date: August 25th, 1795.
Consideration: John Burk to pay all state and other taxes.
Amt. of land: A certain loot of ground in said town of Blountville, Lott. No. 17.
Location: In town of Blountville, County of Sullivan.
Witnesses: Above mentioned Commissioners.
Registered: June 2d, 1796.

(Page)

(57) JAS. GAINES, RICHARD GAMMON, GEORGE RUTLEDGE, JOHN SHELBY, JUNR. COMMISSIONERS, to JOHN BURK : COMMISSIONERS DEED.

Date: August 25th, 1795.
Consideration: John Burk to pay all state and other taxes.
Amt. of land: LOtt No. 19.
Location: Town of Blountville, County of Sullivan.
Witnesses: Above mentioned commissioners.
Registered: June 2d, 1796.

---

(58) JOSEPH COLE to JOB KEY : DEED OF WARRANTY

Date: May 24th, 1796.
Consideration: 10 £ current money of Tennessee.
Amt. of land: 50 acres.
Location: Sullivan County, Tennessee.
Description: One certain tract or parcel of land lying and being in the County of Sullivan aforesaid (boundaries) containing 150 acres more or less.
Witnesses: Benjamin Downs, Stephen Taylor.
Acknowledged: By Joseph Cole in open court Sullivan County May Sessions, 1796.
Test: Matthew Rhea, C. S. C.
Registered: June 2d, 1796.

---

(59) JOHN GENTRY to PETER DRONE : DEED OF WARRANTY

Date: February 23d, 1796.
Consideration: 60 £ Virginia money.
Amt. of land: 240 acres.
Location: Sullivan County, Territory South of the Ohio.
Description: One certain tract or parcel of land lying and being in the County of Sullivan aforesaid containing 240 acres including the part of the plantation where Nicholas Gentry formerly lived.
Witness: John Anderson.
Proven: By the oath of John Anderson Sullivan County, Febr. Sessions 1796.
Test: Mattw. Rhea, C. S. C.
Registered: June 2d, 1796.

---

(59) JOHN CLOWER to JOHN MUSGROVE : DEED OF WARRANTY

Date: March 14th, 1796.
Consideration: $366.66.
Amt. of land 200 ¾ acres.
Location: Sullivan County, Tennessee.

(Page)

Description: Two certain tract or parcell of land lying and being in Sullivan County and state aforesaid, the first containing by estimation 176 acres be the same more or less situated on the waters of Beaver Creek and on both sides of the Watauga road and on the east end of John Bealor's land the other containing

24-3/4 acres be the same more or less and lying on the North side of Holston River.
Acknowledged: In open court of Sullivan County, May Sessions, 1796, by John Clower.
Test: James Rhea, D. C.
Registered: June 3d, 1796.

---

(60) MOSES WEBB : DEED OF WARRANTY
to
JAMES KING & COMPANY

Date: May 24th, 1796.
Consideration: $500.00.
Amt. of land: 200 acres.
Location: Sullivan County, Tennessee.
Description: All that plantation or tract of land herein mentioned to have been sold by the said Stephen Renfro and afterward to Moses Webb. Stephen Renfro sold the said land to John Rhea by deed dated May 21st, 1790, John Rhea later conveying the land to Moses Webb. Said tract of land containing 200 acres.
Witnesses: James Delaney, John Anderson, James Gaines.
Acknowledged: In open court, by Moses Webb, Sullivan County, May sessions, 1796.
Test: Mattw. Rhea, C. S. C.
Registered: June 3d, 1796.

---

(62) JOHN CHRISMAN : DEED OF WARRANTY
to
JOHN STURGIN

Date: May 23d, 1796.
Consideration: 55 £ Virginia currency.
Amt. of land: 72 acres.
Location: Sullivan County, Tennessee.
Description: All that tract of land containing 72 acres be the same more or less lying and being in said County on Holston River.
Acknowledged: In open Court, Sullivan County, May Sessions, 1796.
Test: Matthew Rhea, C. S. C.
Registered: June 3d, 1796.

---

(63) STEPHEN FALLIN : DEED OF WARRANTY
to
PETER BRECKBILL

Date: May 23d, 17 96.
Consideration : 100 £ current money of Tennessee.
Amt. of land: 127.2 acres lying on Sinking Creek.
Location: Sullivan County, North Carolina.
Description: One certain tract otr parcel of land lying and being in the county of Sullivan and state aforesaid 127.2 acres lying on Sinking Creek.
Witness: Stephen Major.

Proven: By the oath of Stephen Major, Sullivan May Sessions, 1796.
Registered: June 4th, 1796.

---

(64) HUGH CUMMINS :
to : DEED OF WARRANTY
THOMAS HUGHES :

Date: May 10th, 1796.
Consideration: $283-1/3/
Amt. of and: 100 acres.
Location: Sullivan County, Tennessee,
Description: A certain tract or parcel of land lying and being in the County of Sullivan aforesaid on Cedar Creek a branch of Beaver Creek containing 100 acres be the same more or less.
Witnesses: James Lane, John Punch.
Proven: By the oath of John Punch in Sullivan County May Sessions, 1796.
Test: Matthew. Rhea, C. S. C.
Registered: June 4th, 1796.

---

(65) JOHN SHELBY, SENR. :
to : DEED OF WARRANTY
ISAAC SHELBY :

Date: May 5th, 1796.
Consideration: $1000.00
Amt. of land: 463 acres.
Location: Sullivan County, Tennessee.
Description: A certain plantation or tract of land in Sullivan C County aforesaid containing 46 3 acres.
Acknowledged: In open Court of Sullivan County May Session 1796, by John Shelby.
Test: James Rhea, D. C.
Registered: June 10th, 1796.

---

(66)
WILLIAM MCCORMACK :
to : DEED OF WARRANTY
STEPHEN WALLING :

Date: May 24th, 1796.
Consideration: 130 L.
Amt. of land: 100 acres.
Location: Sullivan County, Tennessee.
Description: A certain tract or parcel of land containing100 acres be the sa me more or less lying and being in the county of Sullivan lying on the South side of Holston River.
Witness: James Gaines.
Acknowledged: In open court by William McCormack Sullivan County May Sessions, 1796.
Test: Matthw. Rhea, C. S. C.
Registered: June 10th, 1796.

---

(67) STATE OF NORTH CAROLINA :
SAMUEL JOHNSTON, GOV. : LAND GRANT
to NO. 481.
WILLIAM GOAD

(67) Date: July 10th, 179_.
Consideration: 50 shillings for every 100 acres of land.
Amt. of land: 100 acres.
Location: Sullivan County, North Carolina.
Description: A tract of land containing 100 acres lying and being in our County of Sullivan on the head of Lick Creek.
Witness: Samuel Johnston, Gov. By his Excellys Comd. J. Glasgow, Sec.
Registered: August 10th, 1796.

STATE OF NORTH CAROLINA. :
SAMUEL JOHNSTON, GOV. : LAND GRANT
to : NO. 473.
WILLIAM GOAD :

Date: July 10th, 1788.
Consideration: 50 shillings for every 100 acres of land.
Amt. of land: 200 acres.
Location: Sullivan County, North Carolina.
Description: A tract of land containing 200 acres lying and being in our County of Sullivan on the North side of Walkers Fork of Horse Creek.
Witness: Samuel Johnston, Esquire, By his Excellys. Comd. J. Glasgow Sec
Registered: August 10th, 1796.

---

(68) STATE OF NORTH CAROLINA :
ALEXANDER MARTIN, GOV. : LAND GRANT
to : NO. 553
JAMES MORRISON :

Date: Nov. 17th, 179 ___.
Consideration: 50 shillings for every 100 acres of land.
Amt. of land: 100 acres.
Location: Sullivan County, North Carolina.
Description: A tract of land containing 100acres lying and being in our County of Sullivan on the waters of Beech Creek.
Witness: Alexander Martin, Gov. By his Excellys. Comd. J. Glasgow, Sec
Registered: Autust 10th, 1796.

---

(69) THOMAS HUGHES :
to : DEED OF WARRANTY
JOHN KINCHELOE :

Date: April 20th, 1796.
Consideration: 250 £ Current money.
Amt. of land: 136 acres.
Location: Sullivan County, North Carolina.
Description: A certain tract or parcel of land lying and being in Sullivan County on Kindreiks Creek.
Witnesses: Walter Emmerson, Richard Daniel, William Emerson.
Proven: In Sullivan August Sessions, 1796, by oath of Richard Daniel.
Test: Mattw,.Rhea, C. S. C.
Registered: August 29th, 1796.

---

(71)

(71) NATHAN PEOPLES : to : DEED OF WARRANTY JOHN PEOPLES :

Date: August 3d, 1796.
Consideration: 10 £ current money of Tennessee.
Amt. of land: 186 acres.
Location: Sullivan County, North Carolina.
Description: A certain tract or parcel of land containing 186 acres more or less situate lying and being in said county of Sullivan it being the upper end of the part of the land that sd. Nathan Peoples lives on.
Witnesses: Geo. Vincent, John Shoemaker.
Acknowledged: In Court Sullivan County August Sessions, 1796, by Nathan Peoples.
Witnesses: Geo. Vincent, John Shoemaker.
Acknowledged: In Court Sullivan County, August Sessions, 1796 by Nathan Peoples.
Test: Mattw. Rhea, C. S. C.
Registered: Sept. 10th, 1796.

---

(72) GEORGE SIRKLE : to : DEED OF WARRANTY LEWIS SIRKLE :

Date: August 9th, 1796.
Consideration: 150 £ current money,
Amt. of land: 148 acres.
Location: Sullivan County, North Carolina.
Description: A certain tract or parcel of land containing 148 acres lying and being in Sullivan County on the waters of Beaver Creek a branch of Holston River including the plantation whereon the said George Sirckle now lives.
Witnesses: John Vance, Esqr., John Huling.
Proven: In open court, Sullivan August Sessions, 1796. by oath of John Vance.
Test: Matthew Rhea. C. S. C.
Registered: Sept. 2d, 1796.

---

(73) EPHRAIM SMITH, : to : ARCHIBALD BRUMLEY & : DEED OF WARRANTY PETER HICKMAN :

Date: August 23d, 1796.
Consideration: 80 £ current money of Virginia.
Amt. of land: 160 acres.
Location: Sullivan County, Tennessee.
Description: A certain tract or parcel of land containing 160 acres more or less lying and being in our county of Sullivan and State of Tennessee on the waters of Beaver Creek.
Acknowledged: August Sessions, 1796, by Smith.
Test: Mattw. Rhea, C. S C.
Registered: DSepeember 8th, 1796.

(Page) (74)

JOHN RILEY : DEED OF WARRANTY
to
JOHN HUGHES

Date: December 18th, 1794.
Consideration: 50 £ current money of Virginia.
Amt. of land: 200 acres.
Location: Sullivan County, Tennessee.
Description: A certain tract or parcel of land lying in Sullivan County and State aforesaid containing by estimation 200 acres by estimation be it more or less lying on the waters of Holston River on a creek called Indian Creek.
Witnesses: John Scott, William Hughs.
Acknowledged: Sullivan County, August Sessions, 1796, in open court by John Riley.
Test: Mattw. Rhea, C. S. C.
Registered: September 10th, 1796.

(75)

STATE OF NORTH CAROLINA
SAMUEL ASHE, GOV. : LAND GRANT
to : NO. 687.
WILLIAM SNODGRASS

Date: December 9th, 1796.
Consideration: 50 shillings for every 100 acres of land.
Amt. of land: 100 acres.
Location: Sullivan County, North Carolina.
Description: A tract of land containing 100 acres lying and being in our County of Sullivan South of the Ohio.
Witness: Samuel Ashe, Gov. by J. Glasgow, Sec.
Registered: September 20th, 1796.

STATE OF NORTH CAROLINA
RICHARD DOBBS SPAIGHT, GOV. : LAND GRANT
to : NO. 669
WILLIAM WILEY

Date: December 5th, 1794.
Consideration: 50 shillings for every 100 acres of land.
Amt. of land: 150 acres.
Location: Sullivan County, North Carolina.
Description: A tract of land containing 150 acres lying and being in our county of Sullivan on the waters of Horse Creek.
Witness: Richard Dobbs Spaight, Esq. by J. Glasgow, Sec.
Registered: September 20th, 1796.

---

(76) STATE OF NORTH CAROLINA
WILLIAM SHARP : DEED OF WARRANTY
to
HENRY KALBACH

Date: August 25th, 1790.
Consideration: 250 £.
Description: A certain piece of land situate lying and being in the County of Sullivan late Washington and state of aforesaid bound as followeth on both sides of the lower west fork of Indian Creek the waters of Holston including Blevins bottom and his own survey

by virtue of Major Robertson's office. Land grant made to William Sharp by the State December 15th, 1778.
Witnesses: William Cobb, Pharah Cobb, John McKernh.
Acknowledged: February 23d, 1791. J. S. U.
Regst. Sept. 20th, 1796.

---

(78) FRANCES HODGE, SENR. to FRANCES HODGE, SENR. : DEED OF WARRANTY

Date: June 17th, 1796.
Consideration: $100.00.
Amt. of land: 500 acres.
Location: Sullivan County, Tennessee.
Description: All that tract or parcel of land whereon the sd. Francis Hodge, Senr. and Francis Junr. now lives the patent granted by the State of North Carolina to the said Frances Hodge, Senr., and situate lying and being in the state and county aforesaid.
Test: Robert Allison, Thomas King.
Proven: By Robert Allison Sullivan County, August Sessions, 1796.
Test: Mathew Rhea, C. S. C.
Registered: Sept. 20th, 1796.

---

(79) DUDLEY JOLLY to THOMAS MOSLEY : DEED OF WARRANTY

Date: October 17th, 1795.
Consideration: 6 ₤.
Amt. of land: 70 acres.
Location: Sullivan County, North Carolina.
Description: A certain tract or parcel of land containing 70 acres be the same more or less lying and being in sd. county of Sullivan including part of the plantation where said Mosley now lives.
Witnesses: George Vincent, Isaac White, Lewis Corner.
Proven: By the oath of Isaac White in Sullivan County August Sessions, 1796.
Test: Matthew Rhea, C. S. C.
Registered: Sept. 20th, 1796.

(80)

SAMUEL COX to WILLIAM MILLINER : DEED OF WARRANTY

Date: October 24th, 1795.
Consideration: 100 ₤.
Amt. of land: 200 acres.
Location: Sullivan County, Tennessee.
Description: A certain tract or parcel of land containing 200 acres be the same more or less lying and being in the county of Sullivan including the plantation where sd. Samuel Cox now lives on the head waters of Horse Creek and Beech Creek.
Witnesses: Isaac White, James Johnston.
Proven: By the oath of Isaac White, Sullivan August Sessions, 1796.
Registered: Sept. 24th, 1796.

---

(81)

(Page)
(81) CHRISTOPHER CHOATES : to : DEED OF WARRANTY FORRESTER MERCER :

Date: November 10th, 1788.
Consideration: 100 £ current money.
Amt. of land: 300 acres.
Location: Sullivan County, Tennessee.
Description: One certain tract or parcell of land lying and being in Sullivan on Kindrick's Creek and State aforesaid (bounds) containing 300 acres.
Witnesses: John Black, William Wyne, David Webb.
Proven: By the oath of William Black Sullivan County May Sessions, 1795.
Test: Matthew Rhea, C. S. C.
Registered: September 24th, 1796.

---

(82) FORRESTER MERCER : to : DEED OF WARRANTY EDWARD MERCER :

Date: December 6th, 1793.
Consideration: 60 £ current money.
Amt. of land: 164 acres.
Location: Sullivan County, Tennessee.
Description: A certain tract of land lying and being on Kindrick's Creek in the county and state aforesaid (bounds) containing 164 acres.
Witnesses: William Emerson, Walter Emerson. Test: Matw. Rhea, CS.C.
Registered: Sept. 26th, 1796.

---

(83) RICHARD MURRELL : to : DEED OF WARRANTY JOHN SHOEMAKER :

Date: August 20th, 1796.
Consideration: 40 £.
Amt. of land: 85 acres.
Location: Sullivan County, Tennessee.
Description: A certain tract or parcel of land containing 85 acres be the same more or less situate lying and being in the county of Sullivan on the waters of Horse Creek.
Witnesses: Nathan Peoples, John Peoples, Thomas McNary.
Proven: In Sullivan August Sessions, 1796, by Nathan Peoples.
Test: Mattw. Rhea, C. S. C.
Registered: Sept. 26th, 1796.

---

(84) THOMAS RUBEY : to : DEED OF WARRANTY JOHN JONES, JUNR. :

Date: Nov. 27th, 1792.
Consideration: 55 £ Virginia currency.
Amt. of land: 50 acres.
Location: Sullivan County, Tennessee.
Description: One certain tract or parcel of land containing by survey 50 acres be the same more or less being part of the survey

the said Thomas Rubey holds by Patent bearing date Nov. 29th, 1792, lying and being in the County of Sullivan on the waters of Holston River.
Witnesses: Nicholas Howson, John Hadson, Basil Hunt.
Proven: In open Court by the oath of Nicholas Houser, Sullivan County, August Sessions, 1796.
Test: MAttw. Rhea, C. S. C.
Registered: Sept. 27th, 1796.

---

(85) FOSTER MERCER : to : DEED OF WARRANTY THOMAS HUMES :

Date: Dec. 6th, 1793.
Consideration: 100 £ current money.
Amt. of land: 136 acres.
Location: Sullivan County, Tennessee.
Description: One certain tract or parcel of land containing 136 acres lying and being on Kendrick Creek in the county aforesaid.
Witnesses: Nathaniel Mercer, Walter Emmerson,
Proven: By the oath of William Emerson, Sullivan Augusta Sessions, 1796.
Test: Mattw. Rhea, C. S. C.
Registered: Sept. 27th, 1796.

---

(86) ISAAC SHELBY, SHERIFF : to : SHERIFF'S DEED ELIZABETH HUGHS :

Date: Nov. 30th, 1796.
Consideration: $36.89.
Purpose: Pursuant to an execution of firia facias to me directed in the suite of John Robinson on William Hughs on behalf of sd. John Robinson said land directed to be sold.to the highest bidder.
Amt. of land: 280 acres.
Location: Lying in the County of Sullivan and formerly a part of the County of Washington in said state on Austin Choates branch,, being the said tract of land granted to William Hughs by patent dated October 24th, 1782, and No. 126.
Witnesses: John Anderson, Richd. Gammon, Abraham Britton, Hopkins Lacey, D. Braezeal
Proven: In open court, Sullivan November Sessions, 1796, by D. W. Braezeal, a witness thereto.
Test: Mattw. Rhea, C. S. C.
Registered: Mattw. Rhea, C. S. C. December 5th, 1796.

---

(87) STATE OF NORTH CAROLINA : SAMUEL ASHE, GOV. : LAND GRANT to : NO. 695. JAMES BRIGHAM :

Date: July 28th, 1796.
Considersion: 50 shillings for every 100 acres of land.
Amt. of land: 100 acres.
Location: Sullivan County, North Carolina.

Description: A tract of land containing 100 acres lying and being in our county of Sullivan joining the tract of land said Brigham lives on.
Witness: Samuel Ashe, Esquire, By his Excellys. Comd. J. Glasgow, Se
Registered: December 5th, 1796.
No. of warrants 90 entered February 8th, 1780.

---

(88) JOHN KING : to : DEED OF WARRANTY
SAMUEL DUNSMORE :

Date: November 25th, 1796.
Consideration: 100 £.
Amt. of land: 150 acres.
Location: Sullivan County, Tennessee.
Description: All that tract or parcel of land situate lying and being in the county and state aforesaid on the North side of Wataugah joining John Torbett, William Traim and George Smith
Witnesses: Edmund Hawes, Thomas King.
Acknowledged: In open Court Sullivan County, November Sessions, 1796, by John King.
Test: Mattw. Rhea, C. S. C.
Registered: December 14th, 1796.

RICHARD GAMMON, GEORGE RUTLEDGE, :
JOHN SHELBY, JAS. GAINES, :
(89) JOHN ANDERSON, JUNR. COMMISSIONERS : COMMISSIONERS DEED
to :
ROBERT RUTLEDGE :

Date: August 25th, 1795.
Consideration: Robert Rutledge and heairs to pay all taxes.
Amt. of land: Lott No. 7 in the town of Blountville.
Location: Sullivan County.
Witnesses: Above mentioned commissioners.
Acknowledhed: Sullivan County, August Sessions, 1795, by subscribed commissioners.
Test: James Rhea, D. C. S. C.
Registered: Dec. 18th, 1796.

RICHARD GAMMON, GEORGE RUTLEDGE, :
(90) JOHN SHELBY, JAMES KING, JOHN ANDERSON, JUNR. : COMMISSIONERS DEED
COMMISSIONERS, :
to :
GEORGE RUTLEDGE :

Date: August 25th, 1795.
Consideration: George Rutledge and heirs to pay all taxes.
Amt. of land: Lott. No. 6 in the town of Blountville.
Locations Sullivan County,
Witnesses: Above mentioned commissioners.
Acknowledged: In Sullivan County, August Sessions, 1795, by above mentioned Commissioners.
Test: James Rhea, D. C.
Registered: December 18th, 1796.

(Page)

FORRESTER MERCER : to : DEED OF WARRANTY
WILLIAM GOAD :

Date: December 10th, 1792.
Consideration: 98 £ lawful money.
Amt. of land: 100 acres more or less.
Location: Sullivan County, Western Territory.
Description: A certain tract or parcel of land situate lying and being in the Countyaforesaid on Beach Creek opposite the Chimney Top Mountain (bounds) containing by estimation 100 acres more or less.
Witnesses: Nicholas Mercer, David Morrison, William Morrison.
Proven: In open Court Sullivan March Sessions, 1793 by David Morrison.
Test: Mattw. Rhea, C. S. C.
Registered: December 10th, 1796.

---

(92) ANTHONY AGEE : to : DEED OF WARRANTY
SAMUEL MOORE :

Date: November 25th, 1795.
Consideration: $333.33
Amt. of land: 200 acres.
Location: Sullivan County, Tennessee.
Description: A certain tract or parcel of land containing by estimation 200 acres be the same more or less situate lying and being in the county of Sullivan and State aforesaid on the North side of Eaton's Ridge.
Witnesses: John Yancey, William Agee, Isaac Agee.
Proven: In open Court Sullivan November Sessions, 1796, by William Agee,
Registered: Decemvber 18th, 1796. Test: Mattw. Rhea. C. S. C.

---

(93) JAMES BOYD : to : DEED OF WARRANTY
CHARLES JONES :

Date: December 13th, 1795.
Consideration: 50 £.
Amt. of land: 200 acres.
Location: Sullivan County,
Description: One certain tract or parcell of land lying and being on the waters of Kendricks Creek (bounds) containing200 acres.
Witnesses: Richard B askett, William Hughs.
Proven: In open Court, Sullivan County November Sessions, by William Hughs. Test: Mattw. Rhea, C. S. C.
Registered: December 21, 1796.

---

(94) JOHN BEALOR : to : DEED OF WARRANTY
JOHN FASHAM :

Date: August 30th, 1796.

Consideration: $1500.00.
Amt. of land: 200 acres.
Location: Sullivan County, Tennessee.
Description: A certain tract or parcel of land containing 300 acres be the same more or less situate lying and being in the County of Sullivan including the place where the said John Bealor now lives.
Witness: John Vance.
Acknowledged: In open court Sullivan November Session, 1796, by John Bealor.
Test: Mattw. Rhea. C. S. C.
Registered: December 21, 1796.

---

(96) EDMOND PENDLETON & JOHN TAYLOR : to : DEED OF WARRANTY SAMUEL MOORE :

Date: December 30th, 1794.
Consideration: 78 L, 6 s.
Amt. of land: 261 acres.
Location : Sullivan County, Tennessee.
Description: A certain tract or parcel of land containing 261 acres lying and being in the County of Sullivan westof Reedy Creek a branch of Holston River.
Witnesses: Edward Moore, Mattw. Hughes, Gabriel Moore.
Proven: By the oath of Edward Moore Sullivan County May [illegible] Sessions 1796.
Test: James Rhea, D. C.
Registered: December 21, 1796.

****---

(97) STATE OF TENNESSEE, SULLIVAN COUNTY, NOV. 18th, 1796.
WILLIAM GROSS : to : DEED OF WARRANTY EDWARD COX :

Consideration: 95 L.
Amt. of land: 86 acres.
Location: Above mentioned.
Description: A certain tract or parcel of land containing 86 acres.
WitnessEs: Joseph Smith, Joseph Cole.
Test: Matthew Rhea, C. S. C.
Registered: February 12th, 1797.

---

(98) STATE OF NORTH CAROLINA : SAMUEL ASHE, GOV. : to : LAND GRANT DAVID HUGHES : NO. 698

Date: July 10th, 1796.
Consideration: 50 shillings for every 100 acres of land.
Amt. of land: 150 acres.
Location: Sullivan County, North Carolina.
Description: A tract of land containing 150 acres lying and being in our county of Sullivan.
Witness: Samuel Ashe , Gov. By J. Glasgow, Sec.
Registered: February, 20, 1796.

(98) STATE OF NORTH CAROLINA :
SAMUEL ASHE, GOV. :
to :LAND GRANT
MATTHEW RHEA, ASSIGNEE :: NO. 799.
OF JOSEPH WALLACE :

Date: November 17th, 1796.
Consideration: 50 shillings for every 100 acres of land.
Amt. of land: 20 acres.
Location: Sullivan County, North Carolina.
Description: Twnety acres of land lying and being in our County of Sullivan on the North side of Holston River.
Witness: Samuel Ashe, Esqr. By his Excellys. Comd.J.Glasgow,Sec.
Registered: Feb. 12th, 1797.

---

(99) JOHN CARMACK, SENR. :
to : DEED OF WARRANTY
JOHN CARMACK, JUNR. :

Date: February 9th, 1797.
Consideration: 'A certain sum of money.'
Amt. of land: 151 acres.
Location: Sullivan County, Tennessee.
Description: A tract or parcel of land in the said county of Sullivan containing 151 acres being part of a tract of land containing 500 acres granted by John Carmack, Senr. by a patent bearing date the 23d of April, 1794, lying on both sides of Sinking Creek.
Acknowledged: In open Court Sullivan February Sessions, 1797.
Registered: March 1, 1797.

---

(100) JOHN CARMACK, SENR. :
to : DEED OF WARRANTY
JOSEPH GRAY :

Date: February 9th, 1797.
Consideration: 50 £ current money.
Amt. of land: 114 acres.
Location: Sullivan County, Tennessee.
Description: One certain tract of land in the said County of Sullivan containing 114 acres lying on the waters of Sinking Creek a north branch of Holston and is granted to John Carmack by patten bearing date the 23d of April, 1794.
Acknowledged: By John Carmack in open court Sullivan County , February Sessions.
Test: Mattw. Rhea, C. S. C.
Registered: March 1, 1797.

---

(101) UNITED STATES OF AMERICA :
JOHN ANDERSON & WILLIAM SHELLITON : DEED OF WARRANTY
to :
MATTHIAS CLARK :

Date: October 1, 1796.
Consider ation: 110 £ Virginia money.
Amt. of land: 72 acres.

Location: Sullivan County,
Description: A certain tract or parcel of land containing 72 acres be the same more or lesslying and being in the County of Sullivan being part of a tract joining Peter Morrison and granted to Hohn Anderson and William Shelliton.
Witnesses: James Gaines, Peter Morrison, Michael Cleek.
Acknowledged: Sullivan November Sessions, 1796, by John Anderson and William Skellion.
Test: Matthew Rhea, C. S. C.
Registered: March 2d, 1797.

JOHN HALL :
(102) to : DEED OF WARRANTY
RICHARD HICKS :

Date: December 15th, 1794.
Consideration: 5 L.
Amt. of land: 140 acres.
Location: Sullivan County, Tennesse.
Description: A certain parcel of land being part of a deed of 640 acres joining Benjamin Morey's Senr. for 140 acres.
Witness: Joshua Miller.
Proven: In Sullivan County Sessions Nov. 1794 by the oath of Joshua Miller.
Test: Mattw. Rhea, C. S. C.
Registered: March 2d, 1797.

RICHARD GAMMON, JAMES GAINES, GEORGE :
RUTLEDGE, JOHN ANDERSON, ESQ. COMMS. : COMMISSIONERS DEED
to :
ROBERT WORK :

Date: August 23d, 1796.
Consideration: Robert Work and heirs to pay all state and other taxes.
Amt. of land: A certain lott of ground .
Location: In the town of Blountville being Lott No. 3.
Witnesses: John Williams, William McCormack,
Acknowledged: In open Court by John Anderson. Test: Matw. Rhea, C.S.C
Regst. March 2d, 1794.

---

(104) STATE OF NORTH CAROLINA :
SAMUEL ASHE, GOV. : LAND GRANT
to : NO. 306.
JAMES GAINES :

Date: March 12th, 1796.
Consideration: 50 shillings for every 100 acres of land.
Amt. of land: 1000acres.
Location: Sullivan County, North Carolina.
Description: A tract of land containing 1000 acres of land lying and being in our middle District on both sides of a fork of Caney Fork beginning at two beech trees nearthe river about one mile from the foot of Cumberland Mountains including several Indian Camps.

Witness: Samuel Ashe, Gov. By his Excellys. Com. J. Glasgow, Sec.
Registered: March 2d, 1797.

STATE OF NORTH CAROLINA :
SAM ASHE, GOV. : LAND GRANT
to : NO. 685
WILLIAM DOWNS :

Date: December 9th, 1795.
Consideration: Fifty shillings for every 100 acres of land.
Amt. of land: 100 acres.
Location: Sullivan County, North Carolina.
Description: A tract of land containing 100 acres lying and being in our county of Sullivan on the waters of Muddy Creek.
Witness: Sam. Ashe, Gov. By his Excellys. Comd. J. Glasgow, Sec.
Registered: Match 9th, 1797.

---

(105) STATE OF NORTH CAROLINA :
SAMUEL ASHE, GOV. : LAND GRANT
to : NO. 699.
SOLOMON JONES :

Date: July 20th, 1796.
Consideration: 50 shillings for every 100 acres of land
Amt. of land: 240 acres.
Location: Sullivan County, North Carolina.
Description: A tract of land containing 240 acres lying and being in our county of Sullivan on the waters of Mudy Creek.
Witness: Samuel Easho, Gov. By his Excellys. Comd. J. Glasgow, Sec.
Registered: March 10th, 1797.

---

(106) STATE OF NORTH CAROLINA :
SAMUEL ASHE, GOV. : LAND GRANT
to : NO. 728.
GEORGE BROWN :

Date: December 2d, 1796.
Consideration: 50 shillings for every 100 acres of land.
Amt. of land: 400 acres.
Location: Sullivan County, North Carolina.
Description: Four hundred acres of land lying and being in our wounty of Sullivan on Beaver Dam Creek.
Witness: Samuel Ashe, Gov. By his Excellys. Comd. J. Glasgow, Sec.
Registered: April 4th, 1797.

(107)

FORRESTER MERCER :
to : DEED OF WARRANTY
VASHEL WRIGHT :

Date: December ____, 1792.
Consideration: 100£ current money.
Amt. of land: 100 acres.
Location? Sullivan County, Territory South of the Ohio.
Description: A certain tract or parcel of land containing 100 acres be the same more or less situate lying and being in sd. County of Sullivan on Beech Creek including the plantation where

Jame Smith formerly lived,
Witnesses: James Morrison, William Morrison, Nicholas Mercer.
Proven: By the oath of James Morrison, Sullivan County, 1st day of June Sessions, 1793. Test Mattw. Rhea, C. S. C.
Registered: April 10th, 1797.

---

(108) JONATHAN MORRELL to THOMAS MORRELL : DEED OF WARRANTY.

Date: February 15th, 1797.
Consideration: 60 £ current money.
Amt. of land: 106 acres.
Location: Sullivan County, Tennessee.
Description: One certain tract or parcel of land containing 106 acres more or less situate lying and being in the county of Sullivan the South side of Holston River.
Acknowledged: In open court by Jonathan Morrell Sullivan February Sessions, 1797, Test: Mattw. Rhea, C. S. C.
Registered: April 10th, 1797.

---

(109) JOHN SHELBY, GEORGE RUTLEDGE, RICHARD GAMMON, JOHN ANDERSON, JAMES GAINES, to JOHN BROWN : COMMISSIONERS DEED

Date: November 29th, 1796.
Consideration: John Brown and heirs to pay all taxes on lot.
Amt. of land: LOtt No. 23, in the said town of Blountville.
Witnesses: Above mentioned Commissioners.
Executed: In open Court Sullivan County, November Sessions, 1796, by a majority of the Commissioners.
Registered: May 10th, 1797. Test: Mattw. Rhea, C. S. C.

---

(109) JOHN HOLLOWAY to JESSE BOND : DEED OF WARRANTY.

Date: May 22d, 1797.
Consideration: $150.00.
Amt. of land: 43 acres.
Location: Sullivan County, Tennessee.
Description: A certain tract or parcel of land containing 43 acres lying and being in sd. County of Sullivan on the North Fork of Holston River.
Acknowledged: In open Court, May Sessions, 1797.
Registered: May 26th, 1797.

(110)

WILLIAM DUFF to WILLIAM OWEN : DEED OF WARRANTY

Date: May 1st, 1797.
Consideration: 140 £ Virginia money.
Amt. of land: 200 acres.

Location: Sullivan County, Tennessee.
Description: A certain tract of land containing 200 acres lying and being in our county of Sullivan between the lands of John Sharp and William King and William McPharin.
Witnesses: James Montgomery, Willie Duff.
Acknowledged: In open court Sullivan County May Sessions, 1797.
Test: Mattw. Rhea, C. S. C.
Registered: May 27th, 1797.

---

(111) JAMES HARRIS : to : DEED OF WARRANTY ROBERT COWAN :

Date: February 27th, 1797.
Consideration: $.300.— ($300.00)
Amt. of land: 50 acres.
Description: A certain piece or parcel of land part of the plantation whereon sd. James Harris now lives (bounds) containing 50 acres more or less.
Test: John Williams, Alex. Laughlin.
Proven: In open Coutt Sullivan February Sessions, 1797, by John Williams. Test: Mattw. Rhea, C. S. C.
Registered: May 26th, 1797.

---

(112) THOMAS DRIEN : to : DEED OF WARRANTY ROBERT COWAN :

Date: May 22d, 1797.
Consideration: 90 ₤.
Amt. of land: 100 acres.
Location: Sullivan County, Tennessee.
Description: A certain tract or parcel of land containing 100 acres.
Witnesses: James Harris, Henery Harkleroad.
Test: Mattw. Rhea. C. S. C.
Registered: May 26th, 1797.

---

(113) GEORGE BIRDWELL : to : DEED OF WARRANTY WILLIAM SMITH :

Date: Nov. 20th, 1795.
Consideration: 100 ₤.
Amt. of land: 118 acres.
Location: Sullivan County, Territory Souht of the Ohio.
Description: A certain tract of land containing 118 acres lying and being in Sullivan County, Territory South of the Ohio, on the waters of Holston River it being the same tract of land that the said George Birdwell did live on.
Test: William Childress, John Childress.
Proven: In open court Sullivan County, August Sessions, 1796, by the oath of William Childress.
Registered: June 8, 1799. Test: Matw. Rhea, C. S. C.

(Page)

(114) WILLIAM HUGHES : DEED OF WARRANTY
to :
WILLIAM FREAM :

Date: August 13th, 1796.
Consideration: $100.00.
Amt. of land: 50 acres.
Location: Sullivan County, Tennessee.
Description: A certain piece or parcel of land lying in Sullivan County and state aforesaid containing 50 acres by estimation be it more or less lying on the waters of Wataugah.
Witness: Agnes Tarbet, John Scot.
Acknowledged: In open Court Sullivan County, May term, 1797.
Test: Mattw. Rhea, by Hopkins Lacey.
Registered: June 8th, 1797.

---

(115) JOSEPH SMITH : DEED OF WARRANTY
to :
JOHN CHESTER :

Date: August 10th, 1796.
Consideration: 16 £ current money.
Amt. of land: 50 acres.
Location: Sullivan County, Tennessee.
Description: A certain tract or parcel of land be the same more or less laying and being in the county and state aforesaid on the waters of the clear fork of Horse Creek.
Witnesses: Thomas McLein, William Turney, Robert Birdwell.
Proven: In open Court, Sullivan County, May term, 1797.
Registered: June 8th, 1797. Test: Matw. Rhea, by Hopkins Lacey.

---

(116) STATE OF NORTH CAROLINA :
SAMUEL ASHE, GOV. : LAND GRANT
to : NO. 711.
THOMAS MORRELL :

Date: Nov. 18th, 1796.
Consideration: 50 shillings for every hundred acres of land.
Amt. of land: 50 acres.
Location: Sul ivan County, North Carolina.
Description: Fifty acres of land lying and being in our county of Sullivan on the South side of Holston River.
Witness: Samuel Ashe, Esqr. By his Excellys. Comd.J. Glasgow, Sec.
Registered: June 14th, 1797.

---

(117)
STATE OF NORTH CAROLINA :
SAMUEL ASHE, GOV. : LAND GRANT
to : NO. 715.
JAMES BOYD :

Date: December 20th, 1796.
Consideration: 50 shillings for every 100 acres of land.
Amt. of land: 84 acres.
Location: Sullivan County, North Carolina.
Description: Eighty four acres of land lying and being in our county of Sullivan, as by the plat hereunto annexed doth appear.

Witness: Samuel Ashe, Gov. By his Excellys. Comd. J. Glasgow, Sec.
Registered: June 14th, 1797.

---

(118) STATE OF NORTH CAROLINA : LAND GRANT
SAMUEL ASHE, GOV. : NO. 726.
to :
NICHOLAS HOUSER :

Date: December 2d, 1796.
Consideration: 50 shillings for every 100 acres of land.
Amt. of land: 52 acres.
Location: Sullivan County, North Carolina.
Description: 52 acres of land lying and being in our county of Sullivan as by the plat hereunto annexed doth appear.
Witness: Samuel Ashe. Gov. By his Excellys. Comd. J. Glasgow, Sec.
Registered: June 15th, 1797.

JOSEPH SMITH :
to : DEED OF WARRANTY
JAMES DAVIS :

Date: March 26th, 1794.
Consideration: 25 £ Virginia money.
Amt. of land: 50 acres.
Location: Sullivan County, Tennessee.
Description: A certain tract or parcel of land containing 50 acres be the same more oe less lying and being in the county of Sullivan and state aforesaid on the clear fork of Horse Creek.
Witnesses: John Chester, Waletr Emmerson.
Proven: In open court Sullivan County, May term, 1797.
Test: Matthew Rhea, by Hopkins Lacey.
Registered: June 16th, 1797.

---

(119) JOHN CHESTER :
to : DEED OF WARRANTY
JAMES DAVIS :

Date: March 25th, 1794.
Consideration: 125 £ current money of Virginia.
Amt. of land: 100 acres.
Location: Sullivan County, Tennessee.
Description: A certain tract ot parcel of land containing 100 acres of land be the same more or less lying and being in Sullivan on the waters of the Clear Fork of Horse Creek.
Witnesses. Joseph Smith, Walter Emmerson.
Acknowledged: In ope court Sullivan May term, 1797. Test: Mattw. Rhea, C. S. C.
Registered: June 16th, 1797.

---

(120) JOHN SHOEMAKER :
to : DEED OF WARRANTY.
DANIEL SHOEMAKER :

Date: November 10th, 1796.
Consideration: $400.00.

Amt. of land: 100 acres.
Location: Sullivan County, Tennessee.
Description: A certain tract or parcel of land containing 100 acres be the same more or less lying and being in the County of Sullivan on the north side of Holton's Ridge.
Witnesses: Ann Gounes, Samuel Moor.
Proven: In open Court Sullivan County, November Sessions, 1796.
Registered: June 16th, 1797. Test: Matw. Rhea, C. S.C.

---

(121) FRANCIS H. GAINS, DEPUTY SHERIFF, to ANDREW GREER, JUNR. : DEPUTY SHERIFF'S DEED.

Date: May 24th, 1794.
Purpose of sale: To carry out an execution or ferifacias that proceeded from a suit wherein James Kain was plaintive and Charles Hockhold, Defendant.
Description: One tract or parcell of land containing 50 acres be the same more or less which land was taken by virtue of an execution or Ferifacias that proceeded from a suit wherein James Kain was plaintive and Charles Hockhold, defendant, said land being legally advertised and sold according to law.
Witnesses: John Rhea, Hopkins Lacy,
Acknowledged: In open court Sullivan County, May Sessions, 1797.
Test: Mattw. Rhea, C. S. C.
Registered: June 26th, 1797.

STATE OF NORTH CAROLINA SAMUEL ASHE, GOV. to ADAM TROXEL : LAND GRANT NO. 703

Date: July 20th, 1796.
Consideration: 50 shillings for every 100 acres off land.
Amt. of land: 32 3/4 acres.
Location: Sullivan County, North Carolina.
Description: A tract of land containing 323/4 acres lyingand being in our county of Sullivan as by the plat hereunto annexed doth appear.
Witness: Samuel Ashe, Gov. By his Excellys. Comd.J.Glasgow,Sec.
Registered: July 17th, 1797.

---

(122) STATE OF NORTH CAROLINA SAMUEL ASHE, GOV. to JAMES OFFIELD : LAND GRANT NO. 700.

Date: July 20th, 1796.
Consideration: 50 shillings for every 100 acres of land.
Amt. of land: 50 acres.
Location: Sullivan County, North Carolina.
Description: A tract of land containing 50 acres lying and being in our county of Sullivan.
Witness: Samuel Ashe, Gov. By his Excellys. Comd. J. Glasgow,Sec.
Registered: Aug. 24, 1797.

(123)

(Page)

(123) STATE OF NORTH CAROLINA :
SAMUEL ASHE, GOV. : LAND GRANT
to : NO. 714.
MICHAEL MALONE :

Date: November 18th, 1796.
Consideration: 50 shillings for every 100 acres of land.
Amt. of land: 200 acres.
Location: Sullivan County, North Carolina.
Description: A tract of land containing 200 acres lying and being in our county of Sullivan on the North side of Holston River.
Witness: Samuel Ashe, Gov. By his Excellys. Comd. J. Glasgow, Sec.
Registered: August 8th, 1797.

---

(124) STATE OF NORTH CAROLINA :
SAMUEL ASHE, GOV. : LAND GRANT
to : NO. 735.
JOHN SHARP :

Date: July 22d, 1797.
Consideration: 50 shillings for every 100 acres of land.
Amt. of land: 717 acres.
Location: Sullivan County, North Carolina.
Description: A tract of land containing 717 acres lying and being in the County of Sullivan as by the plat hereunto annexed doth appear.
Witness: Samuel Ashe, Gov. By his Excellys. Comd. J. Glasgow, Sec.
Registered: August 22d, 1797.

STATE OF NORTH CAROLINA :
SAMUEL ASHE, GOV. : LAND GRANT
to : NO. 736.
JOHN SHARP :

Date: July 28th, 1797.
Consideration: 50 shillings for every 100 acres of land,
Amt. of land: 100 acres.
Location: Sullivan County, North Carolina.
Description: A tract of land containing 100 acres lying and being in our county of Sullivan as by the plat hereunto annexed doth appear.
Witness: Samuel Ashe, Gov. By his Excellys. Comd. J. Glasgow, Sec.
Registered: August 22, 1797.

---

(126) STATE OF NORTH CAROLINA :
SAMUEL ASHE, GOV. : LAND GRANT
to : NO. 733.
JOHN LAUGHLIN :

Date: July 28th, 1797.
Consideration: 50 shillings for every hundred acres of land.
Amt. of land: 29 acres.
Location: Sullivan County, North Carolina.
Description: A tract of land containing 29 acres lying and being in our county of Sullivan on Holston River.

(Page)

STATE OF NORTH CAROLINA :
SAMUEL ASHE, GOV. : LAND GRANT
to : NO. 740
JOHN LEUGHLIN :

Date: Juoy 28th, 1797.
Consideration: 50 shillings for every 100 acres of land.
Amt. of land: 80 acres.
Location: Sullivan County, North Carolina.
Description: A tract of land containing 80 acres lying in the County of Sullivan entered the 10th of March, 1780, as by the plat hereunto annexed doth appear.
Witness: Samuel Ashe, Gov. By his Excellys. Comd.J.Glasgow,Sec.
Registered: August 24th, 1797.

---

(127) JOHN CHRISMAN : to : DEED OF WARRANTY ADAM KISHLER :

Date: August 28th, 1797.
Consideration: $800.00.
Amt. of land: 300 acres.
Description: A tract or parcel of land containing 300 acres and being in Sullivan County on the South Side of Holston River.
Location: Sullivan County, Tennessee.
Executed: In open court by John Chrisman Sullivan County, August Sessions, 1797.
Registered: Aug. 29th, 1797. Test: Mattw. Rhea. C. S. C.

---

(128) JOSEPH COLE : to : DEED OF WARRANTY WM. WADDELL, THOMAS WADDLE, : DANIEL WADLOW, JOHN WADLOW, : SAMUEL WADLOW, :

Date: October 7th, 1791.
Consideratinn: 40 £.
Amt. of land: Not stated.
Location: Sullivan County, Territory of the United States South of the Ohio River.
Description: One certain tract or parcel of land in the sd.County of Sullivan upon Beaver Creek where the heirs now live.
Witnesses: Joseph Wallace, Robert Whitnel.
Proven: By the oath of Joseph Wallace in Sullivan County, December Sessions, 1795. Test: Mattw. Rhea, C. S. C.
Registered: September 1st, 1797.

---

(129) STATE OF NORTH CAROLINA : SAMUEL ASHE, GOV. : to : LAND GRANT ISAACH HICKS. : NO. 731

Date: July 6th, 1797.
Consideration: 50 shillings for every 100 acres of land.
Amt. of land: 133 acres.

Location: Sullivan County, North Carolina.
Description: A tract of land containing 133 acres lying and being in our county of Sullivan.
Witness: Samuel Ashe, Gov. By his Excellys. Comd. J. Glasgow, Sec.
Registered: September 2d, 1797.

---

(130) STATE OF NORTH CAROLINA :
SAMUEL ASHE, GOV. : LAND GRANT
to : NO. 712.
JOHN PARKER :

Date: Nov. 18th, 1796.
Consideration: 50 shillings for every 100 acres of land.
Amt. of land: 140 acres.
Location: Sullivan County, North Carolina.
Description: 140 acres lying and being in our county of Sullivan as by the plat hereunto annexed doth appear.
Witness: Samuel Ashe, Gov. By his Excellys. Comd. J. Glasgow, Sec.
Registered: September 14th, 1797.

STATE OF NORTH CAROLINA :
SAMUEL ASHE, GOV. : LAND GRANT
to : NO. 710.
MICHAEL DEVAULT :

Date: November 18th, 1796.
Consideration: 50 shillings for every 100 acres of land.
Amt. of land: 50 acres.
Location: Sullivan County, North Carolina.
Description: A tract ofland containing 50 acres lying and being in the county of Sullivan.
Witness: Samuel Ashe, Esquire. By his Excellys. Comd.J.Glasgow,Sec.
Registered: September 15th, 1797.

---

(131) GEORGE SIRKLE :
to : DEED OF WARRANTY
HENDRY JONES :

Date: February 17, 1797.
Consideration: 290 £ Virginia money.
Amt. of land: 148 acres.
Location: Sullivan County, Tennessee.
Description: A certain tract or parcel of land containing 148 acres more or less lying and being in the county of Sullivan on the waters of Beaver Creek a branch of Holston River including the plantation where the sd. Sirkle now lives.
Witnesses: John Vance, James West.
Proven: In open Court, Sullivan County, August Sessions, 1797, by the oath of John Vance.
Registered: September 20th, 1797. Test. Mattw. Rhea, C. S. C.

---

(132) JOHN ANDERSON :
to : DEED OF WARRANTY
WILLIAM KEY :

Date: August 28th, 1797.

(Page)

Consideration: $20.00.
Amt. of land: 16 acres.
Location: Sullivan County, Tennessee.
Description: A tract of land containing 16 acres more or less lying and being on the waters of Reedy Creek.
Executed: In open Open I Sullivan County, August term, 1797, by John Anderson. Test: Mattw. Anderson.
Registered: October 6th, 1797.

(133) STATE OF NORTH CAROLINA : LAND GRANT
RICHARD DOBBS SPAIGHT, GOV. : NO. 683.
to
MATHIAS CLENCK

Date: February 4th, 1795.
Consideration: 50 shillings for every 100 acres of land.
Amt. of land: 46 acres.
Location: Sullivan County, North Carolina.
Description: A tract of land containing 46 acres lying and being in our County of Sullivan lying near the survey he now lives on.
Witness: Richard Dobbs Spaight, Gov. By his Excellys. Comd.J.Glasgow,Sec.
Registered: October 15th, 1797.

STATE OF NORTH CAROLINA : LAND GRANT NO. 712.
SAMUEL ASHE, GOV.
to
THOMAS BARTON

Date: Dec. 2d, 1795.
Consideration: 50 shillings for every 100 acres of land.
Amt. of land: 85 acres.
Location: Sullivan County, North Carolina.
Description: 85 acres of land lying and being in the county of Sullivan joining the tract of land where sd. Barton lives.
Witness: Samuel Ashe, Esq. By his Excellency's Comd.J. Glasgow,Sec.
Registered: Nov. 8th. 1797.

(134) JACOB SHULTZ : DEED OF WARRANTY
to
HENRY WAGONER

Date: January 3d, 1797.
Consideration: $250.00.
Amt. of land: 100 acres.
Location: Sullivan County, Tennessee.
Description: A certain tract or parcel of land lying and being between Holston and Watauga River in the County and State aforesaid joining Alexander Torbett and William Scott's lands.
Witnesses: John Scott, Jonathan Bradley.
Proven: In open court Sullivan County May term.
Test: Mattw. Rhea, by Hopkins Lacey.
Registered: November 14th, 1797.

(135) JOHN WADDLE
to
ROBERT YANCEY
Date: August 27th, 1797.

Consideration: 150 £ current money.
Amt. of land: 150 acres.
Location: Sullivan County, Tennessee.
Description: A certain tract or parcel of land lying and being in the County of Sullivan.
Acknowledged: Sullivan County, August Sessions, 1797.in open court by John Waddle.
Test: Mattw. Rhea, C. S.C.
Registered: Nov. 14th, 1797.

---

(136) ABRAHAM BRITTEN, SENR. to NATHANIEL BRITTEN : DEED OF WARRANTY

Date: August 27th, 1797.
Consideration: $240.00.
Amt. of land: 122 acres.
Location: Sullivan County, Tennessee.
Description: A tract or parcel of land lying and being in the County of Sullivan being on the waters of Fall Creek a branch of Holston River.
Test: Abraham Britten, Junr. Arch Taylor.
Registered: November 14th, 1797.

---

(137) ROSANAH STEPHENS to ALEXANDER WHITLOCK : DEED OF WARRANTY

Date: August 28th, 1797.
Consideration: Omitted through error.
Amt. of land: 123 acres.
Location: Sullivan County, Tennessee.
Description: A certain tract or parcel of land containing 123 acres be the same more or less situate lying and being in the county of Sullivan on the waters of Horse Creek it being part of a 400 acres tract of land.
Executed: In open court Sullivan County, August Sessions, 1797, by Rosanah Stephens.
Registered: Nov. 14th, 1797. Test: Mattw. Rhea, C. S. C.

---

(138) JOHN MUSGROVE to MOSES MUSGROVE : DEED OF WARRANTY

Date: Nov. 26th, 1796.
Consideration: $1000.00.
Amt. of land: 126 acres & 20-3/4 acres or 200 -3/4 acres(200-3/4 acres in one place in deed book; 20-3/4 in another place in deed).
Location: Sullivan County, Tennessee.
Description: Two certain tracts or parcels of land lying and being insd. county of Sullivan and state aforesaid the first containing by estimation 126 acres be the same more or less situate on the waters of Beaver Creek and on both sides of the Wataugah road and on the east end of John Sealor's tract of land that he now lives on. the second tract containing 24-3/4 of and acre be the same more

or less situate and lying on the North side of Holston River.
Witnesses: Thomas Major, Henry Hawkins.
Acknowledged: In open court Sullivan County, June Sessions, 1797, by John Musgrove.
Registered: Nov. 15th, 1797. Test: Mattw. Rhea, C. S. C.

STATE OF NORTH CAROLINAA :
(139) SAMUEL ASHE, GOV. : LAND GRANT
to : NO. 2707
WILLIAM BLEVINS :

Date: November 17th, 1796.
Consideration: 50 shillings few every 100 acres of land.
Amt. of land: 200 acres.
Location: Sullivan County, North Carolina.
Description: A tract of land containing 200 acres lying and being in the County of Sullivan on top of the Iron Mountain.
Witness: Samuel Ashe, Gov. By his Excellys Comd. J. Glasgow, Sec.
Registered: December 4th, 1797.

STATE OF NORTH CAROLINA :
SAMEUL ASHE, GOV. : LAND GRANT
to : NO. 1219.
STEPHEN WHEELER :

Date: Feb. 27th, 1796.
Consideration: 50 shillings for every 100 acres of land.
Amt. of land: 400 acres.
Location: Sullivan County, North Carolina.
Description: A tract of land containing 400 acres lying and being in the County of Sullivan on Beaver Dam Creek including the little Bottom.
Witness: Samuel Ashe, Esq. By his Excellys. Comd. J. Glasgow, Sec.
Registered: December 4th, 1797.

---

(140) STATE OF NORTH CAROLINA :
SAMEUL ASHE, GOV. : LAND GRANT
to :
STEPHEN WHEALAR :

Date: December 2d, 1796.
Consideration: 50 shillings for every 100 acres of land.
Amt. of land: 100 acres.
Location: Sullivan County, North Carolina.
Description: One hundred acres of land lying and being in our county of Sullivan on Beaver Dam Creek.
Witness: Samuel Ashe, Gov. By his Excellys. Comd. J. Glasgow, Sec.
Registered: December 4th, 1797.

---

(141) STATE OF NORTH CAROLINA :
SAMUEL ASHE, GOV. : LAND GRANT
to : NO. 761.
JAMES HUGES :

Date: November 17th, 1797.

Consideration: 50 shillings for every 100 acres of land.
Amt. of land: 200 acres.
Location: Sullivan County, North Carolina.
Description: A tract of land containing 200 acres lying and being in the county of Sullivan on the North side of the Holston River and on White Top Creek.
Witness: Samuel Ashe, Gov. By his Ecellys. Comd.J. Glasgow,Sec.
Registered: December 8th, 1797.

STATE OF NORTH CAROLINA :
SAMUEL ASHE, GOV. : LAND GRANT
to : NO. 747
JAMES GREGG :

Date: Nov. 17th, 1797.
Consideration: 50 shillings for every 100 acres of land.
Amt. of land: 500 acres.
Location: Sullivan County, North Carolina.
Description: A tract of land containing 500 acres lying and being in the county of Sullivan on the head of Lick Branch the waters of Watauga.
Witness: Samuel Ashe,Gov. By his Excellys. Comd. J. Glasgow,Sec.
Registered: December 22d, 1797.

---

(142) JAMES YOUNG & JOSEPH YOUNG :
to : DEED OF WARRANTY
SAMUEL CROCKETT, SENR. :

Date: Sepsember 15th, 1797.
Consideration: $500.00
Amt. of land: 213 acres.
Location: Sullivan County, Tennessee.
Description: One certain tract or parcel of land lying and being in the county of Sullivan and State aforesaid being part of a tract of land granted to the heirs of Young, decd.of No. 248 and dated October 23d, granted by Alex Martinlying on the North side of Holston River including the plantation whereon said Crockett now lives.
Witness: William King.
Proven: Sullivan November Sessions, 1797, the execution of the within deed was proven in open court by the oath of William King.
Test: Mattw. Rhea.CS.S. C.
Registered: Dec. 22d, 1797.

JOHN BROWN :
to : DEED OF WARRANTY
JOHN CASEBOLT :

Date: September 18th, 1797.
Consideration: John Casebolt and heirs to pay all taxes.
Amt. of land: One lot containing 1/4 of an acres.
Description: One certain Lott No. 23 in the town of Blountville containing one quarter of an acre.
Witnesses: John Shelby, Isaac Shelby.
Proven: By the oath of John Shelby in Sullivan Nov. Sessions,1797.
Registered: December 22d, 1797. Test: Mattw. Rhea, C.S.C.

JULIUS HACKER :
(144) to : DEED OF WARRANTY
JAMES KING :

Date: October 10th, 1797.
Consideration: $1813.
Amt. of land: 230 acres.
Location: Sullivan County, Tennessee.
Description: A tract or parcel if land situate lying and being in Sullivan County on both dides of Beaver Creek including 190 acres which was conveyed to James King and Com. by deed of conveyance bearing date the 10th of January 1796 and 40 acres be the same more or less.
Witnesses: John Punch, James Walker.
Provent: In open Court Sullivan County November Sessions, 1797 by the oath of John Punch.
Registered: December 22d, 1797. Test: Mattw. Rhea, C. S. C.

****

JOHN FEGAN :
to : DEED OF WARRANTY
WILLIAM TOWSON :

Date: August 23d, 1796.
Consideration: 25 ₤.
Amt. of land: 25 acres.
Location: Sullivan County, Tennessee.
Description: A certain tract of land containing 25 acres be the same more or less situate lying and being in Sullivan County and State aferesaid.
Witness: John Anderson.
Acknowledged: Sullivan County Augustt Sessions, 1796, the execution of the within deed was acknowledged in open court by John Fegan party thereto. Test: Matw. Rhea.C. S. C.
Registered: Décember 22d, 1797.

(145)

ISAAC BRASHEARS :
to : DEED OF WARRANTY
MICHAEL JOHNSON :

Date: August 29th, 1797.
Consideration: $200.00.
Amt. of land: 100 acres.
Location: Sullivan County, Tennessee.
Description: A certain tract or parcel of land containing 100 acres be the same more or less lying and being in the county of Sullivan and State aforesaid on the North side of Holston River on a branch of Reedy Creek.
Witnesses: James Igou, Samuel Brashears,
Executed: In open Court Sullivan November Sessions, 1797, by the oath of James Igou.
Registered: December 22d, 1797. Test: Matw. Rhea, C. S. C.

(Page)
(146) ROBERT ALISON AND JOHN ALISON : to : DEED OF WARRANTY FINLEY ALISON :

Date: Npvember 23d, 1797.
Comsideration: $326.95.
Amt. of land: 2/3 of 196 acres and 96 poles.
Location: Sullivan County, Tennessee.
Description: Two thirdsof 190 acres and 96 poles of land situate lying and being in the state and county aforesaid on the north side of Watauga River.
Acknowledged: In open Court November Sessions, 1797, Sullivan County by Robert Alison and John Alison.
Registered: December 22d, 1797. Test: Matw. Rhea, C. S. C.

---

(147) FINLEY ALISON, : to : DEED OF WARRANTY ROBERT ALISON :

Date: November 24th, 1797.
Consideration: $85.50.
Amtount of land: 2/3 of 12 and 3/4 of and acre & 12 poles of land.
Location: Sullivan County, Tennessee.
Description: Two thirds of 12-3/4 of an acres and 12 poles of land situate lying and being in the state and county aforesaid on the North side of Watauga River.
Acknowledged: In open Court Sullivan November Sessions, 1797, by Finley Alison. Test: Mattw. Rhea, C. S. C.
Registered: December 22d, 1797.

---

(148)
RICHARD BRITTEN : to : DEED OF WARRANTY JOHN SPURGIN :

Date: Ocotber 11th, 1797.
Consideration: $1400.00.
Amt. of land: 484 acres.
Location: Sullivan County, Tennessee.
Description: A certain tract or parcel of land containing 484 acres be the same more or less lying and being in the county aforesaid on the North side of Holston River & on Abbots Branch.
Witnesses: Solomon Jones, John Anderson, William Touron.
Proven: In open Court Sullivan November Sessions 1797, by John Anderson. Test: Mattw. Rhea, C. S. C.
Registered: December 22d, 1797.

---

(149)
JOHN TORBET : to : DEED OF WARRANTY SAMUEL DUNSMORE :

Date: August 15th, 1792.
Consideration: 10 £.
Amt. of land: 3 cares more or less.
Description: A certain tract or parcel of land lying and being in

the sate and county aforesaid between the rivers Wataugah and Holston being a tract of land where the sd. John Torbet now lives and also to join the lands where the sd. Samuel Dunsmore now lives.
Location: Sullivan County, Tennessee.
Witnesses: Alexander Torbet, Samuel King.
Proven: In open Court Sullivan November Sessions 1797 by John Torbet.
Registered: December 23d, 1797. Test: Mattw. Rhea, C. S. C.

RICHARD BASKET :
to : DEED OF WARRANTY
JOHN JONES, JUNR. :

Date: November 27th, 1797.
Condideration: 40 ₤ current money.
Amt. of land: Supposed to be 60 acres.
Location: Sullivan County, Tennessee.
Description: One certain tract or parcel of land lying and being in the County and state aforesaid.
Witnesses: Thomas Rogers, Roger Cudginton, Morris Baker.
Proven: In open Court Sullivan County, November Sessions, 1797, by Morris Baker. Test: Mattw. Rhea, C. S. C.
Registered: December 23d, 1797.

---

(150) ISAAC SHELBY, SHERIFF, :
to : SHERIFF'S DEED
JOHN ALISON :

Date: August 29th, 1797.
Consideration: $23.00.
Purpose of sale: To satisfy a writ of Tire Facies in the suit of Robert Alison against William Hughs from the Superior Court of law of Washington District.
Description: One tract of land granted to William Hughs from North Carolina said tract of land lying in Sullivan County in the District of Washington in the fork of Watauga.
Executed : By Isaac Shelby in Sullivan August Sessions, 1797.
Registered: December 23d, 1797.

ALEXANDER TORBETT :
to : DEED OF WARRANTY
JOHN TORBETT :

Date: September 21, 1797.
Consideration: $150.00.
Amt. of land: 100 acres by estimation.
Location: Sullivan County, Tennessee.
Description: A certain tract or parcell of land lying and being int eht County and State aforesaid containing100 acres by estimation be the same more or less.
Witnesses: Samuel Dunsmore, Joseph Torbet.
Acknowledged: By Alexander Torbett, Sullivan November Sessions, 1797.
Registered: Decem. 23c, 1797. Test: Mattw. Rhea, C. S. C.

(Page)

(152) JOHN TAYLOR : to : DEED OF WARRANTY WM. ROISE :

Date: November 25th, 1797.
Consideration: 200 £ current money.
Amt. of land: 107 acres.
Location: Sullivan County, Tennessee.
Description: A certain tract or parcel of land containing 107 acres be the same more or less lying and being in sd. County of Sullivan including the plantation where the sd. Taylor now lives.
Witnesses: James Wheelar, James Cunningham.
Proven: In open court by the oath of James Wheelar, Sullivan November Sessions, 1797.
Registered: December 24d, 1797. Test: Mattw. Rhea, C. S. C.

---

(153) NICHOLAS STEPHENSON : to : DEED OF WARRANTY THOMAS ROGERS :

Date: August 19th, 1797.
Consideration: 70 £ current money.
Amt. of land: 100 acres.
Location: Sullivan County, Tennessee.
Description: A certain tract or parcel of land containing 100 acres be the same more or less situate lying and being in the county aforesaid on the waters of Kendrick's Creek it being part of a tract of land granted to Charles Gates containing 370 acres.
Witnesses: Nathan Haile, George Crindington.
Proven: By the oath of George Crindington.
Test: Mattw. Rhea, C. S. C.
Registered: December 23d, 1797.

---

(154) NICHOLAS STEPHENSON : to : DEED OF WARRANTY GEORGE CREEDINGTON :

Date: August 19tH, 1797.
Consideration: 200-£-current money.
Amt. of land: 212 acres.
Location: Sullivan County, Tennessee.
Description: A certain tract or parcel of land containing 212 acres be the same more or less lying and being in the County of Sullivan on the waters of Kendricks Creek including the plantation where the sd. Creedington now lives it being part of a tract of land of 373 acres granted by the state of North Carolina to Charles Yeates.
Witnesses: Thomas Rogers, Nathan Haile.
Proven: In open court Sullivan November Sessions, 1797, by Thomas Rogers.
Registered: December 24th, 1797. Test: Matw. Rhea, C.S.C.

(Page)

(155) STATE OF NORTH CAROLINA : LAND GRANT NO. 748.
SAMUEL ASHE, GOV.
to
WILLIAM BEALY

Date: November 17th, 1797.
Consideration: 50 shillings for every 100 acres of land.
Amt. of land: 250 acres.
Location: Sullivan County, North Carolina.
Description: A tract of land containing 250 acres lying and being in the county of Sullivan on the North side of Holston River and Beaver Creek.
Witness: Samuel Ashe, Esq. By his Excellys. Comd. J. Glasgow, Sec.
Registered: January 12th, 1798.

STATE OF NORTH CAROLINA : LAND GRANT NO. 738.
SAMUEL ASHE, GOV.
to
JACOB MOYERS

Date: July 28th, 1797.
Consideration: 50 shillings for every 100 acres of land.
Amt. of land: 140 acres.
Location: Sullivan County, North Carolina.
Description: A tract of land containing 140 acres lying and being in the County of Sullivan.
Witness: Samuel Ashe, Esq. By his Excellys. Comd. J. Glasgow, Sec.
Registered: January 24th, 1798.

(156)

BENJAMIN BEACHBOARD : DEED OF WARRANTY
to
CHRISTOPHER BEAVERLY

Date: January 24th, 1795.
Consideration: 100 L.
Amt. of land: 100 acres.
Location: Sullivan County, North Carolina.
Description: A certain tract of land containing 100 acres lying and being in the county of Sullivan on the waters of Beaver Creek a branch of Holston River including the improvements whereon sd. Beachboard now lives.
Witness: John Vance.
Proven: In Sullivan August Sessions, 1797, by the oath of John Vance.
Registered: January 3d, 1798. Test: Mattw. Rhea, C. S. C.

---

(157) DANIEL BEALOR : DEED OF WARRANTY
to
NICHOLAS BAUGHT

Date: August 26th, 1797.
Consideration: $30.00.
Amt. of land: 10 acres.
Location: Sullivan County, Tennessee.
Description: A certain tract or parcell of land containing 10 acres be the same more or less and being in the county of Sullivan on the

waters of Beaver Creek abranch of Holston River.
Witness: John Vance: Proven: In open Court Sullivan November Sessions, 1797.
Registered: February 8th, 1798.

(158)

DANIEL BEALOR : DEED OF WARRANTY
to
NICHOLAS BARNET

Date: May 19th, 1797.
Consideration: $396.68.
Amt. of land: 106 acres, 7 poles.
Location: Sullivan County, Tennessee.
Description: A certain tract or parcel of land containing 106 acres and 7 poles lying and being in the county of Sullivan on the waters of Beaver Creek a branch of Holston River being the place where the sd. Barney now lives.
Wintess: John Vance, Henery Harklerod.
Pooven: By the oath of John Vance in open Court Sullivan County, November Sessions, 1797.
Registered: February 8th, 1798.

GEORGE EMMERT : DEED OF WARRANTY
to
JACOB EMMERT AND JOHN EMMERT

Date: February 12th, 1798.
Consideratãon: $500.00.
Amt. of land: 150 acres.
Location: Sullivan County, North Carolina.
Description: A certain tract or parcel of land containing 150 acres lying and being in the county of Sullivan on the north side of Wataugah River known by the name of Black Springs e

---

(159) STATE OF NORTH CAROLINA
SAMUEL ASHE, GOV. : LAND GRANT
to : NO. 766
WILLIAM SNODGRASS

Date: November 17th, 1797.
Consideration: 50 shillings for every 100 acres of land.
Amt. of land: 150 acres.
Location: Sullivan County, North Carolina.
Description: A tract of land containing 150 acres lying and being in the County of Sullivan as by the plat hereunto annexed doth appear.
Wtiness: Samuel Ashe, Esq. By his Excellys. Comd. J. Glasgow, Sec.
Registered: Feb. 22d, 1798.
No. 347 entered March 24, 1780. No. 618 June 25th,

(160)

STATE OF NORTH CAROLINA
SAMUEL ASHE, GOV. : LAND GRANT
to : NO. 768.
WILLIAM SNODGRASS

Date: November 22d, 1797.

(Page)

Consideration: 50 shillings for ever 100 acres of land.
Amt. of land: 600 acres.
Location: Sullivan County, North Carolina.
Description: A tract of land containing 600 acres lying and being in our county of Sullivan as by the plat hereutno annexed doth appear.
Witness: Samuel Ashe, Gov. By his Excellys. Comd. J. Glasgow, Sec.
Registered: February 22d, 1798.

---

(161) STATE OF NORTH CAROLINA : LAND GRANT
SAMUEL ASHE, GOV. : NO. 746.
to
JAMES JOHNSTON

Date: November 17th, 1797.
Consideration: 50 shillings for every 100 acres.
Amt. of land: 81 _.
Location: A tract of land containing 81 - lying and being in the county of Sullivan.
Witness: Samuel Ashe, Esq. By his Excellys. Comd. J. Glasgow, Sec.
Entered: April 1, 1780.
Registered: Feb. 24th, 1798.

---

(162) STATE OF NORTH CAROLINA : LAND GRANT
SAMUEL ASHE, GOV. : NO. 757.
to
BATTICE ROLLER

Date: November 17th, 1797.
Consideration: 50 shillings for every 100 acres of land.
Amt. of land: 100 acres.
Location: Sullivan County, North Carolina.
Description: A tract of land containing 100 acres lyong and being in the County of Sullivan on the North side of Holston River.
Witness: Samuel Ashe, Esq/ By his Excellys. Comd. J. Glasgow, Sec.
Registered: March 4th, 1798.

****

(163) STATE OF NORTH CAROLINA : LAND GRANT
SAMUEL ASHE, GOV. : NO. 762.
to
ELIAS SHENLKER

Date: Nov. 17th, 1797.
Consideration: 50 shillings for ev ry 100 acres of land.
Amt. of land: 198 acres.
Location: Sullivan County, North Carolina.
Sullivan County, North Carolina.
Description: A tract of land containing 194 acres lying and being in our county of Sullivan on the N rth side of Holston River.
Witness: Samuel Ashe, Esq. By his Excellys. Comd. J. Glasgow, Sec.
Registered: March 15th, 1798.

---

(164) STATE OF NORTH CAROLINA : LAND GRANT NO. 732.
SAMUEL ASHE, GOV.
to
RICHARD DAVID

Date: July 6th, 1797.
Consideration: 50 shillings for every 100 acres of land.
Amt. of land: 100 acres.
Location: Sullivan County, North Carolina.
Description: A tract of land containing 100 acres lying and being in the County of Sullivan.
Witness: Samuel Ashe, Esq. By Wm. Hill, Secretary.
Registered: March 16th, 1798.

----

(165) WILLIAM HEDRICK : DEED OF WARRANTY
to
MARTIN BOUGHER

Date: December 22d, 1797.
Consideration: 850 £.
Amt. of land: 447 acres.
Location: Sullivan County, Tennessee.
Description: A certain tract or parcel of land containing 447 acres be the same more or less lying and being in the county of Sullivan.
Witnesses: John Vance, James Harris, John Shelby.
Proven: In open court by the oath of John Shelby, Sullivan February sessions, 1798.
Registered: March 28th, 1798. Test: Matw. Rhea, C. S. C.

----

(164) WILLIAM BUCKNER : DEED OF WARRANTY
to
HENERY SULLIVAN

Date: October 16th, 1797.
Consideration: 100 £ current money.
Amt. of land: 300 acres.
Location: Sullivan County, Tennessee.
Description: One certain tract or parcel of land lying and being in the county of Sullivan containing 300 acres on the waters of Horse Creek being the place where the said Buckner now lives.
Witnesses: Robert Easley, John Moody.
Proven: By the oath of Robert Easley, Sullivan November Sessions, 1797.
Registered: March 16th, 1798. Test: Mattw. Rhea, C. S. C.

----

(168) WALTER JOHNSTON : DEED OF WARRANTY
to
MICHAEL DEVALT

Date: February 2d, 1798.
Consideration: $40.00.
Amt. of land: 32-3/4 acres.
Description: A certain tract or parcel of land containing 32-3/4 acres be the same more or less.
Executed: In Sullivan County Febr. Sessions, 1798 in court by Walter Johnston.
Registered: March 29th, 1798. Test: Matw. Rhea, C. S. C.

(Page)
(167) STATE OF NORTH CAROLINA :
SAMUEL ASHE, GOV. : LAND GRANT
to : NO. 1242.
JOHN BROWN :

Date: April 5th, 1797.
Consideration: 50 shillings for every 100 adres of land.
Amt. of land: 225 acres.
Location: Sullivan County, North Carolina.
Description: A tract of land containing 225 acres of land lying and being in our county of Sullivan.
Witness: Samuel Ashe, Esquire. By his Excellys. Comd. J. Glasgow,Sec.
Registered: Samuel Ashe,Gov. By his Excellys. Comd. J. Glasgow,Sec.
Rn

---

(168) STATE OF NORTH CAROLINA :
SAMUEL ASHE, GOV. : LAND GRANT
to : NO. 728
BENJAMIN BROWN :

Date: April 5th, 1787.
Consideration: 50 shillings for every 100 acres of land.
Amt. of land: 100 acres.
Location: Sullivan County, North Carolina.
Description: A tract of land containing 100 acres lying and being in the county of Sullivan on the Beaver Dam Creek.
Witness: Samuel Ashe, Esquire. By his Ex cellys Comd.J.Glasgow,Sec.
Registered: April 4th, 1798.

STATE OF NORTH CAROLINA :
SAMUEL ASHE, GOV. : LANDGRANT
to : NO. 729
BENJAMIN BROWN :

Date: April 5th, 1797.
Consideration : 50 shillings for every 100 acres of land.
Amt. of land: 100 acres.
Location: Sullivan County, North Carolina.
Description: A tract of land containing 100 acres lying and being in our county of Sullivan on the waters of Bever Dam Creek.
Witness: Samuel Ahe, Esq. By his Excellys. Comd.J.Glasgow,Sec.
Registered: April 4th, 1798.

---

(169) STATE OF NORTH CAROLINA :
SAMUEL ASHE, GOV. : LAND GRANT
to : NO. 727
BENJAMIN BROWN :

DATE: April 5th, 1797.
Consideration: 50 shillings for every 100 acres of land:
Amt. of land: 400 acres.
Location: Sullivan County, North Carolina.
Description: A tract of land containing 400 acres lying and being in our county of Sullivan.
Witness: Samuel Ahse, Gov. By his Excellys. Comd.J.Glasgow,Sec.
Registered: April 4th, 1798.

(Page)

(170) STATE OF NORTH CAROLINA :
SAMUEL ASHE, GOV. : LAND GRANT
to : NO. 1245.
STEPHEN WHEALER :

Date: April 5th, 1797.
Consideration: 50 shillings for every 100 acres. of land.
Amt. of land: 100 acres.
Location: Sullivan County, North Carolina.
Description: A tract of land containing 100 acres lying and being in our sd. County of Sullivan on Beaver Dam Creek.
Witness: Samuel Ashe, Gov. By his Excellys. Comd. J. Glasgow, Sec.
Registered: April 4th, 1798.

STATE OF NORTH CAROLINA :
SAMUEL ASHE, GOV. : LAND GRANT
to : NO. 1243.
STEPHEN WHEALER :

Date: April 5th, 1797.
Consideration: 50 shillings for every 100 acres of land.
Amt. of land: 100 acres.
Location: Sullivan County, North Carolina.
Description: A tract of land containing 100 acres lying andbeing in our county of Sullivan on the waters of Beaver Dam Creek.
Witness: Samuel Ashe, Gov. By his Excellys. Comd. J. Glasgow, Sec.
Registered: April 4th, 1798.

---

(171) STATE OF NORTH CAROLINA :
SAMUEL ASHE, GOV. : LAND GRANT
to : NO. 1244.
STEPHEN WHEALER :

Date: April 5th, 1797.
Consideration: 50 shillings for every 100 acres of land.
Amt. of land: 200 acres.
Location: Sullivan County, North Carolina.
Description: A tract of land containing 200 acres lying in sd. County of Sullivan BEAVER DAM CREEK WATERS.

****

DAVID HUGHS, EXECUTOR :
to : EXECUTOR'S DEED OF
HUGH CHRISLY : WARRANTY

Date: February 20th, 1798.
Consideration: $700.00.
Amt. of land: 200 acres.
Description: A certain tract or parcel of land containing 200 acres be the same more or less.
Witness: Johnn Anderson.
Proven: In open Court, Sullivan County, February Sessions by David Hughs.
Registered: April 16th, 1798. Test: Mattw. Rhea, C. S. C.

(172) STATE OF NORTH CAROLINA : SAMUEL ASHE, GOV. to JAS. KING & COMPANY : LAND GRANT NO. 2689

Date: June 6th, 1796.
Consideration: A reward for services rendered.
Grant: Pursuant to an Act of the General Assembly for the releif of the officers and soldiers in the Continental line and for and in consideration of the signal bravery and persevering Zeal of Able Sullivan, a private in the Continental line do give and grant unto Jas. King and Company assignee of the heirs of the sd. Abel Sullivan 640 acres of land in the county of Sullivan on both sides of Beaver Creek adjoining the land of Julius Hackef and the said. James Jing and Company.
Witness: Samuel Ashe, Esq. By his Excellys. Comd. J.Glasgow,Sec.
Registered: May 17th, 1798.

---

(173) STATE OF NORTH CAROLINA : SAMUEL ASHE, GOV. to JOHN BEALOR : LAND GRANT NO. 694.

Date: July 20th, 1796.
Consideration: 50 shillings for every 100 acres of land.
Amt. of land: 200 acres.
Location: Sullivan County, North Carolina.
Description: A tract of land containing 200 acreslying and being in our county of Sullivan.
Witness: Samuel Ashe, Gov. By his Excellys. Comd. J. Glasgow,Sec.
Registered: May 17th, 1798.

---

(174) JAMES OFFIELD to JAMES JORDAN : DEED OF WARRANTY

Date: Februarty 18th, 1798.
Consideration: $500.00.
Amt. of land: 50 acres.
Location: SULLIVAN COUNTY.
Description: One certain tract or parcel of land containing 50 acres on the North abnk of the Holston River.
Acknowledged: By James Offield Sullivan February Sessions, 1798.
Registered: May 22d, 1798. Test: Mat.w. Rhea. C. S. C.

FREDERICK KEELOR to JACOB ELLER : DEED OF WARRANTY

Date: February 14th, 1798.
Consideration: $250.00.
Amt. of land: 150 acres.
Location: Sullivan County, Tennessee.
Description: A certain tract or parcel of land lying and being in sd. County of Sullivan (bounds) containing 150 acres, lying on a small

branch the waters of Holston River.
Witness: Frederick Keilar.
Registered: May 22d, 1798. Test: Mattw. Rhea, C. S.C.
Registered: May 22d, 1798. Test: Mattw. Rhea, C. S. C.

---

(175) STATE OF NORTH CAROLINA : LAND GRANT
SAMUEL ASHE, GOV. : NO. 756.
to
MICHAEL NICELY

Date: November 17th, 1797.
Consideration: 50 shillings for every 100 acres of land.
Amt. of land: 250 acres.
Location: Sullivan County, North Carolina.
Description: A certain tract of land containing 250 acres lying and being in our county of Sullivan on the North side of Holston River.
Witness: Samuel Ashe, Gov. By his Excellys. Comd. J. Glasgow, Sec.
Registered: June 4th, 1798.

---

(176) STATE OF NORTH CAROLINA : LAND GRANT
SAMUEL JOHNSTON, GOV. : NO. 464
to
JACOB NEDEVER

Date: July 10th, 1788.
Consideration: 50 shillings for every 100 acres of land.
Amt. of land: 400 acres.
Location: Sullivan County, North Carolina.
Description: A tract of land containing 400 acres lying and being in our county of Sullivan to include and Island on Holston River opposite to the mouth of Richland Creek.
Witness: Samuel Johnston, Gov. By his Excellys. Comd. J. Glasgow, Sec.
Registered: June 5th, 1798.

STATE OF NORTH CAROLINA : LAND GRANT
SAMUEL JOHNSTON, GOV. : NO. 465.
to
JACOB NEDEAVER

Date: July 10th, 1788.
Consideration: 50 shillings for every 100 acres of land.
Amt. of land: 150 acres
Location: Sullivan County, North Carolina.
Description: A tract of land containing 150 acres lying and being inour county of Sullivan. on both sides of Indian Creek.
Witness: Samuel Johnston, Esquire, By his Excellys, Comd. J.Glasgow,Sec.
Registered: June 5th, 1798.

---

(177) STATE OF NORTH CAROLINA : LAND GRANT
SAMUEL ASHE, GOV. : NO. 773
to
GEORGE BIRDWELL

Date: November 24th, 1797.
Consideration: 50 shillings for every 100 acres of land.

Amt. of land: 375 acres.
Location: Sullivan County, North Carolina.
Description: A tract of land containing 375 acres lying and being in our county of Sullivan on Kindrick's Creek above the Watauga road called the Maple Botton.
Witness: Samuel Ashe, Gov. By his Excellys. Comd. J.Glasgow,Sec.
Registered: June 11th, 1798.

---

(178) STATE OF NORTH CAROLINA :
RICHARD DOBBS SPAIGHT, GOV. : LAND GRANT
to : NO. 758
WILLIAM JOLLEY :

Date: Nov. 17th, 1797.
Consideration: 50 shillings for every 100 acres of land.
Amt. of land: 200 acres.
Location: Sullivan County, North Carolina.
Description: A tract of land containing 200 acres lying and being in our county of Sullivan on the waters of Reedy Creek.
Witness: Samuel Ashe, Gov. By his Excellys. Comd.J.Glasgow,Sec.
Registered: June 11th, 1798.

---

(179) STATE OF NORTH CAROLINA :
RICHARD DOBBS SPAIGHT, GOV. : LAND GRANT
to : NO. 596
WILLIAM JOLLEY :

Date: June 7th, 1793.
Consideration: 50 shillings for every 100 acres of land.
Amt. of land: 100 acres.
Location: Sullivan County, North Carolina.
Description: A tract of land containing 100 acres lying and being in outrcounty of Sullivan.
Witness: Richard Dobbs Spaight, Gov. By his Excellys. Comd. J.Glasgow,Sec.
Registered: June 11th, 1798.

FRANCIS BIRD :
to : DEED OF WARRANTY
:
JESSE HOLLAND :

Date: November 15th, 1797.
Consideration: 100 £ lawful money.
Amt,of land: 50 acres.
Location: Sullivan County, Tennessee.
Description: A certain tract or parcel of land lying and being in the county of Sullivan containing 50,more or less granted to John Holloway bearing date the 9th of August, 1787 being on the waters of the North Fork of the Holston River.
Witnesses: James Gaines, Edmd. Gaines.
Acknowledged: In open court by Francis Bird Sullivan County May Sessions, 1798.
Registered; June 11th, 1798. Test: Mat'w. Rhea, C. S. C.

(Page)

(180) WILLIAM KEY : to : DEED OF WARRANTY JOHN BOWMER :

Date: November 15th, 1793.
Consideration: 50 £ current money.
Amt. of land: 100 acres.
Location: Sullivan County, Tennessee.
Description: A certain tract ofland containing 100 acres be the same more or less lying and being in the county of Sullivan.
Witness: John Anderson.
Acknowledged: In open Court Sullivan County, August Sessions, 1795, by William Key.
Registered: June 14th, 1798. Test: Mattw. Rhea, C. S. C.

---

(181) JOHN SHARP : to : DEED OF WARRANTY DAVID KING :

Date: May 23d, 1797.
Consideration: $500.00.
Amt. of land: 620 acres.
Location: Sullivan County, Tennessee.
Description: A certain plantation or tract of land situate lying and being in Sullivan County and State of Tennessee (bounds) including 620 acres be the same more or less.
Executed: In open Court Sullivan May Sessions, 1797, by John Sharp.
Registered: June 26th, 1798. Test: Mattw. Rhea. C. S. C.

---

(182)

ABRAHAM BRITTEN, SENR. : to : DEED OF WARRANTY JOSEPH COX :

Date: February 13th, 1798.
Consideration: $400.00.
Amt. of land: 100 acres.
Location: Sullivan County, Tennessee.
Description: A certain tract or parcel of land containing 100 acres be the same more or less lying and being in the county of Sullivan and Statoof Tennessee.
Witnesses: John Fegan, Samuel Britton.
Proven: In open Court Sullivan February Sessions, 1798 by the oath of John Fegan.
Registered: June 26th, 1798. Test: Mattw. Rhea. C. S. C.

MORRIS BAKER : to : DEED OF WARRANTY HUMPHREY JONES :

Date: September 2d, 1793.
Consideration: 6 £ lawful money.
Amt. of land: 50 acres.
Location: Sullivan County, ~~Tennessee~~ Territory South of the Ohio.
Description: A certain tract of land lying and being in Sullivan County containing 50 acres more or less.

Witnesses: Daniel Allen, Garret Moore.
Proven: In open Court Sullivan County, November Sessions, 1794, by the oath of Garret Moore.
Registered: June 27th, 1798. Test: Mattw. Rhea, C. S. C.

---

(183) WILLIAM SNODGRASS : to : DEED OF WARRANTY BARNABAS WAGNER :

Date: February 19th, 1798.
Consideration: $163.00.
Amt. of land: 107 ***_______.
Location: Sullivan County, Tennessee.
Description: A certain tract or parcel of land containing 107 _ be the same more or less lying and being in the county aforesaid.
Witness: James Campbell.
Proven: In open Court by the oath of James Campbell Sullivan Feb. Sessions, 1798.
Registered: June 27th, 1798. Test: Matw. Rhea, C. S. C.

---

(184) DANIEL ALLEN : to : DEED OF WARRANTY BENNET JAMES :

Date: October 12th, 1796.
Consideration: $20.00.
Amt. of land: 43 acres.
Location: Sullivan County, Tennessee.
Description: A tract or parcel of land lying and being in Sullivan County on the south side of Holston River.
Witness: Joseph Denton, William Denton.
Acknowledged: In open court Sullivan Feb. Sessions, 1797, by Daniel Allen.
Registered: June 27th, 1798. Test: Mattw. Rhea, C. S. C.

(185)

STATE OF NORTH CAROLINA : SAMUEL ASHE, GOV. : LAND GRANT to : NO. 739 JOHN SHARP :

Date: July 28th, 1798.
Consideration: 50 shillings for every 100 acres of land.
Amt. of land: 100 acres.
Location: Sullivan County, North Carolina.
Description: A tract of land containing 100 acres lying and being in the County of Sullivan,
Wintess: Samuel Ashe, Esq. By William H Hill, D. Sec.
Registered: June 27th, 1798.

---

(186) STATE OF NORTH CAROLINA : RICHARD DOBBS SPAIGHT, GOV. : LAND GRANT to : NO. 672. WALTER KING, JOHN SEVIER, SENR., : JOHN SEVIER, JUNR.

Date: Aug. 17th, 1 795.

Consideration: 50 shillings for every 100 acres of land.
Amt. of land: 1000 acres.
Location: Sullivan County, North Carolina.
Description: A tract of land containing 1000 acres lying and being in our county of Sullivan on the North side of Holston River on Heatons Ridge.
Witness: Richard Dobbs Spaight, Gov. By His Excellys. Comd.J.Glasgow,Sec .
Registered: July 24th, 1798.

---

(186) MOSES CAVIT to WALTER KING, JOHN SEVEIR, SENR. JOHN SEVEIR, JUNR. : DEED OF WARRANTY

Date: March 3d, 1795.
Consideration: 960 £.
Amt. of land: 585 acres.
Location: Sullivan County, Tennessee.
Description: A certain tract or parcel of land containing by estimation 585 acres be the same more or less situated lying and being in sd. County of Sullivan and State aforesaid on the South side of Holston River and including the mouth of Kendrick's Creek and Iron Works.
Witnesses: Thomas Hambleton, John Funk.
Proven: In oepn Court Sullivan County, August Sessions, 1797, by John Funk.
Registered: Julyx 24th, 1798. Test: Mattw. Rhea, C. S. C.

---

(187) JOHN LYON to WALTER KING : DEED OF WARRANTY

Date: January 15th, 1795.
Consideration: $1000.00.
Amt. of land: 176 acres.
Location: Sullivan County, Tennessee.
Description: A certain tract or parcell of land containing estimation 176 acres be the same more or less lying and being in the county and state aforesaid on the south side of Holston River it being two surveys granted to John Cottwell and from him transferred to sd. Lyon.
Witnesses: Thomas Hamilton, ~~John Funk,~~ Jesse Craft.
Proven: In open Court by the oath of John Funk Sullivan August Sessions, 1797.
Registered: July 24th, 1798. Test: Mattw. Rhea, C. S. C.

JOHN WALDRUP to WALTER KING : DEED OF WARRANTY

Date: December 28th, 1795.
Consideration: 300 £ Virginia money.
Amt. of land: 50 acres.
Location: Sullivan County, Tennessee.
Description: A certain tract or parcel of land containingb y estimation 5o acres be the same more or less lying and being in the county of Sullivan on Jarrots Branch being a part of the grant obtained by sd. Waldrup for 247 acres.

Witnesses: Thomas Waldrupe, Jr., Nicholas Mercer.
Proven: In open Court by the oath of Nicholas Mercer, Sullivan County, August Sessions 1797.
Registered: July 24th, 1798.

---

(188) HENRY JONES : to : DEED OF WARRANTY WM. NATGATE :

Date: June 9th, 1798.
Consideration: 240 £ Virginia money.
Amt. of land: 70 acres.
Location: Sullivan County, Tennessee.
Description: A certain tract or parcel of land lying and being in Sullivan County aforesaid (bounds) containing 70 acres be the same more or less.
Witnesses: James Young, Michael Nicely, David Bushong.
Proven: In open court by the oath of David Bushong Sullivan August Sessions, 1790.
Registered: August 24th, 1798. Test: Mattw. Rhea, C. S. C.

---

(189) HENRY JONES : to : DEED OF WARRANTY DAVID BUSHONG :

Date: August 16th, 1798.
Consideration: $633.33.
Amt. of land: 148 acres.
Location: Sullivan County, Tennessee.
Description: A certain tract or parcel of land containing 200 acres be the same more or less lying and being in Sullivan County and State aforesaid.
Witness: Wm. Natgate, [illegible]
Registered: August 24 th, 1798. Test: Mattw. Rhea, C. S. C.

---

(190) JOHN BEALER : to : DEED OF WARRANTY JAMES KING :

Date: March 10th, 1798.
Consideration: 200 £ Virginia money.
Amt. of land: 200 acres.
Location: Sullivan County, Tennessee.
Description: A certain tract or parcel of land containing 200 acres be the same more or less lying and being in Sullivan County and State aforesaie.
Wintess: Archibald Brumley, George Bealer, J. Punch.
Registered: August 27, 1798. Test: Mattw. Rhea, C. S. C.

---

(191) DANIEL BEALOR : to : DEED OF WARRANTY MARTIN MOYERS :

Date: August 26th, 1797.
Consideration: One dollar., [illegible].

Amt. of land: Not stated.
Location: Sullivan County, Tennessee.
Description: A certain tract or parcel of land lying and being in the county of Sullivan on the waters of Beaver Creek a branch of Holston River.
Witness: John Vance.
Proven: In Sullivan August Sessions, 1798 by the oath of John Vance.
Registered: September 28th, 1798. Test: Mattw. Rhea, C. S. C.

STATE OF NORTH CAROLINA :
SAMUEL ASHE, GOV. : LAND GRANT
to : NO. 172.
WILLIAM SNODGRASS :

Date: Nov. 17th, 1797.
Consideration: 50 shillings for every 100 acres of land.
Amt. of land: 400 acres.
Location: Sullivan County, North Carolina.
Description: A tract of land containing400 acres lying and being in the county of Sullivan on the waters of Reedy Creek.Wintess
Witness: Samuel Ashe, Gov. By his Excellys. Comd. J. Glasgow,Sec.
Registered: October 2d, 1798.

---

(192) JOSEPH MOORE :
to : DEED OF WARRANTY
RICHARD GAMMON :

Date: March 3d, 1798.
Consideration: $650.00.
Amt. of land: 260 acres.
Location: Sullivan County, Tennessee.
Description: A certain tract of land containing 260 acres be the same more or less lying and being in the county of Sullivan in the big bent of Holston River on the North side between Blithe & Leapers.
Witnesses: Joseph Taylor, George Gammon.
Proven: In open Court Sullivan County, May Sessions, 1798, by the oath of Joseph Taylor.
Registered: October 2d, 1798. Test: Mattw. Rhea, C. S. C.

---

(193) WILLIAM COPELAND :
to : DEED OF WARRANTY
RICHARD GAMMON :

Date: May 24th, 1798.
Consideration: $150.00.
Amt. of land: 150 acres.
Location: X Sullivan County, Tennessee.
Description: A certain tr act of land containing 150 acres be the same more or less lying and being in the County of Sullivan on Holston River.
Acknowledged: In open Court State of Tennessee, Sullivan County May Sessions, 1798, by William Copeland.
Registered: October 2d, 1798. Test: Mattw. Rhea, C. S. C.

---

(194) STEPHEN EASLEY : to : DEED OF WARRANTY ELIJAH BUTLER :

Date: May 18th, 1798.
Consideration: 100 £ lawful money.
Amt. of land: 300 acres.
Location: Sullivan County, Tennessee.
Description: One tract or parcel of land containing 300 acres on Holston river below Easley upper survey.
Witnesses: Robert Easley, Henry Sullivan.
Proven: In open court by the oath of Robert Easley Sullivan County, May Sessions, 1790.
Registered: October 2d, 1798. Test: Mattw. Rhea, C. S. C.

---

(195) WILLIAM ROSEBERRY : to : DEED OF WARRANTY JOHN STONE :

Date: March 5th, 1798.
Consideration: 200 £ current money.
Amt. of land: 200 acres.
Location: Sullivan County, Tennessee.
Description: A certain tract or parcel of land containing 200 acres be the same more or less situate lying and being in sd. county of Sullivan on Wakers Fork of horse Creek including the plantation where William Rosenberry now lives.
Witnesses: Thomas Jones, John Roberts.
Proven: By the oath of John Roberts in open Court Sullivan August Sessions, 1798.
Registered: October 2d, 1798. Test: Mattw. Rhea, C. S. C.

---

(196) ISAAC SHELBY, SHERIFF : to : SHERIFF'S DEED. JOHN ALLISON :

Date: May 22d, 1798.
Consideration: $403.00.
Amt. of land: 115 acres.
Location: Sullivan County,
Description: That tract and parcel of land former the property of Alexander Torbet containing as aforesaid be the same more or less lying and being in sd. County of Sullivan.
Acknowledged: In open Court by Isaac Shelby Sullivan County May sessions, 1798.
Registered: October 3d, 1798. Test: Mattw. Rhea, C. S. C.

---

(197) JOHN TOPP : to : DEED OF WARRANTY MATTHEW RHEA :

Date: August 18th, 1798.
Consideration: $1000.00.
Amt. of land: 404 acres.
Location: Sullivan County, Tennessee.

Description: One certain tract or parcel of land containing 404 acres lying and being on the North side of Holston River in Sullivan County aforesaid being the place whereon the said Matthew Rhea now lives.
Witness: Henery Harkleroad. John Rhea.
Proven: In open court by the oath of Henery Harkleorad Sullivan County August Sessions, 1798.
Registered: October 3d, 1798. Test: Mattw. Rhea, C. S. C.

---

(198) MC OZBORN : DEED OF WARRANTY
to
PETER MCINTOST

Date: May 15th, 1798.
Consideration: $200.00.
Amt. of land: 6 acres.
Location: Sullivan County, Tennessee.
Description: A certain tract or parcel of land containing estimation six acres situate lying and being in the county of Sullivan and State aforesaid on the south side of Holston River on Jarrett's branch a part of the tract of land sd. Ozborn now lives on.
Wintess: John Hunt.
Proven: In open court by the oath of Juhn Hunt Sullivan County May sessions, 1798.
Registered: October 3d, 1798. Test: Mattw. Rhea, C. S. C.

---

(199) DANIEL HUFFMAN : DEED OF WARRANTY
to
PETER McINTOSH

Date: January 22d, 1798.
Consideration: $1000.00.
Amt. of land: 150 acres.
Location: Sullivan County, Tennessee.
Description: A certain tract of land containing by estimation 150 acres be the same more or less situate lying and being in Sullivan County and State aforesaid the south side of Holston River on Stuarts Branch.
Wintess: Philip Morris.
Recorded: Carter County, August term, 1798.
Registered: October 3d, 1798. Test: George Williams, C. C.

(200 STATE OF NORTH CAROLINA : LAND GRANT
RICHARD DOBBS SPAIGHT, GOV. : NO. 640.
to
DANIEL HUFFMAN

Date: July 9th, 1794.
Consideration: 50 shillings for every 100 acres of land.
Amt. of land: 150 acres.
Location: Sullivan County, North Carolina.
Description: A tract of land containing 150 acres lying and being in our county of Sullivan on the South side of Holston River on Stuarts Branch.
Witness: Richard Dobbs Spaight, Gov. By his Excellys. Comd.
J. Glasgow, Sec.
Registered: October 23d, 1798. Test: Mattw. Rhea, C. S. C.

(Page)
(200) RICHARD GAMMON, JNO ANDERSON, JOHN ANDERSON, JUNR. to WILLIAM NASH. : COMMISSIONER'S DEED

Date: Nov. 27th, 1797.
Consideration: William Nash and heirs to pay all state and other taxes.
Amt. of land: 1/4 and acre.
Location: Blountville, Sullivan County, Tennessee.
Description: A certain lott of ground in the townof Blountville known in a plan of sd. town by Lott No. 13.
Acknowledged: By Richard Gammon and John Anderson in Sullivan November Sessions, 1797.
Registered: Nov. 23d, 1798. Test: Mattw. Rhea, C. S. C.

---

(201) STATE OF NORTH CAROLINA SAMUEL ASHE, GOV. to WILLIAM NASH : LAND GRANT NO. 751

Date: Nov. 17th, 1797.
Consideration: 50 shillings for every 100 acres of land.
Amt. of land: 200 acres.
Location: Sullivan County, North Carolina.
Description: A tract of_ containing 200 acres lying and being in our county of Sullivan on the waters of Reedy Creek.
Witness: Samuel Adhe Gov. By his Excellys. Comd.J. Glasgow,Sec.
Regst. Nov. 23d, 1798.

---

(202) LAURENCE SNAPP to PHILIP SNAPP : DEED OF WARRANTY

Date: November 15th, 1798.
Consideration: $700.00.
Amt. of land: 2 lotts.
Location: Blountville, Sullivan County, Tennessee.
Description: Two lotts together with all buildings and improvements thereon made or erected, marked in a plan of said town ~~knit~~ by Lotts Nos. 17 & 18.
Acknowledged: In open court in Sullivan November Sessions, 1798, by Laurence Snapp.
Regst. Nov. 24th, 1798.

---

(203) HENRY HARKLEROAD & ISAAC SHELBY, EXECUTOR : MEMORANDUM OF AGREEMENT

Date: November 5th, 1798.
Purpose: To render null and void all writings obligatory made or said to be made heretofore between the sd. Henry Harkleroad and Evan Shelby, deceased, concerning 3 claims to certain lands in Disputes between them on Beaver Creek.
Isaac Shelby is executor for Evan Shelby.

(Page)
Witnesses: John Anderson, Martin Harkleroad, Evan Shelby, Alex Dromgoole.
Acknowledged: In open Court Sullivan County November Sessions, 1798, by Henry Harkleroad and Isaac Shelby and also proven by the oaths of Martin Harkleroad and Evan Shelby.
Registered: December 1, 1798. Test: Mattw. Rhea, C. S. C.

---

(204) HENRY HARKLEROAD : and : DEED OF ADJUSTMENT ISAAC SHELBY, EXECUTOR :

Date: November 9th, 1798.
Purpose: To amicably adjust disputes of many years concerning sundry entrys andtracts of land laying on Beaver Creek belowthe sapling grove tract and above the land fromerly owned by Julius Hacker.
Adjustment: Was made by dusputants having agreed to convey to each other certain parts of the disputed land.
Description:of land: Henery Harkleroad for the consideration of 400 acres of land transferred to him by the sd. Isaac Shelby, having relinquished to him certain parts of the said disputed lands by deed bearing date with these presents "All that tract or parcel of the sd. disputed land laying on both sides of Beaver Creek."
P. S. It is agreed before signing that if any of the aforesaid 286 acres of land should be taken from the sd. Shelby any prior claim then that the said Harkleroad that he is not to be accountable to sd. Shelby for any damage on account thereof.
Witnesses: John Anderson, Martin Harkleroad,
Acknowledged: In court Sullivan November Sessions 1798 by Henry Harkleroad and proved by the oath of Martin Harkleroad and Evan Shelby.
Registered: December 1, 1798. Test: Mattw. Rhea, C. S. C.

---

(205) ALEXANDER LAUGHLIN : to :DEED OF WARRANTY JOHN LAUGHLIN :

Date: February 23d, 1798.
Consideration: $500.00.
Amt. of land: 200 acres.
Location: Sullivan County, Tennessee.
Description: A certain tract of land lying and being in the sd. County of Sullivan (bounds) containing 200 acres be the same more or less.
Witness: John McCroskey, Joseph Gray.
Acknowledged: In open court Sullivan November Sessions, 1798.
Test: Mattw. Rhea, C. S. C.
Registered: December 2d, 1798.

(206)

JOHN [illegible] : to : DEED OF WARRANTY DAVID SMITH :

Date: November 17th, 1798.
Consideration: $1140.00.

(Page)

Amt. of land: 285 acres.
Location: Sullivan County, Tennessee.
Description: A certain tract or parcel of land containing 285 acres lying and being in the county of Sullivan and State aforesaid.
Acknowledged: In open court Sullivan November Sessions, 17 98 by John Vance.
Registered: December 2d, 1798. Test: Mattw. Rhea, C. S. C.

---

(208) JOHN HOLLOWAY : DEED OF WARRANTY
to
JAMES KING

Date: October 17th, 1798.
Consideration: $300.33.
Amt. of land: 73 ½ acres.
Location: Sullivan County, Tennessee.
Description: A certain tract or parcel of land situate lying and being on Beaver Creek in the county aforesaid containing 73 ½ acres be the same more or less.
Witnesses: John Goodson, John Punch.
Proven: In open court Sullivan November Sessions, 1798, by the oath of John Punch.
Registered: December 2d, 1798.

---

(207)
JAMES GREGG : DEED OF WARRANTY
to
DAVID HUGHS

Date: August 16th, 1798.
Consideration: 17 £ current money.
Amt. of land: 133 acres.
Location: Sullivan County, Tennessee.
Description: A certain tract or parcel of land lying and being in the county of Sullivan and State of Tennessee (bounds) containing 133 acres.
Acknowledged: Sullivan November Sessions, 1798, in open court by James Gregg.
Registered: December 2d. Test: Mattw. Rhea, C. S. C.

---

(209) JOHN SHELEY, JUNR. : DEED OF WARRANTY
to
CONROD SHARRETL

Date: October 1, 1798.
Consideration: $3917.00.
Amt. of land: 500 acres.
Location: Sullivan County, Tennessee.
Description: A certain tract of land containing 500 acres be the same more or less lying in Sullivan County.
Witnesses: William Natgate, Hen Harkleroad.
Acknowledged: In open court by the oath of William Natgate Sullivan November Sessions, 1798.
Retistered: December 2d, 1798. Test: Mattw. Rhea, C. S. C.

---

(210) JOHN SHELEY

(Page)

(210) JOHN SHELBY, SENR. : DEED OF WARRANTY
to
JOHN SHELBY, JUNR.

Date: September 10th, 1798.
Consideration: $500.00.
Amt. of land: 500 acres.
Location: Sullivan County,
Desdription: A tract or parcel of land lying and being in the County of Sullivan, containing by estimation 500 acres or more.
Witness: Alex. Greer, Isaac Shelby.
Proven: In open court by the oath of William Natgate Sullivan November Sessions, 1798.
Registered: December 2d, 1798. Test: Mattw. Rhea, C.S.C.

---

(211) SAMUEL CARRATHERS : DEED OF WARRANTY
to
JOHN SPURGIN

Date: September 15th, 1798.
Consideration: $300.00.
Amt. of land: 100 acres.
Location: Sullivan County, Tennessee.
Description: A certain tract or parcel of land containing 100 acres be the same moreor less sd. land lying and being in the County of Sullivan on the west fork of Muddy Creek.
Witness: John Tipton, John Williams.
Proven: In open court by the oath of John Williams Sullivan November sessions 1798.
Registered: December 3d, 1798. Test: Mattw. Rhea, C. S. C.

---

(212) JOSEPH MOOR, : DEED OF WARRANTY
to
JOHN SPURGIN

Date: September 18th, 1798.
Consideration: $150.00.
Amt. of land: 12½acres.
Location: Sullivan County, Tennessee.
Description: A certain tract or parcel ofland containing 12½acres be the same more or less lying and being in the county aforesaid on theNorth side of Holston River.
Witness: William Scott, Rubin Barned.
Proven: In open court by the oath of William Scott, Sullivan November Sessions, 1798.
Registered: December 3d, 1798. Test: Mattw. Rhea, C. S. C.

---

(212) JESSE PURDUE : DEED OF WARRANTY
to
WILLIAM BOND

Date: August 19th, 1798.
Consideration: $358.00.
Amt. of land: 300 acres.
Location: Sullivan County, Tennessee.
Description: A certain tract or parcel of land lying and being in

Sullivan County aforesaid on the head spring of Divers Run.
Signed: By Micajah Adams, his lawful authority.
Proven: In open court by Micajah Adams, Sullivan August Sessions, 1798.
Registered: December 4th, 1798. Test: Mattw. Rhea, C. S. C.

---

(213) BARNABAS WAGGONER : to : DEED OF WARRANTY PETER SHELLY :

Date: November 1th, 1798.
Consideration: $400.00.
Amt. of land: 107 acres.
Location: Sullivan County, Tennessee.
Description: A certain piece or parcel of land situate lying and being in Sullivan County aforesaid (bounds) containing 107 acres of land:
Proven: In open Court by the oath of Barnabas Waggoner Sullivan November Sessions, 1798.
Registered: December 4th, 1798.

---

(214) ISAAC SHELBY, EXECUTOR, : & : EXECUTOR'S DEED OF ADJUSTMENT HENRY HARKLEROAD :

Date: Nov. 6th, 1798.
Consideration: 286 acres of land.
Purpose: Whereas disputes have existed for many years between Evan Shelby, deceased, and Henry Harkleroad concerning entrys and tracts of land lying on Beaver Creek in Sullivan County between the Sapling Grove tract and the land formerly owned by Julius Hacker and whereas Isaac Shelby and Henry Harkleroad have mutually agreed to settle these disputes and have agreed to convey to each other certain parts of land. Henry Harkleroad conveys to Isaac Shelby 286 acres of the disputed land lying in Sullivan County on both sides of Beaver Creek. Isaac Shelby conveys to Henry Harkleroad 649 acres of land lying on both sides of Beaver Creek.
Witnesses: JohnAnderson , Martin Harkleroad, Evan Shelby.
Acknowledged: In open Court by Isaac Shelby Sullivan November Sessions, 1798.
Registered: December 4th, 1798. Test: Mattw. Rhea, C. S. C.

---

(215)

ALEXANDER BRAY : to : DEED OF WARRANTY EXECUTOR OF JOSEPH ROOS, DECD. :

Date: October 6th, 1795.
Consideration: 175 L.
Amt. of land: 200 acres.
Location: Sullivan County, Tennessee.
Description: A tract of land containing 200 acres be the same more or less lying and being in the county of Sullivan.
Witness: James Gaines, Samuel Gass.
Proven: By the oath of James Gaines, Sullivan November Sessions, 1795.
Registered: December 4th, 1798. Test: Mattw. Rhea, C. S. C.

(216) STATE OF NORTH CAROLINA : LAND GRANT
SAMUEL ASHE, GOV. : NO. 778.
to
ABRAHAM BRITTON

Date: Nov. 17th, 1797.
Conisderation: 50 shillings for every 100 acres of land.
Amt. of land: 100 acres.
Location: Sullivan County, North Carolina.
Description: A tract of land containing 100 acres lying and being in our county of Sullivan.
Witness: Samuel Ashe. Gov. By his Excellys. Comd.J. Glasgow,Sec.
Registered: January 24th, 1799.

---

(217) STATE OF NORTH CAROLINA : LAND GRANT
SAMUEL ASHE, GOV. : NO. 708.
to
RICHARD BRITTAIN

Date: Nov. 17th, 1796.
Consideration: 50 shillings for every 100 acres of land.
Amt. of land: 400 acres.
Location: Sullivan County North Carolina.
Description: 400 acres of land lying and being ine ourcounty of Sullivan on Abbots. Branch.
Witness: Samuel Ashe, Gov. By his Excellys. Comd. J. Glasgow,Sec.
Registered: January 24th, 1797.

---

(218) STATE OF NORTH CAROLINA : LAND GRANT
RICHARD DOBBS SPAIGHT,GOV. : NO. 634.
to
ANDREW MCCLALAND

Date: July 9th, 1794.
Consideration: 50 shillings for every 100 acres of land.
Amt. of land: 400 acres.
Location: Sullivan County, North Carolina.
Description: A tract of land containing 400 acres be the same more or less lying and being in our county of Sullivan on the South Side of the North Fork .
Witness: Richard Dobbs Spaight, Gov. By his Excellys. Comd.J/Glasgow Secretary.
Registered: Feb. 22d, 1799.

---

(219) STATE OF NORTH CAROLINA : LAND GRANT
SAMUEL ASHE, GOV. : NO. 716
to
ELIJAH CROSS

Date: December 2d, 1796.
Consideration: 50 shillings for every 100 acres of land.
Amt. of land: 100 acres.
Location: Sullivan Connty, North Carolina.
Description: 100 acres of land lying and being in our county of Sullivan.
Witness: Samuel Ashe, Gov. By his Excellys. Comd. J. Glasgow,Sec
Retistered: Feb. 22d, 1799.

(Page)

STATE OF NORTH CAROLINA :
SAMUEL ASHE, GOV. : LAND GRANT
to : NO. C 722
SOLIMON SMALLING :

Date: December 2d, 1796.
Consideration: 50 shillings for every 100 acres of land.
Amt. of land: 100 acres.
Location: Sullivan County, North Carolina.
Description: 100 acres of land lying and being in the county of Sulliv an.
Witness: Samuel Ashe, Esq. By his Excellys. Comd. J. Glasgow,Sec.
Registered: Feb. 22d, 1799.

---

(220) STATE OF NORTH CAROLINA :
SAMUEL ASHE, GOV. : LAND GRANT
to : NO. 762.
PHILIP FOUST :

Date: ____ 17th, 1797.
Consideration: 50 shillings for every 100 acres of land.
Amt. of land: 47 acres.
Location: Sullivan County, North Carolina.
Description: A tract of land containing47 acres lying and being in the county of Sullivnn on the north side of Holston River.
Witness: Samuel Ashe, Gov. By his Exwellys. Comd. J. Glasfow,Sec.
Registered: Feb. 22d, 1799.

---

(221) STATE OF NORTH CAROLINA :
SAMUEL ASHE, GOV. : LAND GRANT
to : NO. 741.
JACOB YORK :

Date: August 12th, 1797.
Consideration: 50 shillings for every 100 acres of land.
Amt. of land: 142 acres.
Location: Sullivan County, North Carolina.
Description: A tract of land containing 142 acres lying and being in the county of Sullivan.
Witness: Samuel Ashe, Gov. By his Excellys. Comd.J. Glasgow, Sec.
Registered: Feb. 22d, 1797.

---

(222) STATE OF NORTH CAROLINA :
SAMULE ASHE, GOV. : LAND GRANT
to : NO. 730.
WILLIAM GOAD :

Date: July 6th, 1797.
Consideration: 50 shillings for every 100 acres of land.
Amt. of land: 300 acres.
Location: Sullivan County, North Carolina.
Description: A tract of land containin300 acres lying and being in the County of Sullivan on Walkers Fork.
Witness: Samuel Ashe. Gov. By his Excellys. Comd. J. Glasgow,Sec.
Registered: Feb. 22d, 1799.

(Page)

STATE OF NORTH CAROLINA :
SAMUEL ASHE, GOV. : LAND GRANT
to : NO. 750.
JOHN FOUST :

Date: Nov. 17th, 1796.
Consideration: 50 shillings for every 100 acres of land.
Amt. of land: 8 acres.
Location: Sullivan County, North Carolina.
Description: A tract of land containing 8 acres lying and being the county of Sullivan on the waters of Reedy Creek.
Registered: Feb. 22d, 1799.

---

(223) STATE OF NORTH CAROLINA :
RICHARD DOBBS SPAIGHT, GOV. : LAND GRANT
to : NO. 648.
ALEXANDER FORD :

Date: December 5th, 1794.
Consideration: 50 shillings for every 100 acres of land.
Amt. of land: 100 acres.
Location: Sullivan County, North Carolina.
Description: A tract of land containing 100 acres lying and being in our county of Sullivan.
Witness: Richard Dobbs Spaight, Gov. By J. Glasgow, Sec.
Registered: December 5th, 1794.

(224)

JOHN BEALOR :
to : DEED OF WARRANTY
EDWARD RICHARTS :

Date: November 23d, 1798.
Consideration: $250.00.
Amt. of land: 60 acres.
Location: Sullivan County, Tennessee.
Description: A certain tract or parcel of land containing 60 acres more or less lying in the county of Sullivan & State of Tennessee on the waters of Beaver Creek a branch of Holston River known by the name of Petree's tract a part of the east end of John Bealor's old patent.
Witnesses: Henry Harkleroad, Sullivan County, February Sessions, 1797.
Registered: Feb. 23d, 1799. Test: Mattw. Rhea, C. S. C.

JOSEPH OWEN :
to : DEED OF WARRANTY
NATHAN OWEN :
Date: Feb. 27th, 1797.
Consideration: $120.00.
Location: Sullivan County, Tennessee.
Description: A certain parcel of land containing 197 acres be the same more or less sd. land lying and being in the county and state aforesaid.
Witnesses: David Hughes, John Williams.
Registered: Feb. 23d, 1797. Test: Mattw. Rhea, C. S. C.

(Page)
(226) JOHN ROLLER : QUIT CLAIM DEED
to
BATTICE ROLLER :

Date: Feb. 18th, 1799.
Consideration: 150.00.
Amt. of land: 146 acres.
Location: Sullivan County, Tennessee.
Description: Said land lying and being in the county aforesaid (bounds) containing 146 acres.
Witnesses: John Anderson, Peter McIntosh.
Acknowledged: By John Roller in Sullivan County, February Sessions. 1799.
Registered: Feb. 24th, 1799.

BATTICE ROLLER :
(227) to : QUIT CLAIM DEED
JOHN ROLLER :

Date: February 18th, 1799.
Consideration: $200.00.
Amt. of land: 254 acres.
Location: Sullivan County, Tennessee.
Description: A certain tract of land containing 254 acres lying in the county of Sullivan.
Witnesses: John Anderson, Peter McIntosh.
Acknowledged: In open court Sullivan County Feb. Sessions, 1799, by Battice Roller.
Registered: Feb. 24th, 1799. Test Mattw. Rhea

STATE OF NORTH CAROLINA :
SAMUEL ASHE, GOV. : LAND GRANT
to : NO. 723.
GEORGE CRUMLEY :

Date: December 2d, 1796.
Consideration: 50 shillings for every 100 acres of land.
Amt. of land: 34 acres.
Location: Sullivan County, North Caolina.
Description: 34 acres of land lying and being in the county of Sullivan.
Witness: Samuel Ashe, Gov. By his Excellys. Comd. J. Glasgow, Sec.
Registered: Feb. 25th, 1799.

---

(228) JOHN BOWIE :
to : DEED OF WARRANTY
ROBERT McCULLEY :

Date: February 15th, 1799.
Consideration: 150 £ current money.
Amt. of land: 195 acres.
Location: Sullivan County, Tennessee.
Description: A certain tract of land or part of my tract of land on which I live 195 acres being in Sullivan County,
Acknowledged: By John Bowie Sullivan County, Febr. Sessions, 1799.
Registered: Feb. 25th, 1799. Test: Mattw. Rhea, C. S. C.

---

(229) JOHN KING : to : DEED OF WARRANTY THOMAS KING :

Date: February 18th, 1799.
Consideration: $100.00.
Amt. of land: 28 acres.
Location: Sullivan County, Tennessee.
Description: A certain parcel of land lying and being on the North side of Wataga in the county of Sullivan.
Acknowledged: In open Court by John King Sullivan Febr. Sessions, 1799.
Registered: Feb. 25th, 1799. Test: Mattw. Rhea, C. S. C.

---

(230) JAMES KING : to : DEED OF WARRANTY JOHN KING :

Date: Feb. 18th, 1794.
Consideration: $100.00.
Amt. of land: 25 acres.
Location: Sullivan County, Tennessee.
Description: A certain parcel of land lying and being on the North side of Wataugha River in the county aforesaid being part of a tract of land whereon the said James King now lives.
Acknowledged: In the open Court by James King Sullivan Febr. Sessions, 1799.
Registered: Feb. 25th, 1799. Test: Mattw. Rhea, C. S. C.

---

(229) THOMAS KING : to : DEED OF WARRANTY JOHN KING :

Date: Feb. 18th, 1799.
Consideration: $100.00.
Amt. of land: 17 acres.
Location: Sullivan County, Tennessee.
Description: A certain parcel of land lying and being inthe county aforesaid on the north side of Watauga River being part of the tract whereon the sd. King now lives.
Acknowledged: Sullivan County, February Sessions, 1799, by Thomas King.
Registered: Feb. 25th, 1799. Test: Mattw. Rhea, C. S. C.

---

(231) JOHN KING : to : DEED OF WARRANTY JAMES KING :

Date: Feb. 18th, 1799.
Consideration: $70.00.
Amt. of land: 3-1/2 acres, 30 poles.
Location: Sullivan County, Tennessee.
Description: A certain parcel of land lying and being in Sullivan County on the North side of Wataga River being part of the land the sd. John King purchased from Thomas King and joining the lands of the sd. James King.

(Page)

Proven: In open court Sullivan February Sessions, 1799, by John King.
Test: Feb. 25th, 1799. Mattw. Rhea, C. S. C.

---

(232) ANDREW GREER & JOHN SEVIER : to : DEED OF WARRANTY ISAAC SHELBY :

Date: December 27th, 1798.
Consideration: $200.00.
Amt. of land: 200 acres.
Location: Sullivan County, Tennessee.
Description: All that tract or parcel of land situate in the sd. County of Sullivan on the North side of Holston River known by the name of the Sugar Hollow, beginning on the bank of the Holston River.
Witnesses: Joseph Sevier, Chatty Sevier.
Oath Made: By Chatty Sevier Sullivan County February Sessions, 1799, the third day of Sessions that John Sevier acknowledged deed before her & Greer also acknowledged execution of same.
Registered: May 8th, 1799. Test: Mattw. Rhea, C. S. C.

---

(233) JACOB NEDEAVER : to : DEED OF WARRANTY JOHN FRUTZMAN :

Date: May 8th. 1799.
Consideration: $2000.00.
Amt. of land: 550 acres.
Location: Sullivan County, Tennessee.
Description: Two certain tracts of land containing 550 acres be the same more or less lying and being in the county of Sullivan being a grant to said Jacob Nedeaver No. 464 to include an Island in the Holston River opposite to the mouth of Richland Creek, then beginning in grant No. 455 granted to sd. Nedeaver containing 150 acres on both sides of Indian Creek land including a fine mill Seat thereon and spring on Dry Run.
Witnesses: Isaac Shelby, Mary Shelby.
Proven: In open court Sullivan County, Febr. Sessions, 1799, by Isaac Shelby.
Registered: May 8th, 1799. Test: Mattw. Rhea, C. S. C.

---

(234) WILLIAM HEDRICK & JOHN CARBAGE : to : DEED OF WARRANTY JOHN MUSGROVE :

Date: May 5th, 1797.
Consideration: 70 £ current money.
Amt. of land: 39 acres, 27 poles.
Location: Sullivan County, Tennessee.
Description: A certain parcel of land lying and being in Sullivan County (bounds) containing 39 acres, 27 poles, be the same more or less.
Witness: John Vance.
Proven: In open court by the oath of John Vance.
Registered: May 9th, 1797. Test: Mattw. Rhea, C. S. C.

(Page)
(235) JOHN SHELBY, JUNR. :
to : DEED OF WARRANTY
ALEXANDER MCCRABB :

Date: Feb. 2d, 1797.
Consideration: Subject to state and other taxes.
Amt. of land: LOtt. No. 19 in the town of Blountville.
Description: A certain lott of ground in the town of Blountville marked and numbered in a plan of the said town by LOtt. No. 19, in Sullivan County, Tennessee.
Acknowledged: In open court by John Shelby, Junr. Sullivan County August Sessions, 1798.
Registered: May 15th, 1799. Test: Mattw. Rhea, C. S. C.

JOHN ANDERSON, JOSEPH WALLACE, :
JOHN ANDERSON, COMMISSIONERS : COMMISSIONER'S DEED
to :
ALEX MCCRABB :

Date: May 21st, 1798.
Consideration: Clear and discharged from all incumbrances except taxes.
Amt. of land: A certain lott of ground.
Location: Blountville, Sullivan County, Tennessee.
Description: A certain lott of ground in the town of Blountville marked Lott No. 12.
Proven: In open court by John Anderson, Sullivan November Sessions, 1798.
Registered: May 15th, 1799. Test: Mattw. Rhea, C. S. C.

---

(236) GEORGE RUTLEDGE, RICHARD GAMMON, :
JOHN ANDERSON, COMMISSIONERS, : COMMISSIONER'S DEED
to :
JAMES RHEA :

Date: November 21, 1798.
Consideration: Subject to such taxes as Lotts are subject now or may be hereafter.
Amt. of land: A certain lott.
Location: Blountville, Sullivan County, Tennessee.
Description: A cetyain lott of ground in the said town of Blountville marked and numbered in a plan of saif town by Lott No. 14.
Acknowledged: In open court by Richard Gammon and John Anderson Sullivan County, February Sessions, 1799.
Registered: May 17th, 1799. Mattw. Rhea, C. S. C.

STATE OF NORTH CAROLINA :
(237) SAMUEL ASHE, GOV. : LAND GRANT
to : NO. 750.
ANDREW CROCKETT

Date: November 17th, 1797.
Consideration: 50 shillings for every 100 acres of land.
Amt. of land: 149 acres.
Location: Sullivan County, North Carolina.

(Cont.)
Description: A tract of land containing 140 acres lying and being in our county of Sullivan.
Witness: Samuel Ashe, Esq. By his Excellys. Comd. J. Glasgow, Sec.
Registered: May 18th, 1799.

---

(238) STATE OF NORTH CAROLINA : LAND GRANT
SAMUEL ASHE, GOV. : NO. 759
to
JONATHAN OWEN

Date: March 17th, 1797.
Consideration: 50 shillings for every 100 acres of land.
Amt. of land: 40 acres.
Location: Sullivan County, North Carolina.
Description: A tract of land containing 40 acres lying and being in the county of Sullivan on the north side of Holston River.
Witness: Samule Ashe, Esq. By his Excellys. Comd. J. Glasgow, Sec.
Registered: May 23d, 1797.

---

(239) CHRISTLEY BEALER : DEED OF WARRANTY
to
JOHN HICKMAN

Date: Feb. 3d, 1798.
Consideration: $133-1/3
Amt. of land: 40 acres more or less.
Location: Sullivan County, Tennessee.
Description: A certain tract or parcel of land containing 40 acres more or less lying and being in Sullivan County and State of Tennessee on the waters of Beaver Creek.
Witnesses: James King, John Punch.
Proven: In open court Sullivan Sessions, 1798 by the oath of James King.
Registered: June 3d, 1799. Test: Mattw. Rhea, C. S. C.

---

(240) STATE OF NORTH CAROLINA : LAND GRANT
SAMUEL ASHE, GOV. : NO. 691
to
ROBERT GRAY, JUNR.

Date: December 9th, 1795.
Consideration: 50 shillings for every 100 acres of land.
Amt. of land: 200 acres.
Location: Sullivan County, North Carolina.
Description: A tract of land containing 100 acres lying and being in the county of Sullivan.
Witness: Samuel Ashe, Esq. By his Excellys. Comd. J. Glasgow, Sec.
Registered: June 7th, 1799.

STATE OF NORTH CAROLINA : LAND GRANT
SAMUEL JOHNSTON, GOV. : NO. 474.
to
MATTHIAS LITTLE

Date: July 10th, 1788.
Consideration: 50 shillings for every 100 acres of land.

Amt. of land: 100 acres.
Location: Sullivan County, Tennessee.
Description: A tract of land containing 100 acres lying and being in our county of Sullivan.
Witness: Samuel Johnston, Gov. By his Excellys. Comd.J.Glasgow,Sec.
Registered: June 7th, 1799.

(241)

JOHN TAP :
to : DEED OF WARRANTY
ANDREW CROCKETT :

Date: August 18th, 1798.
Consideration: $600.00.
Amt. of land: 300 acres.
Location: Sullivan County, Tennessee.
Description: A certain tract or parcel of land containing 300 acres lying and being in the said county of Sullivan on the North side of Holston River being the land on which the sd. Andrew Crockett now lives.
Witnesses: Henry Harkleroad, Daniel Troxel.
Registered: June 7th, 1799. Test Mattw. Rhea, C. S. C.

(242) STATE OF NORTH CAROLINA :
RICHARD DOBBS SPAIGHT, GOV. : LAND GRANT
to : NO. 675.
JOHN HALL :

Date: Nov. 12th, 1795.
Consideration: 50 shillings for every 100 acres of land.
Amt. of land: 135 acres.
Location: Sullivan County, North Carolina.
Description: A tract of land containing 135 acres lying and being in our county of Sullivan on the South side of Holston River.
Witness: Richard Dobbs Spaight, Gov. By his Excellys. Comd. J. Glasgow, Sec.
Registered: June 7th, 1799.

(243) HENRY HARKLEROAD :
to : DEED OF WARRANTY
GEORGE EMERT

Date: November 20th, 1798.
Consideration: $4000.00.
Amt. of land: 430 acres.
Location: Sullivan County, Tennessee.
Description: A certain tract or parcel of land containing 430 acres more or less lying in the County of Sullivan and State aforesaid on Beaver Creek a branch of Holston River.
Witnesses: Martin Harkleroad, Adam Hickman.
Acknowledged: In open Court Sullivan County, November Sessions, 1798 by Martin Harkleroad.
Registered: June 17th, 1799. Test: Mattw. Rhea, C. S. C.

(244) JOHN HAKK : to : DEED OF WARRANTY HENRY STALLER :

Date: January 15th, 1799.
Consideration: $157.90.
Amt. of land: Not stated.
Location: Sullivan County, Tennessee.
Description: A certain tract or parcel of land lying and being the county aforesaid.
Witnesses: John Anderson, Solomon Jones.
Proven: In open court by the oath of John Anderson, Sullivan County, M May Sessions, 1797.
Registered: June 17th, 1799. Test: Mattw. Rhea, C. S. C.

ROBERT SAMUEL BRASHERS : to : DEED OF WARRANTY SAMUEL BRASHERS :

Date: February 24th, 1798.
Consideration: $100.00.
Amt. of land: 230 acres.
Location: Not stated.
Description: A certin tract or parcel of land containing 230 acres be the same more or less lying and being int he State and County aforesaid.
Note: Person selling land liv s in Knox County, Purchaser lives in Sullivan County, both of Tennessee.
Witnesses: Wm. Anderson, John Anderson.
Proven: In open court by the oath of John Anderson, Sullivan May Sessions, 1799. Test: Mattw. Rhea, C. S. C.
Registered: June 17th, 1799.

ANTHONY AGEE :
(245) to : DEED OF WARRANTY
MARTIN WADDLE :

Date: May 31st, 1798.
Consideration: 150 £.
Amt. of land: 299 acres.
Location: Sullivan County, Tennessee.
Description: A certain tract or parcel of land containing 299 acres be the same more or less lying and being in the county of Sullivan and state aforesaid on the south side of Reedy Creek joining Pendleton's patent line.
Witnesses: Ambrose Gaines, Sam'l Moore.
Proven: In open court by the oath of Ambrose Gaines, Sullivan May Sessions, 1797.
Registered: June 17th, 1799. Test: Mattw. Rhea, C. S.C.

---

(246) PHILIP HORN : to : DEED OF WARRANTY JAMES DAWSON

Date: November 23d, 1798.
Consideration: $150.00.
Amt. of land : 103 acres.
Location: Sullivan County, Tennessee.
Description: All that tract or parcel of land lying in Sullivan

County and State of Tennessee (bounds) containing 103 acres be the same more or less it being part of 109 acres which North Carolina granted to John Coughron August 9th, 1788, who granted the same to John Long who granted the same to Walter King and David Ross who granted the same to William Smith who deeded the same to William Horn.
Witnesses: William Dawson, Aaron Dawson, Ben Scyphers.
Proven in open court by the oath of Aaorn Dawson, Sullivan County May Sessions, 1799.
Registered: June 17th, 1799. Test: Mattw. Rheam C. S. C.

---

(248) HENRY HARKLEROAD : DEED OF WARRANTY
to
JACOB SUSONG

Date: Novembdr 20th, 1798.
Consideration: 10 shillings per acre.
Description: A certain tract or parcel of land containing 455 acres lying in the County of Washington and State of Virginia on the waters of Beaver Creek a branch of Holston River known by the name of of the barron spart of the tract of land known by the name of the Sapling Grove tract.
Witnesses: Philip Snapp, George Emert.
Acknowledged: In open court by Henry Harkleroad, Sullivan November Sessions, 1799.
Registered: June 17th, 1798. Test: Mattw. Rhea, C. S. C.

---

(249) FRANCIS H. GAINS, DEPUTY SHERIFF, : DEPUTY SHERIFF'S DEED.
to
JOHN SEVEIR

Date: May 22d, 1799.
Consideration: $12.54.
Amt. of land: 100 acres.
Location: Sullivan County, Tennessee.
Description: A certain tract of land lying and being in Sullivan County aforesaid containing 100 acres.
Purpose: to satisfy cost in the suit of the state against Jacob Ellom.
Witness: Walter King, John Clark, Mattw. Rhea.
Acknowledged: By Francis H. Gains, Deputy Sheriff, Of Sullivan County May Session, 1799.
Registered: July 8th, 1799. Test: Mattw. Rhea, C. S. C.

---

(250) STATE OF NORTH CAROLINA : LAND GRANT
SAMUEL ASHE, GOV. : NO. 724
to
WILLIAM WIRICK

Date: December 2d, 1796.
Consideration: 50 shillings for every 100 acres of land.
Amt. of land: 50 acres.
Location: Sullivan County, North Carolina.
Description: 50 acres of land lying and being in our county of Sullivan including the plantation where he now lives.
Witness: Samuel Ashe, Esq. By his Excellys. Comd.J.Glasgow, Sec.

(Page)
(251) JAMES YOUNG : to : DEED OF TRUST JOHN SHARP :

Date: August 20th, 1799.
Consideration: $900.00 with lawful interest for the same on or before the first of August next together with such sum or sums of money as the sd. John Sharp may be put to respecting such land. The land to stand security as a mortgage for the payment of sd. money.
Location: Sullivan County, Tennessee.
Description: A certain plantation or tract of land situate lying and being in Sullivan county aforesaid.
Acknowledged: In open court by James Young Sullivan County, August Sessions, 1799.
Registered: August 27th, 1799.

---

(252) HENRY HAUCK : to : DEED OF WARRANTY ELISHA HARBOUR :

Date: May 2d, 1799.
Consideration: 80 L.
Amt. of land: 100 acres.
Location: Sullivan County, Tennesse.
Description: A certain tract of and containing 100 acres lying and being in the county aforesaid.
Acknowledged: In open court Sullivan May Sessions, 1799, by Henry Mauk.
Registered: August 27th, 1799. Test: Matt / Rhea, C. S. C.

---

(253) STATE OF NORTH CAROLINA : SAMUEL ASHE, GOV. : LAND GRANT to : NO. 754. NATHAN LEWIS :

Date: November 17th, 1797.
Consideration: 50 shillings for every 100 acres of land.
Amt. of land: 100 acres.
Location: Sullivan County, North Carolina.
Description: A tract of land containing 100 acres lying and being in the county of Sullivan on Holston River.
Witness: Samuel Ashe, Gov. By his Excellyse Comd.J.Glasgow,Sec.
Registered: September 22d, 1799.

---

(252) CHARLES KEESEE : to : DEED OF WARRANTY HENRY VARNER :

Date: May 22d, 1799.
Consideration: $400.00.
Amt. of land: 200 acres.
Location: Sullivan County, Tennessee.
Description: A certain tract or parcel of land situate lying and being in Sullivan County and State of Tennessee.
Registered: August 28th, 1799.

(254

(Page)

(254) JAMES KING : DEED OF WARRANTY
to
JOHN RHEA

Date: Feb. 11th, 1799.
Consideration: $750.00.
Amt. of land: 200 acres.
Location: Sullivan County, Tennessee.
Description: A certain tract of land containing 200 acres lying and being in the county of Sullivan on the North side of Holston River at the mouth of Beaver Creek.
Witness: Richard Gammon, James Rhea.
Acknowledged: In open court Sullivan County August Sessions, 1799 by James King.
Registered: September 25th, 1799. Test: Mattw. Rhea, C.S.C.

NATHAN LEWIS : DEED OF WARRANTY
to
(255) JOHN RHEA

Date: July 25th, 1799.
Consideration: $400.00.
Amt. of land: 100 acres.
Location: Sullivan County, Tennessee.
Description: A certain tract or parcel of land containing 100 acres lying and being in the county of Sullivan on Holston River.
Witnesses: Samuel Rhea, James Rhea.
Acknowledged: In open court by Nathaniel Lewis August Sessions, 1799.
Registered: Sept. 25th, 1799. Test: Mattw. Rhea, C. S. C.

---

(256) JOHN TIPTON : DEED OF WARRANTY
to
PHILIP SNAP

Date: August 15th, 1799.
Consideration: $30.00
Amt. of land: A lott.
Location: Blountville, Sullivan County, Tennessee.
Description: A certain lott of ground in the town of Blountville known by the name of No, 2 half acre lot.
Acknowledged: In open court by John Tipton Sullivan County August Sessions, 1799.
Registered: October 12th, 1799. Test: Mattw. Rhea, C. S. C.

---

(257) JOHN CASEBOLT : DEED OF WARRANTY
to
ELKANAH DULANEY

Date: August 7th, 1797.
Consideration: $85.00.
Amt. of land: A lott.
Location: Blountville, Sullivan County, Tennessee.
Description: All that tract or parcel of land lying and being in the county of Sullivan and town of Blountville known by the name of Brown's lott N. 23.

(Page)

Witnesses: Nath Taylor, Alex Greer, Andrew Greer.
Proven: In open court by the oath of Andrew Greer Sullivan County August Sessions, 1799.
Registered: October 12th, 1799. Test: Mattw. Rhea, C. S. C.

---

(259) PETER FEAR : to : DEED OF WARRANTY MATTHIAS FEAR :

Date: June 11th, 1799.
Consideration: $110.00.
Amt. of land: 66 acres.
Description: A certain tract or parcel of land containing 66 acres be the same more or less lying and being in the county of Sullivan on the waters of Beaver Creek adjoining the plantation of William Snodgrass.
Witnesses: George Rutledge, William Snodgrass.
Proven: In open court by the oath of William Snodgrass Sullivan August Sessions, 1799.
Registered: October 12th, 1799. Test: Mattw. Rhea, C. S. C.

THOMAS HUGHS : to : DEED OF WARRANTY SIMON HOLT :

Date: August 21st, 1799.
Consideration: 20 £ current money.
Amt. of land: 100 acres.
Location: Sullivan County, Tennessee.
Description: A certain plantation or tract of land lyingand being in Sullivan County (bounds) containing 100 acres more or less.
Acknowledged: In open court by Thomas Hughs Sullivan August Sessions, 1799.
Explanation: This deed made to correct error in deed dated Sept.24, 1793, in running the lines of which sd. line an error has been commited.
Registered: Oct. 10th, 1799. Test: Mattw. Rhea, C. S. C.

---

(260) JACOB EMERT : to : DEED OF WARRANTY JOHN EMERT :

Date: February 20th, 1799.
Consideration: $500.00.
Amt. of land: 250 acres.
Location: Sullivan County, Tennessee.
Description: Two certain tracts or parcels of land in sd. County of Sullivan lying on the North side of Holston River known by the name of the black spring containing 250 acres.
Witnesses: Michael Montgomery, Henry Harkleroad.
Acknowledged: In open court by Jacob Emert Sullivan County, Feb. sessions, 1799.
Registered: Novemr. 12th, 1799.
Test: Mattw. Rhea, C. S. C.

MOSES MUSGROVE
to
JOHN EGAN & JACOB THOMAS : DEED OF WARRANTY

Date: Aug. 24th, 1799.
Consideration: $400.00.
Amt. of land: Two certaintracts or parcels.
Description: Two certain tracts or parcels of land lying and being in the county of Sullivan and state aforesaid the first containing by estimation 170 acres be the same more or less situated on the waters of Beaver Creek and on the sides of the Watauga road & on the east end of the tract of land formerly the property of John Bealot's kins whereon John Wassom now lives. The other containing 200-? acres be the same more or less situate and lying on the North side of Holston River.
Witnesses: James Rhea, John Thomas, Samuel Carithers.
Acknowledged: Before David Campbell one of the Judges of the Suprtior Court of Law and Equity for the state of Tennessee by Samuel Carrithers who made oath that he saw Moses Musgrave execute and acknowledge the within instrument, Sept. 13th, 1797.
Registered: Nov. 12th, 1799. Test: David Campbell.

---

(261) WILLIAM COCKE
to
JACOB MOYERS : DEED OF WARRANTY

Date: September 4th, 1799.
Consideration: $1000.00.
Amt. of land: 170 acres. Also shown as 190 acres according to the courses of a deed granted from the State of North Carolina to John Smith.
Description: A certain tract of parcel of land containing 170 acres.
Witnesses: John Carter, Walter King, Christopher Myers.
Proven: In open court by the oath of Christopher Myers Sullivan November Sessions, 1799.
Registered: Nov. 21, 1799. Test: Mattw. Rhea, C. S. C.

---

(262) JACOB MYERS TO
to
JOHN CLAR : DEED OF WARRANTY

Date: Septmeber 14th, 1797.
Consideration: $790.00.
Amt. of land: 237 acres.
Location: Sullivan County, Tennessee.
Description: A certain tract or parcell of land containing 237 acres of land be the same more or less.
Witnesses: Jas. Gaines, Philip King, Chrostopher Myers.
Proven: In open court Sullivan County, November Sessions, 1799, by the oath of Christopher Myers.
Registered: Nov. 21, 1799. Test: Mattw. Rhea, C. S. C.

(Page)

(263) JACOB MYERS : to : DEED OF WARRANTY JOHN OLAR :

Date: Sept. 14th, 1799.
Consideration: $500.00.
Amt. of land: 150 acres.
Location: Sullivan County, Tennessee.
Description: A certain tract of land containing 150 acres be the same more or less.
Witnesses: Jas. Gaines, Philip King, Christopher Myers.
Proven: In open Court Sullivan County, Nov. Sessions, 1799, by the oath of Christopher Myers. Test: Mattw. Rhea, C. S. C.
Registered: Nov. 21, 1799.

---

(264) JACOB MYERS : to : DEED OF WARRANTY GASPER MYERS :

Date: Sept. 14th, 1799.
Consideration: $200.00.
Amt. of land: 120 acres.
Location: Sullivan County, Tennessee.
Description: A certain tract or parcel of land containing 120 acres be the same more or less.
Witnesses: John Anderson, Philip Kiter.
Proven: In open court by the oath of John Anderson Sullivan County Novr. Sessions, 1799.
Registered: November 21st, 1799. Test: Mattw. Rhea, C. S .C.

MOSES MUSGROVE : to : DEED OF WARRANTY MARY JOHNSTON :

Date: July 31, 1799.
Consideration: $200.00.
Amt. of land: 208 acres.
Location: Sullivan County, Tennessee.
Description: A tract of land situate lying and being in the county of Sullivan and State aforesaid on the waters of Beaver Creek on the main road from Abingdon to Jonesborough containing 208 acres.
Witnesses: John Robinson, Landon Carter, Samuel Musgrove.
Signed by mark: Moses Musgrove.
Note: The above deed land was sold for value received unto John Vance by Mary Johnston, Sept. 22, 1799.
Witnesses: Wm. N. Gale, Alex Laughlin, Fr. Perry.
Proven: The assignment of the above mortgage of land is proven in open court by the oath of Alex Laughlin.
Registered: Nov. 21, 1799. Test: Mattw. Rhea, C. S. C.

---

(265) MOSES MUSGROVE : to : DEED OF MORTGAGE JOHN VANCE :

(Moses Musgrove to Mary Johnston)

(Page)

Date: Nov. 20th, 1799.
Consideration: $ 200.00 to be paid within two years from date.
Amt. of land: 208 acres.
Location: Sullivan County, Tennessee on the waters of Beaver Creek.
Explanation: Moses Musgrove on July 31st, 1799, sold Mary Johnston 208 acres of land for the sum of $200.00 this land being on the main road from Abingdon to Jonesborough said sum secured by mortgage on said land.
Witnesses: John Robertson, Landon Carter, Samuel Musgrove.
Signed: Moses Musgrove.
Note: Said land now being sold by sd. Moses Musgrove to sd. John Vance was sold to Mary Johnston by Moses Musgrove for aforesaid sum secured by mortgage on sd. land, which was defaulted)

(267) MARY JOHNSTON : to : MEMORANDUM OF MORTGAGE JOHN VANCE :

Date: Sept. 2d, 1799.
Memo: Deed of mortgage duly proven in the Court of Pleas and Quarter Sessions held in and for the sd. county of Sullivan on the 3d Monday of November in the sd. year 1799 and ordered to be registered and the same was registered in sd. county and whereas sd. Mary Johnston Sept. 2d, 1799 did for a valuable consideration signed by her assignee all her right title and interest over to John Vance.
Witness: William N. Gale, Alex Laughlin.
Signed: Mary Johnston.
Which sd. assignment is indorsed on the sd. indenture and deed of mortgage provided in the sd. court of Sullivan County and is there registered.

MOSES MUSGROVE : to : DEED OF WARRANTY JOHN VANCE :

Date: August_______, 1799.
Consideration: $400.00.
Amt. of land: 208 acres and 24-3/4 acres.
Location: Sullivan County, Tennessee.
Description: The sd. tract of 208 acres of land situate lying and being in the county of Sullivan and State of Tennessee on the waters of Beaver Creek on the main road from Abingdon to JonesBorough , the other tract containing 24-3/4 acres.
Note: In one part of the description first tract is referred to as containing 176 acres. Both tracts also referred to as 208 acres.
Witnesses: Alex Laughlin , Wm. Willson.
Proven: By the oath of Alexander Laughlin in open court Sullivan County November Sessions, 1799.
Registered: Nov. 21, 1799. Test: Matthw. Rhea, C. S. C.

DAVID SHIPMAN & BENJAMIN DOWNS, ATTY. : to : DEED OF WARRANTY PETER HUMMEL :

Date: Feb. 20th, 1799.

(Page)

(269) Consideration: $175.00.
Amt. of land: 115 acres.
Location: Sullivan County, Tennessee.
Description: A certain plantation or parcel of land int the county of Sullivan and state of Tennessee (bounds) containing 115 acres be the same more or less.
Witnesses: John Williams, Samuel Henyrton.
Proven: By the oath of John Williams Sullivan County August Sessions 1798, in open court.
Registered: November 28th, 1799. Test: Mattw. Rhea, C.S.C.

---

(270) ARNOLD SHELL :
to : DEED OF WARRANTY
EDWARD COX :

Date: November 22d, 1798.
Consideration: $500.00.
Amt. of land: 162 acres.
Location: Sullivan County, Tennessee.
Description: A certain tract or parcel of land lying and being in the county aforesaid and on the south side of Holston River (bounds) containing 162 acres.
Witnesses: Hebert York, John Anderson, Thos. Beard.
Proven: In open court Sullivan November Sessions, 1798, by Arnold Shell.
Registered: December 4th, 1799. Test: Mattw. Rhea, C. S. C.

---

(271) ROBERT WHITNAL :
to : DEED OF MORTGAGE
JAMES COOK :

Date: August 28th, 1797.
Consideration: $100.00.
Amt. of land: 48 acres.
Location: Sullivan County, Tennessee.
Description: A certain tract or parcel of land containing 48 acres be the same more or less lying and being in the county of Sullivan.
Witnesses: John Anderson, John McElderry.
Proven: In open court by the oath of John Anderson Sullivan County November Sessions, 1799.
Registered: December 26th, 1799. Test: Mattw. Rhea, C. S. C.

---

(272) JAMES COOK :
to : DEED OF WARRANTY
RICHARD SMITH :

Date: September 28th, 1799.
Consideration: $200.00.
Amt. of land: 92 acres.
Location: Sullivan County, Tennessee.
Description: Two tracts or parcels of land situate lying and being on the waters of Reedy Creek in the county aforesaid and containing together 92- towit one tract containing 44 acres which was conveyed by Joseph Cook to James Cook August 28th, 1797. The other tract joining the above mentioned tract containing 48 acres conveyed by Robert Whitnal to James Cook, August 28th, 1797.

Witnesses: James Wear, John Smith, John Punch.
Acknowledged: In open court by James Cook, State of Tennessee, Sullivan County, November Sessions, 1799.
Registered: December 26th, 1799. Test: Mattw. Rhea, C. S. C.

---

(273) JAMES HARRIS : to : DEED OF WARRANTY JAMES KING :

Date: May 28th, 1799.
Consideration: $250.00.
Amt. of land: 100 acres.
Location: Sullivan County, Tennessee.
Description: One hundred acres of land including the Oar bank known by the name of Harris Oar Bank.
Witnesses: John Punch, John Goodson.
Proven: In open court by the oath of John Punch Sullivan County, November Sessions, 1799. Test: Mattw. Rhea, C. S. C.
Registered: December 12th, 1799.

---

(274) JOHN ANDERSON, SHERIFF : to : SHERIFF'S DEED JOHN GOODSON :

Pursuant to awrit of Fiere Facois isued from the Supreme Court of Law for Mero District in sd. county on a judgment obtained in sd. court at May term, 1798, by John Overton against James King which judgment was confirmed by the Court of Equity for Washington District at March term, 1799, by my deputy, Francis Hugh Gains. levied on 1200 and 1/2 acres of land including the Beaver Creek Iron Works. Sold at public sale to highest bidder on Tuesday the 1st day of August at the Court house of Sullivan County, John Goodson being the highest bidder.
Consideration: $1700.00.
Description: The following tracts or parcels of land lying in Sullivan County aforesaid to wit one tract containing 200 acres which was conveyed by James King and Com. by Henery Harkelroad by indenture bearing date Jan. 4th, 1796. One tract containing 190 acres which was conveyed to Julius Hacker to James King and Com. January 10th, 1796. One tract containing inclusive of the above mentioned 190 acres 640 acres which was conveyed by Julius Hacker to James King October 10th, 1797. One tract containing 200 acres adjoining the above mentioned tract which was conveyed by John Bealor to James King March 10th, 1798. One tract containing 73-½ acres which was conveyed by John Hollow to James King October 20th, 1798 and lastly one tract containing 100 acres including the Oar bank known by the name of Harris Ore Bank conveyed by James Harris to James King May 28th, 1799.
Witnesses: John Punch, John Williams.
Acknowledged: In open court by John Anderson High Sheriff of Sullivan County, Sullivan County August Sessions, 1799.
Registered: December 27th, 1799. Test: Mattw. Rhea, C. S. C.

(Page)
(278) JOHN GOODSON : DEED OF WARRANTY
to
HIS NEPHEWS,
WILLIAM KING, JAMES KING
& HIS SON, SAMUEL GOODSON

Date: October 1st, 1799.
How deeded: To them jointly and equally.
Date: Ocotber 1st, 1799.
Consideration: Good will and affection.
Amt. of land: 1200 $\frac{1}{2}$ acres, purchased from John Anderson,Sheriff.
Description: One tract containing 200 acres which was conveyed to James King and Com. by Henry Harkleroad by indenture bearing date January 4th, 1796. On tract containing 190 acres which was conveyed by Julius Hacker to James King and Company January 10th, 1796. One contract containing inclusive of the above mentioned 190 acres 640 acres which was conveyed by Julius Hacker to James King October 10th, 1797. One containing 200 acres adjoining the above mentioned tract which was conveyed by John Dealor to James King March 10th,1798. One tract containing 73$\frac{1}{2}$ acres which was conveyed by John Holloway to James King ___ 17th, 1798 and lastly one tract containing 100 acres including the Oare Bank known by the name of Harris Ore Bank conveyed by James Harris to James King May 28th, 1799.
Witnesses: Henry Swingle, R. Elliot, John Punch.
Proven: In open court by the oath of John Punch Sullivan County Nov. Sessions, 1799.
Registered: Dec, 27th, 1799. Test: Mattw. Rhea, C. S. C.

---

(281) JAMES ANDERSON : DEED OF WARRANTY
to
JOHN SHIPLEY

Date: April 19th, 1798.
Consideration: 33 £.
Description: All that messuage or tenement and all those lands where he now lives lying and being in the county of Sullivan and State of Tennessee adjoining the lands of James Cain and Peter Hempl.
Witnesses: John McEldery, George Roller.
Proven: In open court by the oaty of George Roller, Sullivan May Sessions, 1798.
Note: In one place 33 £ is acknowledged as paid and a few lines further down in the deed the condition of the sale is if the 33 £ is paid on or before April 19th,1799, then this obligation to be null and void.
Registered: January 21st, 1800. Test: Mattw. Rhea, C.S.C.

STATE OF NORTH CAROLINA : LAND GRANT
ALEXANDER MARTIN, GOV. : NO. 343
to
JAMES PATTERSON

Date: Nov. 17th, 1790.
Consideration: 10 £ for every 100 acres.
Amt. of land: 2500 acres.
Location: In our Western District on the Massipia.
Description: A tract of land containing 2500 acres lying and being

in our Wester District on the Massipia.
Witnesses: Alex Martin, by his Excellys. Comd. J. Glasgow, Sec.
Knok County state of Tennessee this grant was registered in Book B page 125 Sept. 1, 1796, taxes paid. Thos Chapman, Reg.
Registered in the registers office of Sullivan County Feb. 25th, 1800.

---

(282) STATE OF NORTH CAROLINA : RICHARD DOBBS SPAIGHT, GOV. to JAMES PATTERSON : LAND GRANT NO. 396

Date: November 27th, 1793.
Consideration: 10 ₤ for every 100 acres.
Amt. of land: 5000 acres.
Located: In our Western District on the waters of the Massippia.
Witness: Richard Dobbs Spaight, Gov. By his Excellys, Comd. J. Glasgow, Sec
This grant was registered in Knox county in Book E page 520 October 2d, 1799, and tax paid. Thomas Chapman, Regst.
Registered: In Sullivan County, Feb. 25th, 1800.

---

(284) JAMES PATTERSON to WILLIAM TYRRELL : DEED OF WARRANTY

Date: July18th, 1796.
Consideration: $6200.00.
Amt. of land: 5000 acres.
Location: & Description: In the Western District on the waters of the Massippia River which said tract of land was granted to sd. Patterson and Company by the State of North Carolina Nov. 27th, 1793, Grant No. 396.
Witnesses: Alex Swagerty, Christian Rhods.
Signed by his attorney, Stockley Donelson.
Registered in Knox County on record page 255. Thos. Chapman.
Registered: Feb. 25th, 1800.

---

(286) WILLIAM TYRRELL to JOHN RHEA : DEED OF WARRANTY

Date: October 26th, 1797.
Consideration: $500.00.
Amt. of land: 2500 acres.
Location: Western District and State of Tennessee.
Description: A certain tract or parcel of land containing 2500 acres being an undivided moiety of a tract of 5000 acres of land lying and being in Western District and state aforesaid on the waters of the Misippia River which sd. tract of land was granted to James Patterson by the state of North Carolina Nov. 27th, 1793. Patent No. 385.
Conveyed: To William Tyrrell by James Patterson by his attorney Stokely Donelson. Power of attorney bearing date July 12th, 1796.
Power of attorney given for the purpose of transacting the above sale of land.
Witnesses: David Squire, J. H. Mteel.
Acknowledgement: State of Tennessee, Hamelton District.

William Tyrrell personally appeared before me and acknowleged this to be his deed. Paid the tax to let it be registered October 26th, 1797. Archibald Roan.
Knox County: Registered in page 256 October 30th, 1797 & taxes paid Tennessee Sullivan (county) February 25th, 1800, then registered in the Registers office in page 543.

(287) WILLIAM TYRRELL : to : DEED OF WARRANTY JOHN RHEA :

Date: April 2d, 1798.
Consideration: $500.00.
Amt. of land: 5000.00 acres.
Location and description: A certain tract or parcel of land containing 5000 acres lying and being in the Western District now part of the State of Tennessee on the waters of the Missippia River.
Witnesses: Robert Forgunr, Geo. Roulston.
Acknowledged: Before David Campbell one of the Judges of the Superior Court of Law and Equity in and for the state of Tennessee. Signed at Knoxville April 2d, 1798.
Registered: Feb. 25th, 1800. Let it be Regst. David Campbell.

WILLIAM TERRELL : to : DEED OF WARRANTY JOHN RHEA :

Date: March 27th, 1798.
Consideration: $1000.00.
Amt. of land: 2500 acres.
Location: & Description: A certain tract or parcel of land containing 2500 acres lying and being in Western District formerly part of the State of North Carolina and now part of the State of Tennessee and the waters of the Massippia or Missippia River, which tract was granted to James Patterson by the State of North Carolina by Patent dated Nov. 17th, 1790. No. 343.
Witnesses: Nat R. Markland, James Christolm.
State of Tennessee. Acknowledged before Archibald Roan one of the Judges of the Superior Court of Law and Equity by William Tyrrell, March 28th, 1798. Archiblad Roan.
Registered: In Knox County in Book E. & page 41, April 11th, 1798 & tax paid. Thos. Chapman, Regst.
Regst. 25th day of February, 1800.

BENJAMIN ROYSTON : to : DEED OF GIFTS JOSHUA ROYSTON, BENJAMIN ROYSTON, S : SARAH ROYSTON, SUSANNAH ROYSTON :

Date: Februarty 17th, 1800.
Consideration: Natural love and affection.
Land: The tract of land whereon I now live situate lying and being on Holston River in Sullivan County, Aforesaid.
Individually: To my son Joshua Royston 100 acres of said tract of land adjoining Jacob Boys land and also a negro boy called Nicholas during the lifetime of the said Nicholas.

To my son Benjamin Royston 200 acres part of the sd. tract being that part whereon I now resid and to contain the dwelling house, outbuildings orchard and spring and I give unto the sd. Benjamin a negro woman called Fan during the natural life of the sd. Fan. I give unto my daughter Sarah Royston 50 acres of land next adjoining my son Benjamin's part Lower down on the River. I give unto my daughter Susanah Royston 50 acres part of the sd. tract lower down on the River bounded in part by George Little and Opesit Shells Mill. I also give unto my said daughter Susannah a certain negro girl called Judy during the sd. Judy's life time.
Benjamin Royston reserved the right to revoke any part or all of his deed at any time he desired to do so.
Acknowledged: In open court by Benjamin Royston, Sullivan County, Febr. Sessions, 1800.
Registered: Feb. 28th, 1800. Mattw. Rhea, C. S. C.

---

(291) JOHN BROWN to SAMPSON COLE : DEED OF WARRANTY

Date: February 18th, 1799.
Consideration: 80 £.
Amt. of land: 225 acres.
Location: Sullivan County, Tennessee.
Description: All that tract or parcel of land containing 225 acres laying in the county of Sullivan and state aforesaid.
Acknowledged: In open court Sullivan County, February Sessions, 1799, by John Brown.
Registered: Feb. 28th, 1800. Test: Mattw. Rhea, C. S. C.

---

(292) SAMUEL COLE to GEORGE BROWN : DEED OF WARRANTY

Date: February 18th, 1799.
Consideration: $500.00.
Amt. of land: 400 acres.
Location: Sullivan County, Tennessee.
Description: All that tract or parcel of land containing 400 acres lying in the county of Sullivan and State of Tennessee on Beaver Dam Creek.
Acknowledged: In open court Sullivan County, February Session, 1799 by George Brown.
Registered: Feb. 28th, 1800. Test: Mattw. Rhea, C. S. C.

---

(293) HENRY HARKLEROAD to MARTIN HARKEL : DEED OF WARRANTY

Date: February 1st, 1799.
Consideration: $3000.00
Amt. of land: 349 acres.
Location: Sullivan County, Tennessee.
Description: A certain tract or parcel of land containing 349 acres

be the same more or less in the county and state aforesaid on Bevar Creek a Branch of Holston River known by the name of the mill tract.
Witnesses: John Henry Sieiling, Andrew Emert.
Acknowledged: By Henry Harkleroad Sullivan February Sessions, 1799.
Registered: Feb. 28th, 1800. Test: Mattw. Rhea, C. S. C.

---

(294) JOHN TORBET : to : DEED OF WARRANTY JACOB EMMERT :

Date: February 15th, 1800.
Consideration: $80.00.
Amt. of land: 149 acres.
Location: Washington County, Tennessee.
Description: A certain tract or parcel of land containing 149 acres lying and being in our county of Washington on the dreams of Wautagah River.
Acknowledged: Sullivan County, February Sessions, 1800 in open court by John Torbet.
Registered: March 11th, 1800. Test: Mattw. Rhea, C. S. C.

---

(295) CHARLES ALLEN : to : DEED OF WAR RANTY JOHN ALLEN :

Date: August 16th, 1799.
Consideration: $22.00.
Amt. of land: 48 acres.
Location: Sullivan County, Tennessee.
Description: A parcel of land part of a tract of land originally granted to Henry Goucher from the State of North Carolina bearing date 1782 No. 51(bounds) containing 48 acres.
Witnesses: Daniel Allen, John Hunt, William Denton.
Proven: In open court by the oath of Daniel Allen Sullivan County August Sessions, 1799. Test: Mattw. Rhea, C. S. C.
Regst. March 11th, 1800.

---

(296) WILLIAM SNODGRASS : to : DEED OF WARRANTY PETER SHELLY :

Date: January 24th, 1800.
Consideration: $1000.00.
Amt. of land: 293 acres.
Location: Sullivan County, Tenn.
Description: A certain piece or parcel of land situated lying and being in Sullivan aforesaid (bounds) containing 293 acres.
Witnesses: Peter Hickman, Peter McClain, John Drake.
Proven: In open court by the oath of Peyer Hickman. State of Tennessee Sullivan County February Session 1800.
Regst. March 11th, 1800. Test: Matthew Rhea, C. S. C.

---

(298) JOHN ROWLER : to : DEED OF WARRANTY CONRAD ISLEY :

Date: January 20th, 1800.

Consideration: $33.33.
Amt. of land: 338 acres.
Location: Sullivan County, Tennessee.
Description: A certain tract or parcel of land containing 338 acres be the same more or less.
Witnesses: John Anderson, George Vincent.
Acknowledged: Execution of the within deed acknowledged in open court, State of Rennessee, Sullivan County by John Foller Feb. Sessions, 1800. Test: Mattw. Rhea, C. S. C.
Registered: March 13th, 1800.

---

(298) SHADRACH HICKS to EDWARD COX : DEED OF WARRANTY

Date: Jan. 20th, 1800.
Consideration: $66.66.
Amt. of land: 184 acres.
Location: Sullivan County, Tennessee.
Description: A certain tract or parcel of land containing 184 acres be the same more or less sd. land lying and being in the county aforesaid.
Witnesses: John Anderson, Wm. Carr, George Millerd.
Proven: Sullivan County, February Sessions, 1800, by the oath of John Anderson. Test: Mattw. Rhea, C. S. C.
Registered: March 20th, 1800.

---

(299) ANDREW MCCLAND to HENRY CLEECK : DEED OF WARRANTY

Date: February 14th, 1800.
Consideration: 100 £.
Amt. of land: 100 acres.
Location: Sullivan County, Tennessee.
Description: A cettain tract of land laying and being in the county and state afcresaid and containing 100 acres lying on the north side of the North Fork.
Proven: By the oath of George Morrison in open court, Tennessee Sullivan County, February Session, 1800.
Registered: March 20th, 1800. Mattw. Rhea, C. S. C.

---

(300) JOHN MOIERS to JACOB THOMAS : DEED OF WARRANTY

Date: November 22d, 1799.
Consideration: $400.00.
Amt. of land: 104 acres.
Location: Sullivan County, Tennessee.
Description: A certain tract of land containing 104 acres be the same more or less laying and being in the county and State aforesaid on Sinking (Creek ?)
Witnedd: Wm. N. Gale.
Proven: Inopen court by William N. Gale State of Tennessee, Sullivan County, Feb. Session 1800. Test: Mattw. Rhea, C. S. C.

Registered: March 20th, 1800.

(Page)

(302) PATRICK CREALY : to : DEED OF WARRANTY JACOB HAWKS :

Date: September 4th, 1799.
Consideration: 100 £.
Amt. of land: 100 acres.
Location: Sullivan County, Tennessee.
Description: A certain tract or parcel of land containing 100 acres be the same more or less lying and being in the county of Sullivan on the waters of Bever Creek.
Witness: John Vance.
Proven: In open court by the oath of John Vance, State of Tennessee, Sullivan County, February Session, 1800.
Regst: March 20th, 1800. Test: Mattw. Rhea, C. S. C.

****

(303) THOMAS ROCKHOLD : to : DEED OF WARRANTY JACOB HAWKS :

Date: September 4th, 1799.
Consideration: $107.70.
Amt. of land: 32-3/4 acres.
Location: Sullivan County, Tennessee.
Description: One certain tract or parcel of land containing 32-3/4 acres lying and being on the North side of Holston River and in Sullivan County.
Acknowledged: In open court by Thomas Rockhold Sullivan County, February Sessions 1799. Test: Mattw. Rhea, C. S. C.
Registered: March 20th, 1800.

****

(304) JAMES MCNARE : to : DEED OF WARRANTY DAVID ROSS :

Date: July 1st, 1799.
Consideration: 200 £.
Amt. of land: 200 acres.
Description: One certain tract or parcel of land situate lying and being on the fork of Holston & North Holston containing 200 acres be the same more or less.
Witnesses: Wm. Varison, Thomas Hopkins.
Acknowledgement: State of Tennessee- Thomas Hopkins personally appeared before me one of the Jusges of the said State and made oath that Sam James McNare the grantee therein mentionedsigned and delivered the same as his act July 10, 1799. Archabale Roan.
Registered: March 20th, 1800.

****

(305) JOSEPH COLE, JUNR. : to : DEED OF WARRANTY PHILIP HOBACH :

Date: February 8th, 1800.
Consideration: $1746.00.
Amt. of land: 262 acres.
Location: Sullivan County, Tennessee.

Description: A certain tract or parcel of land containing 262 acres be the same more or less lying and being in the county of Sullivan and on both sides of Beaver Creek.
Witness: Conrad Sharitz, State of Tennessee, Sullivan County and ordered to be registered: Test: Mattw. Rhea, C. S. C.
Registered: March 20th, 1800.

---

(307) STATE OF NORTH CAROLINA :
SAMUEL ASHE, GOV. : LAND GRANT
to : NO. 704.
ZACHARIAS WICKS :

Date: July 20th, 1796.
Consideration: 50 shillings for every 100 acres of land.
Amt. of land: 143 acres.
Location: Sullivan County, Tennessee.
Description: A tract of land containing 143 acres lying and being in our county of Sullivan.
Witness: Samuel Ashe, Gov. By his Excellys. Comd. J. Glasgow, Sec.
Registered: March 20th, 1800.

---

(308) STATE OF NORTH CAROLINA :
SAMUEL ASHE, GOV. t : LAND GRANT
to : NO. 715.
JOHN WICKS :

Date: July 20th, 1796.
Consideration: 50 shillings for every 100 acres of land.
Amt. of land: 46 acres.
Location: Sullivan County, Tennessee.
Description: A tract of land containing 46 acres lying and being in our county of Sullivan.
Witness: Samule Ashe, Gov. By his Excellys. Comd. J. Glasgow, Sec.
Registered: March 20th, 1800.

---

(309) JACOB EMMERT :
to : MORTGAGE
GEORGE LINDENBERGER & :
CHRISTOPHER LINDENBERGER :

Date: May 4th, 1799.
Consideration: 552 £, 18 shillings, 6 d.
Amt. of land: 640 acres.
Location: Sullivan County, Tennessee.
Description: All his the sd. Jacob Emmert's plantation lying in sd. county of Sullivan & State of Tennessee containing about 640 acres adjoining the land of Henry Massengale, David Hughes, William Fremo and Samuel Dinsmore and the following negro slaves to wit Molatto Same aged about 21 years, negro Molly about 24 years of age, her children Kate Agge a girl about 14 years of age, Jude a woman about 17 or 18 years of age, Boy Ned about 14 years of age and a girl Milly about 11 years of age, to have and to hold the sd. land and premises and the increase of such of them as females.
Condition of sale: If said 552 £, 18s,6d be not paid on or before November 4th, 1799, this deed of mortgage becomes null and void.

Witnesses: Jacob Stitcher, George Henry.
State of Merryland, City of Baltimore: Acknowledged before James Calhoun, Mayor of the City of Baltimore by Jacob Emmert, May 4th. 1790. James Calhoun, Mayor of the City of Baltimore.
TO ALL TO WHOM IT DOTH OR MAY CONCERN:
that at ourt of Oarss, and Termier and Goal delivery held for the c ounty aforesaid (Baltimore County) at the court house in the same county on March 20th, 1800, personally appeared Jacob Stetcher one of the sd. subscribing witnesses to the above instrument of writing and made oath on the holy Evangelas of Almighty God that he saw Jacob Emmert sign the foregoing instrument of writing.
William Gibson, Clk. Baltimore County.
Attest: Walter Dorsey, Chief Justice Court of Oyer and Termier and Goal Delivery for Baltimore County May 24th, 1800.
then registered.

---

(312) WALLACE WILLOUGHBY to CONROD SHARATZ : DEED OF WARRANTY

Date: May 19th, 1800.
Consideration: $15.00.
Amt. of land: A lot of land Number 50 lying and being in the County of Sullivan on the West Bank of Sinking Creek containing 40 poles.
Acknowledged: In open court by Wallace Willoughby Sullivan May Session 1800.
Regst: June 2d, 1800. Test: Mattw. Rhea, C. S. C.

---

(313) WALLACE WILLOUGHBY to WILLIAM N. GALE : DEED OF WARRANTY

Date: May 19th, 1800.
Consideration: Amt. not stated.
Amt. of land: 30 acres.
Location: Sullivan County, Tennessee.
Description: A certain piece or parcel of land lying on Sinking Creek, Sullivan County.
Acknowledged: In open court Sullivan County May Sessions, 1800, by Wallace Willoughby.
Registered: June 2d, 1800. Test: Mattw. Rhea, C. S. C.

---

(314) WILLIAM N. GALE to WALLACE WILLOUGHBY : DEED OF WARRANTY

Date: May 19th, 1800.
Consideration: Full satisfaction to him made.
Amt. of land: 25 acres.
Location: Sullivan County, Tennessee.
Description: A certain parcel of land lying in Sullivan County (bounds) containing 25 acres be the same more or less.
Acknowledged: In open court by William N. Gale, Sullivan County May Sessions, 1800.
Registered: June 2d, 1800. Test: Mattw. Rhea, C. S. C.

ANDREW WILLOUGHBY & WIFE ELIZABETH, to WALLACE WILLOUGHBY : DEED OF WARRANTY

Date: April 18th, 1800.
Consideration: Full satisfaction to them made .
Amt. of land: 272 acres.
Location: Sullivan County, Tenn.
Description: A certain piece or parcel of land lying in Sullivan County Tennessee(bounds) containing on the whole 272 acres be the same more or less.
Proven: In open court by the oath of William M. Gale Sullivan County May Session, 1800.
Regst: June 2d, 1800. Test: Matw. Rhea, C. S. C.

---

(316) HANNAH PARKER to THOMAS ROGERS : DEED OF WARRANTY

Date: October 25th, 1799.
Consideration: $300.00.
Amt. of land: 47 acres.
Location: Sullivan County, Tennessee.
Description: One certain tract or parcel of land lying in the county aforesaid on the south side of Holston River.
Witnesses: Robert Esley, Peter McInter.
Proven: In open court by the oath of Robert Esley Sullivan County May Session, 1800. Test: Mattw. Rhea, C. S. C.
Regst. June 7th, 1800.

---

(317) GEORGE SMITH, SENR. to PHILIP KING : DEED OF WARRANTY

Date: August 25th, 1797.
Consideration: $700.00.
Amt. of land: 201 acres.
Location: Sullivan County, Tennessee.
Description: A certain tract or parcel of land lying and being in Sullivan County and State aforesaid south side of the Holston River on Jarrett's Branch.
Witnesses: Walter King, John Talley.
Proven: In open court by the oath of Walter King, Sullivan County May Session, 1800.
Registered: June 7th, 1800. Test: Mattw. Reha, C. S. C.

---

(318) MICHAEL CRAFT to THOMAS TITSWORTH : DEED OF WARRANTY

Date: May 16th, 1800.
Consideration: $500.00.
Amt. of land: 192 acres.
Location: Sullivan County, Tennessee.

Description: A certain tract of land containing by estimation 192 acres be the same more or less situate lying and being in Sullivan County and State of Tennessee on the South side of Holston River opesate the Long Island of Holston including the sd. Richard Craft plantation/
Witnesses: Walter King, Daniel Ealy.
Proven: In open court b y the oath of Walter King Sull van $C_o$unty May Sessions, 1800.
Registered: June 7th, 1800.

---

(319) HENRY SULLIVAN : to : DEED OF WARRANTY AARON BACON :

Date: August 19th, 1799.
Consideration: 40 ₤.
Amt. of land: 128 acres.
Location: One certain tract of land 128 acres situate lying and being in the sd. County of Sullivan on the waters of Hors. Creek including the plantation where William Buckner formerly lived.
Witnesses: George Vincent, Peter Easley, Tabitha Siloiark.
Proven: By the oath of George Vincent Sullivan Co unty May Session 1800. Test: Mattw. Rhea, C. S. C.
Registered: June 7th, 1800.

---

(321) ROBERT GRAY : to : DEED OF WARRANTY JOHN STURGEN :

Date: April 14th, 1800.
Consideration: 200 ₤.
Amt. of land: 400 acres.
Location: Sullivan County, Tennessee.
Description: A certain panteltion or tract of land situate lying and being in Sullivan County (bounds) containing 400 acres.
Witnesses: John Williams and Moses Barbra.
Proven: By the oath of John Williams Sullivan County May Session, 1800.
Registered: June 7th, 1800.

---

(322) THOMAS RAMSEY : to : DEED OF WARRANTY FELTY POPE :

Date: May 11th, 1784.
Consideration: 400 ₤.
Amt. of land: 500 acres.
Location: Sullivan County, North Carolina.
Description: A certain piece or parcel of land containing by estimation:500 acres be the same more or less situate lying and being in sd. county of Sullivan.
Signed: Thomas Ramsey, Ann Ramsey.
Witnesses: Evan Shelby, James Weaver.
Proven: By hte oath of Evan Shelby Sullivan County December Session, 1789.
Registered: June 7th, 1800. Test: Mattw. Rhea, C. S.C.

(324) JOHN ROLLER : to : DEED OF WARRANTY JOHN HANK :

Date: May 19th, 1800.
Consideration: $166.67.
Amt. of land: 138 acres.
Location: Sullivan County, Tennessee.
Description: A certain tract or parcel of land containing 138 acres be the same more or less.
Witness: John Anderson.
Acknowledged: In open court by John Roller Sullivan County May Session, 1800.
Regst: June 10th, 1800. Test: Matthew Rhea, C. S. C.

---

(325) ALEXANDER FORD : to : DEED OF WARRANTY SAMUEL BILLINGSBY :

Date: March 3d, 1800.
Consideration: $246.75.
Amt. of land: 100 acres.
Location: Sullivan County, Tennessee.
Description: A certain Tract or parcel of land lying and being in our county of Sullivan containing 100 acres lying on the North side of Holston River.
Witnesses: Jacob Slaughter, Benjamin Vanvacter.
Proven: In open court by the oath of Jacob Slaughter, Sullivan County May Session, 1800.
Registered: June 10th, 1800. Test: Mattw. Rhea, C. S. C.

---

(327) JACOB ELLER : to : DEED OF WARRANTY JOHN SEVEIR :

Date: Sept. 12th, 1799.
Consideration: $80.00.
Amt. of land: 150 acres.
Location: Sullivan County
Description: A certain tract or parcel of land lying and being in Sullivan County containing 150 acres originally granted to Frederick Keller.
Witness: James Gordon, Moses Minson.
Proven: In open court Sullivan County May Session, 1800.
Regst: June 10th, 1800. Test: Mattw. Rhea. C. S. C.

---

(328) WALLACE WILLOUGHBY : to : DEED OF WARRANTY MARTIN BOOHER, SENR. :

Date: May 19th, 1800.
Consideration: $15.00 to be pd. at the expiration of 3 years.
Amt. of land: A certain lott containing 40 poles.
Location: Sullivan County.
Description: A certain lott containing 40 poles being in Sullivan county on the West bank of Sinking Creek.

Acknowledged: Sullivan County May Sessions, 1800. in open court by Waliace Willoughby. Test: Mattw. Rhea, C. S. C.
Regst: July 27th, 1800.

---

(328) PETER SHELLEY : DEED OF WARRANTY
to
MARTIN BOCHER

Date: March 1st, 1800.
Consideration: $428.00.
Amt. of land: 107 acres.
Location: Sullivan County, Tennessee.
Description: A certain piece or parcel of land situate and lying in Sullivan County aforesaid (bounds) containing 107 acres.
Witness: Stephen Major, George Shilley.
Acknowledged: In open court Sullivan County May Sessions, 1800, by Peter Shelley.
Regst: July 27th, 1800. Test: Mattw. Rhea, C. S. C.

---

(330)

EDMUND WARREN : DEED OF MORTGAGE
ro
ALEX MCCRABB

Date: Aug. 19th, 1800.
Consideration: $110.00.
Amt. of land: 400 acres.
Location: Sullivan County, Tennessee.
Description: A certain plantation or tract of land whereon the sd. Edmund resides in Sullivan County aforesaid (bounds) containing 400 acres be the same more or less.
Note: The said $110.00 to be paid to Alex McCrabb with interest thereon on or before December 1st, next enshing the date hereof.
Acknowledged: In open Court Sullivan County Aug. Sessions, 1800, by Edmund Warren.
Regst: September 1, 1800. Test: Mattw. Rhea, Clerk Sullivan County.

---

(331) COL. JAMES KING : DEED OF WARRANTY
to
ALEXANDER MCCRABB

Date: August 21st, 1800.
Consideration: $75.00.
Amt. of land& description: One certain lott of land in said town of Blountville containing 1/4 of an acre.
Acknowledged: By James King Sullivan County, August Sessions, 1800.
Regst: September 1st, 1800. Test: Mattw. Rhea, C. S.C.

---

(332) SANDFORD BIRDWELL : DEED OF WARRANTY
to
WM. COPELAND

Date: May 31st, 1800.
Consideration: $1000.00.
Amt. of land: 300 acres.
Location: Sullivan County, Tennessee/

Description: A certain tract of land containing 300 acres be the same more or less lying and being in the sd. county of Sullivan on the waters of Holston River.
Witnesses: Jacob Leake, John Yoakley, Richard Gammon.
Proven: In open court by the oath of Jacob Leake Sullivan County August Sessions, 1800.
Regst: September 2d, 1800. Test: Matw. Rhea, C. S. C.

---

(333) JABEZ GIFFORD : to : DEED OF WARRANTY WILLIAM GIFFORD :

Date: August 15th, 1800.
Consideration: $200.00.
Amt. of land: 174 acres.
Location: Sullivan County, Tennessee.
Description: A certain tract or parcel of land containing 174 acres be the same more or less lying and being in the ciunty of Sullivan and State aforesaid and inaluding the plantation whereon the sd. Wm. Gifford, Junr. now lives.
Witnesses: George D. Edge, Robert Pallet.
Proven: In open court Sullivan County August Sessions, 1800. by the oath of Robert Pallet.
Registered: September 2d, 1800. Yest: Mattw. Rhea, C. S. C.

---

(334) JOHN SHOEMAKER : to : DEED OF WARRANTY DANIEL SHOEMAKER :

Date: December 27th, 1799.
Consideration: $50.00.
Amt. of land: 27 acres and 42 poles.
Location: Sullivan County, Tennessee.
Description: All that tract or parcel of land situate, lying and being in the county of Sullivan (bounds) containing 27 acres and 42 poles be the same more or less.
Witnesses: William Anderson~~, John Yancey~~.
Proven: In open court by the oath of William Anderson, Sullivan County August Sessions, 1800.
Registered: September 2d, 1800. Test: Mattw. Rhea, C. S. C.

---

(335) DAVID BUSHONG : to : DEED OF WARRANTY EDWARD RICHART :

Date: August 18th, 1800.
Consideration: $100.00.
Amt. of land: 15 acres.
Location: Sullivan County, Tennessee.
Description: A certain tract or parcel of land situate lying and being in Sullivan County containing 15 acres be the same more or less and part of a tract of 248 acres whiach was granted by the state of North Carolina to Daniel Miller and by him conveyed to George Syrkle and is part of the plantation whereon David Bushong now lives.
Witnesses: Henry Harkleroad, Daniel Harkleroad.

Registered: September 2d, 1800. Test: Mattw. Rhea, C. S. C.

---

(336) WM. PIRICK
to
EDWARD COX
: DEED OF WARRANTY

Date: September 28th, 1799.
Consideration: $140.00.
Amt. of land: 67 acres.
Location: Sullivan County, Tennessee.
Description: A certain tract of land containing 67 acres be the same more or less situate lying and being in the county and state aforesaid and on south side of Holston River.
Witnesses: Joseph Wallace, George Wallace.
Proven: In open court by the oath of Joseph Wallace Sullivan County August Session, 1800.
Registered: September ~~4th, 1800. Test:~~ Mattw. Rhea, C. S. C.

---

(337) JOHN NASH
to
EDWARD COX
: DEED OF WARRANTY

Date: September 26th, 1799.
Consideration: $250,00.
Amt. of land: 50 acres.
Location: Sullivan County, Tennessee.
Description: A certain tract or parcel of land containing 50 acres be the same more or less situate lying and being in the county of Sullivan and state aforesaid on the south side of Holston River.
Witnesses: Joseph Wallace, Benjamin Ristone.
Proven: In open court by the oath of Joseph Wallace, Sullivan County August Session 1800.
Regst: September 4th, 1800. Test: Mattw. Rhea, Clk. Sullivan Cty.

---

(338) ABLE EDWARDS
to
RICHARD GLOVER
: DEED OF WARRANTY

Date: May 15th, 1798.
Consideration: 50 £ Virginia money.
Amt. of land: 50 acres.
Location: Sullivan County, Tennessee.
Description: A certain tract of land in the county aforesaid containing 50 acres more or less on the siuth side of Holston River.
Witnesses: Thomas Jones, Jacob Crumley, John Buckles.
Proven: In open court by the oath of Thomas Jones Sullivan County May Sessions, 1798.
Regst: November 12th, 1800. Test: Mattw. Rhea, C. S.C.

---

(339) JOE MCFARLAN FOR DAVID ROSS
to
WILLIAM McCORMACK &
MICHAEL MONTGOMERY
: LEASE

Date: November 12th, 1795.
Property leased: Publick House and the farm thereunto belonging

on Reedy Creek.
Length of lease: 30 years from December 1st, 1795.
Terms of lease: Sd. McCormack and Montgomery or either of them are to pay to the said John McFarlan for the use of the sd. David Ross the sum of 30 Ꝉ money of Virginia each and every year during the term of the said agreement. McFarlan reserves for his employer the frute in the sd. orchard in the sd. farm. Also the priviledge of making roads through or erecting buildings in any field in the sd. farm, he, McFarlan to pay sd. McCormack and Montgomery the damage the same will make to be decided by 2 neutral men chosen by each party and they are to repair said publick house at their own expense, sow grain on the fields of the sd. farm every other year, and to keep the fences in good repair.
Witness: Ephraim Dunlap.
Proven: In open court Sullivan County November Sessions, 1800, by the oath of Ephraim Dunlap.
Regst: November 20th, 1800. Test: Mattw. Rhea, C. S. C.

---

(340) JAMES DENTON : to : DEED OF WARRANTY JOHN JONES :

Date: August 19th, 1799.
Consideration: $424.00.
Amt. of land: 113 acres.
Location: Sullivan County, Tennessee.
Description: A certain tract or parcel of land containing 113 acres be the same more or less lying in sd. county of Sullivan on Kindricks Creek including the plantation where the said Jones now lives.
Witnesses: John Denton, William Denton, James Jones.
Proven: In open court by James Jones Sullivan County November Sessions 1799.
Registered: December 4th, 1800. Test: Mattw. Rhea, C. S.C.

STATE OF TENNESSEE : JAMES YOUNG AND JOSEPH YOUNG : DEED OF WARRANTY to : JAMES KING :

Date: October 7th, 1797.
Consideration: $400.00.
Amt. of land: Bank of ore on the tract of land which was granted to Elizabeth Young in trust for the orphans of James Young who were the aforesaid James and Joseph Young.
Agreement: James King was given the privilege of digging and hauling ore from the bank aforesaid also cutting and keeping open road to the great road for the purpose of hauling ore and sd. King is not to encroach on the land in possession of Samuel Crocket.
Witnesses: John Crothers , J. Punch.
Assignment: For the sum of $400.00 James King assigned to John Goodson all said Kings right and title to the within mentioned ore bank and the within mentioned priviledge granted to sd. King by James Young and Joseph Young September 13th, 1799.
Witness: John Punch.
Proven: The within bill of Seal and assignment proven in open court

by the oath of John Punch Sullivan County, August Sessions, 1800.
Regst: December 4th, 1800. Test: Mattw. Rhea, Clk. Sullivan Cty.

---

(342) SIMON HOLT : to : DEED OF WARRANTY HUGH CRISTY :

Date: August 19th, 1800.
Note: This deed was written to correct error in deed dated Sept. 1, 1793 from Thomas Hughs to Simon Holt.
Consideration: $50.00.
Amt. of land: 10 acres.
Location: Sullivan County, Tennessee.
Description: Ten acres of land part of the said tract of land whereon sd. Simon Holt now lives.
Acknowledged: In open Court by Simon Holt Sullivan County August Sessions, 1800.
Regst: December 4th, 1800. Test: Mattw. Rhea, Clk. Sullivan County.

---

(343) PHILLIP SNAPP : to : DEED OF WARRANTY ELKANAH DULANEY :

Date: May 21st, 1800.
Consideration: $20.00.
Amt. of land: 170 acres.
Location: Sullivan County, Tennessee.
Description: A certain tract or parcel of land containing 170 acres.
Witness: Hohn Anderson.
Acknowledged: In open court by Phillip Snapp State of Tennessee Sullivan County, May Sessions, 1800.
Registered: December 4th, 1800. Test: Mattw. Rhea, C. S. C.

---

(344) STATE OF NORTH CAROLINA : SAMUEL ASHE, GOV. : LAND GRANT to : NO. 745. JOHN ANDERSON :

Date: Nov. 17th, 1797.
Consideration: 50 shillings fro ev ry 100 acres of land.
Amt. of land: 75 acres.
Location: Sullivan County, North Carolina.
Description: A tract of land containing 75 acres lying and being in our County of Sullivan on the waters of Reedy Creek.
Witness: Samuel Ashe, Esquire, By his Excelly. Comd. J.Glasgow,Sec.
Registored: December 4th, 1800.

---

(345) STATE OF NORTH CAROLINA : SAMUEL ASHE, GOV. : LAND GRANT to : NO. 693 JOHN ANDERSON :

Date: July 20th, 1796.

Consideration: 50 shillings fro ev ry 100 acres of land.
Amt. of land: 54 acres.
Location: Sullivan County, North Carolina.
Description: A tract of land containing 54 acres laying and being in our county of Sullivan.
Witness: Samuel Ashe, Esquire. By his Excellys.Comd.J.Glasgow,Sec.

---

(346) STATE OF NORTH CAROLINA : LAND GRANT
SAMUEL ASHE, GOV. : NO. 749.
to
ALEXANDER FORD

Date: November 17th, 1797.
Consideration: 50 shillings for every 100 acres of land.
Amt. of land: 40 acres.
Location: Sullivan County, North Carolina.
Description: A tract of land containing 40 acres lying and being in the county of Sullivan on the North side of Holston River.
Witness: Samuel Ashe, Gov. By his Excellys. Comd. J. Glasgow,Sec.
Registered: December 4th, 1800.

---

(347) STATE OF NORTH CAROLINA : LAND GRANT
SAMUEL ASHE, GOV. : NO. 769
to
ARCHABALD TAYLOR

Date: November 17th, 1799.
Consideration: 50 shillings for every 100 acres of land.
Amt. of land: 50 acres.
Location: Sullivan County, North Carolina.
Description: A tract of land containing 50 acres lying and being in Sullivan County.
Witness: Samuel Ashe, Gov. By his Excellys. Comd. J. Glasgow,Sec.
Registered: December 4th, 1800.

---

(348) JESSE EVERT : DEED OF WARRANTY
to
WILLIAM SMITH

Date: October 2d, 1800.
Consideration: $1000.00.
Amt. of land: 199 acres.
Location: Sullivan County, Tennessee.
Description: A certain tract or parcel of land lying and being in the state and county aforesaid on the waters of fall creek containing 199 acres be the same more or less.
Witnesses: Riachard Gammon, George Gammon.
Acknowlegdd: In open court November Session 1800.
Test: James Gaines, Deputy for Matthew Rhea.
Registered: December 5th, 1800.

---

(349) JONATHAN PHILLIPS : DEED OF WARRANTY
to
JOHN PHILLIPS

Date: March 31, 1800.

(Page)

Condideration: 300 £.
Amt. of land: 248 acres.
Description: A certain tract or parcel of land lying and being on the south side of Holston River it being the plantation where said Jonathan Phillips now lives.on.
Witnesses: Daniel Allen, Asher Crockett.
Proven: In open court Sullivan County May Sessions, 1800, by the oath of Daniel Allen.
Registered: December 5th, 1800. Test: Mattw. Rhea, C. S.C.

JONATHAN PHILLIPS : to : DEED OF WARRANTY JOHN PHILLIPS :

Date: March 31, 1800.
Consideration: 300 £.
Amt. of land: 100 acres.
Location: Sullivan County, Tennessee.
Description: One certain tract or parcel of land lying and being on the south side of Holston River (bounds) containing 100 acres more or less.
Witnesses: Daniel Allen, Asher Crockett.
Proven: In open court by the oath of Daniel Allen Sullivan County May Sessions, 1800.
Registered: December 5th, 1800. Test: Mattw. Rhea, C. S. C.

---

(350) JOHN HALL : to : DEED OF WARRANTY JOHN BISHOP :

Date: October 10th, 1800.
Consideration: 40 £.
Amt. of land: 135 acres.
Location: Sullivan County, Tennessee.
Description: All that tract and parcel of land in Sullivan County surveyed for 135 acres more or less.
Witness: Ruben Barnard, Richard Hicks.
Proven: In open court State of Tennessee Sullivan County, November Sessions, 1800. James Gains, Deputy Clerk for Mattw. Rhea, Clerk of Sullivan County.
Registered: December 5th, 1800.

---

(351) JACOB SUSONG : to : DEED OF WARRANTY ANDREW SUSONG :

Date: May 20th, 1800.
Consideration: $300.00.
Amt. of land: 75 acres.
Location: Sullivan County, Tennessee.
Description: A certain tract or parcel of land containing 75 acres be the same more or less.
Witness: John Anderson.
Acknowledged: In open court Sullivan County May Sessions, 1800.
Registered: December 27th, 1800. Test: Mattw. Rhea, C. S.C.

(Page)
(352) JAMES ANDERSON :
to : MORTGAGE
JAMES KAIN :

Date: September 18th, 1799.
Consideration: $233.33.
Amt. of land: 250 acres.
Description: One certain tract or parcel of land containing 250 acres surveyed by the sd. James Anderson and granted to him by the state of North Carolina by virtue of a patent dated July 29th, 1793, located in Sullivan County, Tennessee.
Terms: James Anderson and his heirs are to pay sd. James Kain $233.33 with interest from date, to be paid on or before February 18th, 1800. This deed is also to give an injunction in court with bond and sufficient security conditioned as the law directs to secure the payment of $233.33 with interest also all costs and damages which shall be awarded against the sd. James Anderson. Should default be made in the performance of this conditions said property is to revert peaceably to said James King. Until default be made in performance of this deed James Anderson to have peaceable possession of said property.
Witness: James Gaines.
Proven in open court by the oath of Gaines, Nover. Session, 1799.
Registered: Feb. 3d, 1801.

---

(354) JAMES ANDERSON :
to : MORTGAGE
JAMES KAIN :

Date: February 18th, 1799.
Consideration: 70 ½ dollars rated at six shillings each.
Amt, of land: 250 acres.
Description: One certain tract or parcel of land in the county of Sullivan State of Tennessee containing 250 acres surveyed for the sd. James Anderson and granted to him by the State of North Carolina, July 29th, 1793.
Terms: James Anderson is to pay James Kain the above sum with interest on or before Feb. 18th, 1800. An injunction is to be obtained in the court of Sullivan County to secure the payment of this sum with all cost and damages which shall be awarded against said Anderson. Should default be made in payment of said sum James Kanin and his heirs are to have peaceful possession of sd. property. Until default shall be made James Anderson to have and to hold and enjoy peaceful possession of same.
Witness: James Gaines. John McElderry, D. M. Crow.
Proven: In open court by the oath of James Gaines State of Tennessee, Sullivan County, November Session 1799.
Regst. Dec. 3d, 1801. Test: Mattw. Rhea, C. S. C.

---

(356) JOHN SHELBY, JUNR. :
to : DEED OF WARRANTY
JOHN SHELBY, SENR. :

Date: May 3d, 1797.
Consideration: $100.00.

Amt. of land: 200 acres.
Location: Sullivan County, Tennessee.
Description: One certain tract and parcel of land supposed to containing 200 acres be the same more or less lying and being in Sullivan County.
Witnesses: Alexander Greer, Thomas Shelby.
Proven: In open court Sullivan May Sessions, 1799, by Thomas Shelby.
Regst. February 4th, 1801. Regst. Test: Matthew Rhea, C. S. C.

---

(357) ANDREW GREER : to : DEED OF WARRANTY THOMAS ROCKHOLD :

Date: April 11th, 1797.
Consideration: $350.00.
Amt. of land: 400 acres.
Location: Sullivan County, Tennessee.
Description: A certain tract or parcel of land situated lying and being in the county of Sullivan on the North side of Holston River including Womack's olaf fort (bounds) containing 400 acres more or less agreeable to an original patent granted from the state of North Caolina to Andrew Greer No. 581, dated July 1793.
Witnesses: Landon Carter, John Molins.
Executed: In open court Sullivan May Session 1799 by Andrew Greer.
Regst. February 13th, 1801, Test: Mattw. Rhea, C. S. C.

---

(358) JAMES ANDERSON : to : MORTGAGE JAMES KAIN :

Date: April 22d, 1800.
Consideration: $64.24.
Amt. of land: 39 acres.
Description: Two certain tracts or parcels of land containing 39 acres one tract granted to him the sd. James Anderson by the state of North Carolina dated July 27th, 1793; one other tract containing 14 acres conveyed to the said James Anderson by John McDonald dated December 2d, 1793.
Condition: That the sd. James Anderson is to pay or cause to be paid unto the sd. James Cain, His heirs and assigns on or before May 1st, 1801 the aforesai sum of $64.24 with interest from the date hereof. This indenture is to secure the payment of said sum to the said James Kain. If said sum be not paid on or before the 4th day of May, 1801, said James Kain is to recover the said sum as is usual in mortgages of like nature without hindrance from sd. James Anderson. Until default is made in payment sd. James Anderson to hold and enjoy the sd. premises.
Witnesses: Francis H. Gains, Zachariah Wells, Sullivan County Febr. Session, 1801.
Regst. February 17th, 1801. Test: Mattw. Rhea, C. S. C.

(Page)
(360) GEORGE LITTLE : to : DEED OF WARRANTY JOHN GOSSAGE :

Date: August 20th, 1798.
Consideration: $20.00.
Amt. of land: 100 acres.
Location: Sullivan County, Tennessee.
Description: A certain tract of land containing 100 acres situated lying and being in the state and county aforesaid on the south side of Holston River.
Acknowledged: By George Little in Sullivan County August Session 1798.
Registered: February 18th, 1801. Test: Mattw. Rhea, C. S. C.

---

(361) THOMAS COOPER, ANDREW COOPER, ANDREW BEATY : to : DEED OF WARRANTY WILLIAM KING, JAMES KING, SAMUEL GOODSON :

Date: October 25th, 1800.
Consideration: $1000.00. $333-1/3 each to Thomas Cooper, Andrew Cooper, Andrew Beaty.
Amt. of land: 180 acres.
Location: Sullivan County,
Description: A certain tract or parcel of land lying and being on Beaver Creek in Sullivan County which was granted to John Cooper by the State of North Carolina November 10th, 1784; prpowrty devolved on sd. Thomas Cooper, Andrew Cooper and Andrew Beaty by marriage with Elizabeth Cooper as co-heirs of John Cooper containin180 acres be the same more or less.
Witnesses: Benjamin White, John Punch.
Proven: In open court by the oath of John Punch Sullivan County February Session, 1801.
Registered: February 28th, 1801. Test: Mattw. Rhea, C. S. C.

---

(362) JOHN CAROTHERS : to : DEED OF WARRANTY SAMUEL CAROTHERS :

Date: February 24th, 1795.
Consideration: Natural love and affection for my son Samuel and the sum of $5.00.
Amt. of land: 220 acres.
Location: Sullivan County, Territory South of the River Ohio.
Description: A certain tract or parcel of land containing 220 acres be the same more or less lying and being in the county of Sullivan on thr North side of Holston River.
Witness: John Scott.
Proven: In open court Sullivan County, February Session, 1801, by the oath of John Scott.
Registered: March 4ty, 1801, Test: Mattw. Rhea, C. S. C.

(Page)

(363) JACOB WORK : to : DEED OF WARRANTY CHARLES NEWTON :

Date: January 17th, 1801.
Consideration: $1000.00.
Amt. of land: 300 acres.
Location: Sullivan County, Tennessee.
Description: A certain tract or parcel of land situate lying and being in Sullivan county (bounds) containing 300 acres.
Acknowledged: In open court Sullivan County February Sessions 1801 by Jacob Work.
Registered: March 4th, 1801. Test: Mattw. Rhea, C. S. C.

JOHN YANCEY : to : DEED OF WARRANTY JOHN VANCE :

Date: February 16th, 1808.
Consideration: Love and affection.
Amt. of land: 450 acres.
Location: Sullivan County, Tennessee.
Description: All my land or lands lying and being in the county of Sullivan In particular a tract or tracts or parcel of land deeded to James Hollis and sold by James Eaton to the aforesaid Yancey supposed to contain 450 acres more or less; also one negro boy named Frank aged four years.
Reservation: Grantor of this land reserves natural life of living on land not to be disturbed by his son nor any other person; at his death said son to receive said land.
Proven: In open court by the oath of William Anderson, Sullivan County February Session, 1801.
Regst: March 4th, 1801. Test: Mattw. Rhea, C. S. C.

---

(365) PHILIP ISLEY : to : DEED OF WARRANTY FREDERICK DECK :

Date: February 16th, 1801.
Consideration: $190.00.
Amt. of land: 59 acres.
Location: Sullivan County, Tennessee.
Description: A certain tract or parcel of land containing 59 acres be the same more or less said land lying and being in the county aforesaid on the waters of Reedy Creek.
Witness: John Anderson.
Acknowledged: In open court Sullivan County, February Sessions, 1801, by Philip Isley.
Regst: March 10th, 1801. Test: Mattw. Rhea, C. S. C.

---

(366) ABLE EDWARDS : to : DEED OF WARRANTY THOMAS JONES :

Date: April 31st, 1798.

(Page)

(366) Consideration: 60 ₤ current money.
Amt. of land: 50 acres.
Location: Sullivan County, Tennessee.
Description: A certain tract of land in the county aforesaid containing 50 acres more or less on the south side of Holston River
Witnesses: Richard Glover, Jacob Crumley, John Buchles.
Proven: In open court May Sessions, 1798, by the oath of Jacob Crumley and Richard Glover.
Regst: March 10th, 1801. Test: Mattw. Rhea, C. S. C.

WILLIAM BAILEY :
to : DEED OF WARRANTY
MARTIN WADDLE :

Date: January 3d, 1801.
Consideration: 100 ₤ Virginia. (money)
Amt. of land: 200 acres.
Location: Sullivan County, Tennessee.
Description: A certain tract or parcel of land containing 200 acres be the same more or less.
Witness: Phillip King, James T. P. Gaines.
Proven: In open court by the oath of James T. Gains, State of Tennessee, Sullivan County, February Sessions, 1801.
Registered: April 3d, 1801. Test: Mattw. Rhea, C. S. C.

(368)

NATHAN OWEN :
to : DEED OF WARRANTY
THOMAS MCCHESNEY :

Date: Jannary 17th, 1801.
Consideration: £173.00.
Amt. of land: 43 acres.
Location: Sullivan Cunty, Tennessee.
Description: Sullivan County, Tennessee.
Witnesses: Wm. King, John Sharp.
Proven: In open court by the oath of John Sharp Sullivan County February Sessions, 1801.
Registered: April 20th, 1801. Test: Mattw. Rhea, C. S. C.

---

(368) MICHAEL MELONE :
to : DEED OF WARRANTY
CHARLES PHILLIPS :

Date: September 21, 1789.
Consideration: 30 ₤ current money of North Carolina.
Amt. of land: 97 acres.
Location: Sullivan County, Tennessee.
Description: A certain tract or parcel of land lying in the county of Sullivan on the North side of Beaver Creek the waters of Holston River contqining 97 acres.
Witnesses: Joseph Wallace, John Carponter, Jean Wallace.
Proven: By the oath of Joseph Wallace in Sullivan County December Session, 1789.
Registered: April 20th, 1801. Test: Matthew Rhea, C. S. C.

---

(370) JOSEPH COLE : to : DEED OF WARRANTY CHARLES PHILLIPS :

Date: August 28th, 1797.
Consideration: $9,37.
Amt. of land 11 ¼ (acres).
Description: A certain tract or parcel of land containing 11-1/4 be the same more or less said land being-Bevor Creek.
Witness: John Anderson.
Acknowledged: In open court by the oath of Joseph Cole Sullivan August Session 1797.
Registered: April 20th, ~~1801.--Test:~~ Mattw. Rhea, C. S. C.

---

(371) MICHAEL MALONE : to : DEED OF WARRANTY CHARLES PHILLIPS :

Date: November 28th, 1797.
Consideration: 100. _____ in hand paid.
Amt. of land: 69 acres.
Location: Sullivan County, Tennessee.
Description: A certain tract or parcel of land containing 69 acres be the same more or lesslying and being in the county aforesaid on the waters of Bevor Creek.
Witness: John Anderson.
Acknowledged: In open court by Michael Malone Sullivan November Session 1797.
Registered: April 20th, 1801. Test: Mattw. Rhea, C. S. C.

---

(372) WILLIAM NASH, JUNR. : to : DEED OF WARRANTY HENRY BORDEN :

Date: May 18th, 1801.
Consideration: Subject to such taxes as may come due for same.
Amt. of land: 1/4 of and acre.
Location& Description: A certainlott of ground in the town of Blountville known in a plqn of said town by LOtt No. 13.
Witnesses: James T. Gaines, Frances W. Gaines.
Registered: May 26th, 1801. Test: Mathew Rhea, Clerk of Sullivan County.

JOHN BISHOP : to : DEED OF WARRANTY HENRY DEVAULT :

Date: September 25th, 1797.
Consideration: 400£ current money of Virginia.
Amt. of land: 400 acres.
Location: Sullivan County, Tennessee.
Description: Part of a tract of land in the County of Sullivan and state of Tennessee on the csouth side of Holston River containing 400 acres be the same more or less.

(Page)
(372) Witnesses: Stephen Moiars, Jacob Thomas.
Proven: In open court by the oath of Stephen Moiars Sullivan February Session, 1798.
Regst: June 4th, 1801. Test: Mattw. Rhea, C. S. C.

---

(374) JOHN BISHOP : DEED OF WARRANTY
to
HENRY DEVAULT

Date: November 29th, 1800.
Consideration: $400.00.
Amt. of land: 135 acres.
Location: Sullivan County, Tennessee.
Description: All that tract and parcel of land in Sullivan County aforesaid for 135 acres be the same more ow less.
Witness: James Gragg.
Proven: In open court by the oath of James Gragg Sullivan County, February Session, 1801.
Registered: June 4th, 1801. Test: Matthew Rhea, B. S. C.

---

(375) JACOB MEYERS : DEED OF WARRANTY
to
THOMAS FORGESON

Date: September 14th, 1800.
Consideration: $400.00.
Amt. of land: 140 acres.
Location: Sullivan County, Tennessee.
Description: A certain tract of land lying and being in the county of Sullivan ahd state aforesaid on the south side of Holston River the plantation whereon the said Forgeson now lives being suposed to be 140 acres be the same more or less.
Witness: Stephen Moyars, John Richardson.
Proven: State of Tennessee, Sullivan County, November Session, 1800. Proven in open court and ordered to be registered.
Registered: June 4th, 1801. Test: James Haines, Deputy Clerk for Mathw. Rhea, Clerk of Sullivan County.

---

(376) JOHN BILLINGSBY : DEED OF WARRANTY
to
JESSE BILLINGSBY

Date: February 15th, 1800.
Consideration: Natural love and affection foar his son.
Amt. of land: 160 acres.
Location: Sullivan County, Tennessee.
Description: All that tract or parcel of land situate in the county of Sullivan aforesaid on Sinking Creek (bounds) containing 160 acres.
Witness: Nathaniel Shipley, Alexanvder Hail.
Acknowledged: By John Billingsby In court Sullivan County, February Session, 1800.
Test: Mathew Rhea, C. S. C. Regst. June 4th, 1801.

(Page)

(377) ALEXANDER HAIL : to : DEED OF WARRANTY JESSE BILLINGSBY :

Date: February 15th, 1800.
Consideration: $25.00.
Amt. of land: 7-1/2 acres.
Location: Sullivan County, Tennessee.
Description: All that tract or parcel of land situated in the county of Sullivan on Sinking Creek.(bounds) containing 7-½ acres.
Witnesses: John Billingsby, Na. Shipley.
Proven: In open court by the oath of John Billingsby Sullivan County February Session, 1800.
Registered: June 4th, 1801. Test: Mattw. Rhea, C. S. C.

---

(378) GEORGE BRIDWELL : to : DEED OF WARRANTY JAMES BRIDWELL :

Date: December 16th, 1800.
Consideration: 50 ℔.
Amt. of land: 178 acres.
Location: Sullivan County.
Description: A certain tract of land containing 178 acres be the same more or less lying in the county aforesaid on Kindricks Creek being part of the tract that the said James Bridwell now lives on.
Witnesses: Vencel Allen, William Bridwell.
Proven: In open court by the oath of William Bridwell, State of Tennessee, Sullivan County, May Session, 1801.
Regst: June 8th, 1801. Test: Matthew Rhea, C. S. C.

ELISHA COLE : to : DEED OF WARRANTY JOHN ALEXANDER :

Date: October 8th, 1800.
Consideration: $500.00.
Amt. of land: 110 acres.
Location: Sullivan County, Tennessee.
Description: A certain tract or parcel of land containing 110 acres laying and being in the county of Sullivan.
Witnesses: William King, Joseph Cole, Johnston Taylor.
Acknowledgement: State of Tennessee, Sullivan County, May Session, 1801, acknowledged in open court by Elisha Cole,
Regst: June 4th, 1801. Test: Mattw. Rhea, C. S. C.

---

(379) GEORGE BIRDWELL : to : DEED OF WARRANTY WILLIAM CHILDRESS :

Date: December 8th, 1800.
Consideration: 40 ℔.
Amt. of land: 100 acres.
Location: Sullivan County, Tennessee.

Description: A certain tract of land containing 100 acres be the same more or less lying in the county aforesaid on fall creek.
Witnesses: William Smith, James Smith.
Proven: In open court by the oath of William Smith.
Regst: June 4th, 1801. Test: Mathw Rhea, Clek of Sullivan County.

---

(380) JOHN MUSGROVE to MARTIN BOCHER : DEED OF WARRANTY

Date: February 10th, 1801.
Consideration: 40 shillings for every acre of land.
Amt. of land: 39 acres and 27 poles.
Description: That certain tract or parcel of land that is adjoining Wallery Dealor(bounds) containing 39 acres 27 poles.
Witnesses: William N. Gale, W. Willoughby.
Proven: Sullivan County, State of Tennessee, May Session, 1801, proven in open court b y the oath of William N. Gale,.
Test: Matthew Rhea. Clk. of Sullivan County.
Registered: June 5th, 1801.

---

(381) JAMES PATTERSON& ALEXANDER PATTERSON to JAMES KAIN : DEED OF WARRANTY

Date: May 1st, 1801.
Consideration: $1150.00.
Amt. of land: 398 acres.
Location: Sullivan County, Tennessee.
Description: A certain tract or parcel of land containing398 acres be the same more or less said land lying and being int ehe county aforesaid and on the waters of fall creek.
Witnesses: John Anderson, James T. Gaines.
Proven: In open court by the eath of John Anderson, Stateof Tennessee Sullivan County, May Session, 1801.
Regst: June 16th, 1801. Test: Mathew Rhea, Clerk of Sullivan Court.

---

(382) JOHN MCELDERRY to GEORGE LEDICK : DEED OF WARRANTY

Date: April 8th, 1801.
Consideration: $1744.00.
Amt. of land: 218 acres.
Location: Sullivan County, Tennessee.
Description: A certain tract or parcel of land containing 218 acres be the same more or less lying and being in the county of Sullivan as aforesaid on the waters of fall creek.
Witnesses: James Kain, George Ledecah.
Proven: In open court by the oath of James Kain and George Ledecah.
Regst: June 17th, 1801. Test: Matthew Rhea, Clerk of Sullivan Co.

---

(383) JACOB JOB to SAMUEL JOB : DEED OF WARRANTY

Date: August 14th, 1800.

Condsideration: The sum of $1.00 and love for his son.
Amt. of land: 116 acres.
Location: Sullivan County, Tennessee.
Description: All that tract or parcel of land situated in the county aforesaid on a branch of Kindrick Creek (bounds) containing 116 acres be the same more or less.
Witnesses: William Jackson, Nathan Shipley.
Proven: By the oath of William Jackson, State of Tennessee, Sullivan County in open court May Session, 1801.
Regst: May 19th, 1801. Test: Mattw. Rhea, C. S. C.

---

(384) JACOB JOB : to : DEED OF WARRANTY : WILLIAM JACKSON

Date: August 15th, 1800.
Consideration: $200.00.
Amt. of land: 75 acres.
Location: Sullivan County, Tennessee.
Description: All that tract or parcel of land situated in the county of Sullivan aforesaid on Kindrick Creek (bounds) containing 75 acres be the same more or less.
Witnesses: Samuel Job and Nathan Shipley.
Proven: State of Tennessee, Sullivan County, May Session, 1800.
Proven in open court by the oath of Samuel Job.
Regst: June 24th, 1801. Test: Mattw. Rhea, Clerk of Sullivan County.

---

(385) ROBERT GRAY, JUNR. : to : DEED OF WARRANTY : JOHN STURGEN

Date: March 7th, 1801.
Consideration: $150.00.
Amt. of land: 200 acres.
Location: Sullivan County, Tennessee.
Description: A certain tract of land laying and being in Sullivan County (bounds) containing 200 acres be the same more or less.
Witnesses: John Acuff, William Sissteer.
Regst: June 24th, 1801. Test: Mathew Rhea, Clerk of Sullivan County

---

(386) THOMAS WALLACE : to : DEED OF WARRANTY : JOB KEY

Date: October 15th, 1800.
Consideration: $200.00.
Amt. of land: A certain tract or parcel of land lying and being on Bever creek in Sullivan County which was granted by the state of North Carolina to the said Thomas Wallace for 200 acres by Patent No. 358 bearing date the 10th day of November, 1784.
Signed: Thomas Wallace, Rebeckah Wallace.
Witnesses: Joseph Wallace, Abram Cross.
Proven: In open court by the oath of Joseph Wallace, Sullivan County November Session, 1800. Test: Mattw. Rhea, Clerk of Sullivan County.
Regst: August 11th, 1801.

(Page)

(387) FRANCIS HENRY GAINS, SHERIFF to IRESON LONGACRE : SHERIFF'S DEED

Date: August 19th, 1801.
Consideration: $300.00.
Amt. of land: 168 ½ acres.
Location: Sullivan County, Tennessee.
Purpose of sale: To satisfy a writ of Fire Faciss dated May 27th, 1800, at the suit of John and William Alexander against James Young isued from th the county court of pleas and quarters Session for the county of Sullivan directed to the sheriff of the county aforesaid to be made of the goods and chattels, lands and tenements of James Young the sum of $357.355 besides othe endorsed fees which fees makes the further sum of $13.60/
Description of land sold: The land granted to Elizabeth Young in trust for the orphans of James Young on the North side of Holston River. Said tract of landsupposed to be 168 acres &1/2/
Acknowledged: In open court by Francis H. Gains, State of Tennessee, Sullivan County August Session, 1801. Test: Mattw. Rhea, Clerk of Sullivan County.
Registered: October 20th, 1801.

---

(388) JOSEPH COCK to DAVID TULLIS : DEED OF WARRANTY

Date: August 19th, 1801.
Consideration: $196.66.
Amt. of land: 60 acres.
Description: A certain tract of land containing 60 acres be the same more or lesslying and being on the waters of Reedy Creek.
Witness: John Anderson.
State of Tennessee, Sullivan County, August Session, 1801, in open court at said session acknowledged by Joseph Cook.
Regst: November 2d, 1801. Test: Mattw. Rhea, C. S. C.

---

(389) HENRY MAUK to JACOB COCK : DEED OF WARRANTY

Date: August 17th, 1801.
Consideration: $480.00 in hand paid.
Amt. of land: 144 acres.
Location: Sullivan County, Tennessee.
Description: A certain tract or parcel of land containing 144 acres be the same more or less.
Witness: John Anders.
Acknowledged: In open court by Henry Mauk State of Tennessee, Sullivan County, August Session, 1801, by Henry Mauk.
Regst: November 2d, 1801. Test: Mathw. Rhea, Clerk of Sullivan County.

(Page)
(390) EDWARD DAVID : to : DEED OF WARRANTY
JOHN QUEENER :

Date: February 15th, 1800.
Consideration: $46.00.
Amt. of land: 56 acres.
Location: Sullivan County, Tennessee.
Description: A certain tract or parcel of land containing 56 acres be the same more or less.
Witnesses: John Anderson, John Lowry.
Proven: State of Tennessee, Sullivan County, February Session, 1800. by the oath of John Anderson.
Regst: November 2d, 1801. Test: Mattw. Rhea, Clerk of Sullivan County.

---

(391)
ROBERT EASLEY & JAMES GAINES : to : DEED OF WARRANTY
MARTIN ROLLER :

Date: August 17th, 1801.
Consideration: 300 £ current money of the state of Virginia.
Amt. of land: 500 acres.
Description: A certain tract of land lyong on West Reedy Creek in the county of Sullivan and state of Tennessee (bounds) containing 500 acres more or less.
Acknowledged: In open court by James Gaines & Robert Easley State of Tennessee Sullivan County, August Sessions, 1802.
Regst. November 4th, 1801. Test: Mattw. Rhea, Clerk of Sullivan Co.

---

(392) HENRY MAUK : to : DEED OF WARRANTY
THOMAS MORRISON :

Date: August 17th, 1801.
Consideration: $100.00.
Amt. of land: 96 acres.
Location: Sullivan County, Tennessee.
Description: A certain tract or parcel of land containing 96 acres be the same more or less.
Witness: John Anderson.
Acknowledged: In open court by Henry Mauk State of Tennessee, Sullivan County August Session, 1801.
Regst: Nov. 5th, 1801. Test: Mattw. Rhea, C. S. C.

EDWARD DAVID : to : QUIT CLAIM DEED
JOHN QUEENER :

Date: February 15th, 1800.
Consideration: $100.00.
Amt. of land: 142 acres.
Location: Sullivan County, Tennessee.
Description: A certain tract or parcel of land containing 142 acres be the same more or less.

Witnesses: John Anderson, John Lowery.
Proven: In Sullivan County, open court February Session, 1800, by the oaths of John Anderson, John Lowery.
Regst: Nov. 5th, 1801. Test: Mathew Rhea, Clerk of Sullivan County.

---

(393) ISAAC HICKS, SENR. : to : DEED OF GIFT
HIS DAUGHTER JAMIMA :

Date: August 12th, 1801.
Consideration: Natural love and affection.
Amt. of land: 136 acres.
Negroes: My negro man named Tobe and my negro girl caled Elie.
Reservations: Reserving to my wife Elizabeth, the full, quiet and peaceable possession of the dwelling house I now live in for and during her natural life and also reserving to my said wife for the term of her life as aforesaid a fullmaintenance of the land hereby given and granted to my said daughter Jamima to consist of such necessaries as my said wife shall chuse.
Land: The plantation or tract of land whereon I noe reside situate in Sullivan County aforesaid in as full and ample a manner as I now hold and enjoy same and containing 136 acres be the same more or less.
Witnesses: John Spurgin, William Morgan.
Proven: In open court by the oath of John Spurgin, State of Tennessee, Sullivan County August Session, 1801.
Regst: Nov. 5th, 1801. Test: Mathew Rhea, Clerk of Sullivan County.

---

(394) NICHOLAS HAWKINS : to : DEED OF WARRANTY
ROBERT GRAY :

Date: January 15th, 1799.
Consideration: $500.00.
Amt. of land: 400 acres.
Location: Sullivan County.
Description: All that plantation or tract of land containing 400 acres more or less laying and being in said county on the head of King Branch.
Witnesses: John Williams, David Webb.
Proven: In open court Sullivan County August Session, 1801 by the oath of John Williams.
Regst: November 5th, 1801. Test: Mathew Rhea, Clerk of Sullivan County.

****

(395) HENRY SMITH : to : DEED OF WARRANTY
WALTER JAMES :

Date: November 29th, 1798.
Consideration: $400.00.
Amt. of land: 200 acres.
Location: Sullivan County, Tennessee.
Description: A certain plantation or tract of land situated and being in Sullivan County aforesaid (bounds) containing 200 acres.
Witnesses: John Williams, Job Key.
Ackno

Acknowledged: In open court by Henry Shrite Sullivan County November Session, 1799.
Regst: November 7th, 1801. Test: Mathew Rhea, Clerk Sullivan County.

---

(396) JOHN HOLLOWAY, JUNR. to DAVID ROSS : DEED OF WARRANTY

Date: December 1st, 1795.
Considetation: 42 ₤ money of Virginia.
Amt. of land: 200 acres.
Location: Sullivan County, Territory South of the River Ohio.
Description: A certain tract or parcel of land containing 200 acres be the same more or less lying and being in the county of Sullivan near Bullock Pen Run.
Witnesses: Chris Harris, Benjamin Smith, Thomas Hopkins.
Proven: In open court by Thomas Hopkins Sullivan August Session, 1796.
Regst: Nov. 10th, 1801. Test: Mattw. Rhea, Clerk of Sullivan County.

---

(397) GREENBURY DIXON to THOMAS MIRICK : DEED OF WARRANTY

Date: March 13th, 1801.
Consideration: $300.00.
Amt. of land: 100 acres.
Location: Sullivan County, Tennessee.
Description: All that tract or parcel of land situate lying and being in Sullivan County south side of Holston River on the waters of Horse Creek.
Witness: Daniel Huff, Henry Allison.
Proven: In open court, State of Tennessee, Sullivan County by the oath of Henry Alison.
Regst: Nov. 10th, 1801. Test: Mathew Rhea, Clerk of Sullivan County.

---

(398) JACOB FLEENOR to SAMUEL MCCORKLE : DEED OF WARRANTY

Date: May 19th, 1800.
Consideration: $300.00.
Amt. of land: 150 acres.
Location: Sullivan County, Tennessee.
Description: A certain tract or parcel of land containing 150 acres taken out of the tract the said David Perry now lives on.
Witness: Benjamin Birdwell, Jeremiah Chase.
State of Tennessee, Sullivan County, May Session, 1801, Proven in open court by the oath of Benjamin Birdwell.
Registered: November 12th, 1801. Test: Mattw. Rhea, C. S. C.

---

(400) MARTIN MYERS to JOHN LINDENBARGER : DEED OF WARRANTY

Date: April 14th, 1800.

Consideration: $5.00.
Amount of land: 74 ½ acres.
Location: Sullivan County, Tennessee.
Description: 74 ½ acres of the upper part of the tract whereon the said Martin now lives.
Witness: Henry Harkleroad, Michael Lindamood.
Regst: Nov. 16th, 1800. Test: Mattw. Rhea, C. of S. C.

---

(401) JOHN STROUT : to : DEED OF WARRANTY GEORGE WOLFORD :

Date: November 14th, 1801.
Consideration: $430.33.
Amt. of land: 100 acres.
Location: Sullivan County, Tennessee.
Description: A certain tract -parcel of land laying and being between Holston and Wattaugar Rivers on the waters of Wattaugar in the county and state aforesaid.
Acknowledged: State of Tennessee, Sullivan County, November Session 1801. Acknowledged in open court by John Strout.
Regst: Nov. 16th, 1801. Test: Mattw. Rhea, C. S. C.

---

(402) JAMES AND JOSEPH YOUNG : AGREEMENT

Date: October 16th, 1800.
Object of agreement: They agree on a conditional line between them to start from Samuel Crockett's line, said line has been run by Henry Harkleroad Ocotber 16th, 1800.
State of Tennessee, Sullivan County November Session, 1801. The within was proven in open court by the oath of Henry Harkleroad and ordered to be registered.
Regst: Nov. 16th, 1800. Test: Mattw. Rhea, Clk. of Sullivan County.

JOHN SEVEIR : to : DEED OF WARRANTY STEPHEN WALLIN :

Date: September 11th, 1799.
Consideration: $266.66.
Amt. of land: 100 acres.
Locatinn: Sullivan County, Tennessee.
Description: A certain tract or parcel of land containing 100 acres lying and being in Sullivan County.
Witnesses: Samuel McCorkle, Thomas Morrell.
Proven: In open court by the oath of Thomas Morrell.
Regst: Nov. 16th, 1801. Test: Mattw. Rhea, C. S. C.

LAURENCE SNAPP : to : DEED OF WARRANTY JOHN TIPTON :

Date: September 13th, 1798.
Consideration: $4000.00.
Amt. of land: 600 acres.

Location: Sullivan County, Tennessee.
Description: The plantation or tract of land whereon the said John Tipton now lives situated lying and being in Sullivan County aforesaid (bounds) Containing 600 acres.
Witnesses: John Williams, Hugh Barton.
Acknowledged: In open court Sullivan County, November Session, 1798 by Laurence Snapp.
Regst: Nov. 16th, 1801. Test: Mattw. Rhea, C. S. C.

---

(404) LEVI MULLINEX to HUGH MARTIN : DEED OF WARRANTY

Date: Jan. 12th, 1801.
Considerations 45 L ten shilling.
Amt. of land: 50 acres.
Location: Sullivan County, Tennessee.
Description: A certain tract or parcel of land lying and being in the county of Sullivan and State of Tennessee south side of Holston River on the waters of Hors Creek containing 500 acres.
Witnesses: Robert Birdwell, John Birdwell.
Proven: In open court State of Tennessee, Sullivan County, by the oath of John Birdwell.
Registered: November 24th, 1801. Test: Mattw. Rhea, C. S. C.

---

(405) JOHN JONES to EZEKIEL JONES : DEED OF WARRANTY

Date: September 15th, 1801.
Consideration: Natural love and affection for his son.
Amt. of land: 80 acres.
Location: Sullivan County, Tennessee.
Description: One certain tract or parcel of land lying and being in the county and state aforesaid supposed to be 80 acres be the same more or less lying on a branch known by the name of Garret's Branch.
Witnesses: William Copass, John Stidman.
Proven: In open court Sate of Tennessee, Sullivan County, by the oath of John Stedman. Regst. Nov. 24th, 1801.
Test: Mathew Rhea, C. S. C.

---

(406) THOMAS ROGERS to BENJAMIN BIRDWELL : DEED OF WARRANTY

Date: May 18th, 1801.
Consideration: $1000.00.
Amt. of land: 97 acres.
Location: Sullivan County, Tennessee.
Description: A certain tract or parcel of land containing by estimation 97 acres be the same more or less situated lying and being in the couty and state aforesaid on the southside of Holston River on Jerrot's Branch.
Witnesses: Rowland Perry, Jeremiah Chase.
Proven: State of Tennessee, Sullivan County, May Session 1801. The execution of the within deed is proven in open court by the oath of Rowland Parry and Jeremiah Chase.

(Page)
(406) HENRY WAGONER
to
JOHN STROUT

: DEED OF WARRANTY

Date: September 1st, 1798.
Consideration: $426.66.
Amt. of land: 100 acres.
Location: Sullivan County, Tennessee.
Description: A certain piece or parcel of land lying between Holston and Watauga River on the waters of Watauga in the county and state aforesaid (bounds) containing 100 acres.
Witnesses: John Scott, Jonathan Bradley.
Proven: In open court State of Tennessee, Sullivan County, by the oath of Jonathan Bradley.
Regst: Nov. 28th, 1801. Test: Mattw. Rhea, Clk. of Sullivan County.

---

(407) SIMON BARKER
to
JOHN RHEA

: DEED OF WARRANTY

Date: February 20th, 1800.
Consideration: $330.00.
Amt. of land: 70 acres.
Location: Sullivan County, Tennessee.
Description: One certain tract or parcel of land laying and being in Sullivan County in the State aforesaid on the sitth side of Holston River containing 70 acres more or less.
Witnesses: Francis H. Gains, James Rhea.
Proven: State of Tennessee, Sullivan County, November Sessions, 1801, The execution of the within deed is proven in open court by the oath of Francis H. Gaines.
Regst: Nov. 28th, 1801. Test: Matw. Rhea, Clerk of Sullivan County.

---

(408) MARTIN WIRICK
to
HENRY SIGLAR

: DEED OF WARRANTY

Date: November 8th, 1800.
Consideration: $500.00.
Amt. of land: 150 acres.
Description: One certain tract or parcel of land lying and being in Sullivan County and State of Tennessee and on the south side of Holston River containing 150 acres.
Witnesses: Joseph Wallace, George Wallace.
Proven: Sullivan County, February Session, 1801, proven in open court by the oath of Joseph Wallace.
Regst: Nov. 28th, 1801. Test: Mathw. Rhea, C. S. C.

---

(409) ISAAC HICKS
to
ABRAHAM HUTSON

: DEED OF WARRANTY

Date: November 16th, 1801.
Consideration: $285.00.
Amt. of land: 86 acres.

Location: Sullivan County, Tennessee.
Description: A tract of land containing 86 acres be the same more or less lying and being in the county aforesaid.
Witness: John Anderson.
Acknowledged: State of Tennessee, Sullivan County, acknowledged in open court by Isaac Hicks.
Regst: November 28th, 180. Test: Matw. Rhea, Clerk of Sullivan County.

---

(409) ABLE MORGAN : to : DEED OF WARRANTY JOHN LOWDERBACK :

Date: November 17th, 1801.
Consideration: $300.00.
Amt. of land: 33 acres.
Location: Sullivan County, Tennessee.
Description: A tract of land containing 33 acres be the same more or less lying and being in Sullivan County on the south side of Holston River including the first botton below the mouth of Horse Creek.
Signed, Sealed and Delivered in open court. State of Tennessee, Sullivan County, November Session, 1801. Test: John Kennedy, for Mathew Rhea, Clerk of Sullivan County.

---

(410) JOHN TIPTON : to : DEED OF WARRANTY JACOB STURM :

Date: February 14th, 1800.
Consideration: $75.00.
Description: A certain piece or lott of ground in the town of Blountville in sd. County on the north side of the town of Blountville and to contain 3/4 of an acre.
Acknowledged: In open court by John Tipton, Sullivan County, May Session, 1800.
Regst: Nov. 29th, 1801. Test: Mathew Rhea, C. S. C.

---

(411) JOHN GRUBB, JOHN CLAYMAN, CHRISTIAN GRUBB : to : DEED OF WARRANTY JOHN BOCHER :

Date: November 30th, 1801.
Consideration: $500.00.
Amt. of land: 200 acres.
Location: Sullivan County, Tennessee.
Description: A certain tract or parcel of land laying and being in the county and state aforesaid on both sides of little Sinking Creek.
Witnesses: Willaim N. Gale, Wm. Owens, Alex Laughlin.
Proven: Sullivan County, Tennessee, February Session, 1802, in open court by the oath of Wm. N. Gale.
Regst: Feb. 17yh, 1802. Test: Matw. Rhea, C.L.K. of Sullivan County.

---

(412) JOSEPH CROCKETT : to : DEED OF WARRANTY JEAN MOSS :

Date: October 2d, 1800.

Consideration: $4.00 per acre.
Amt. of land: 96 acres.
Location: Sullivan C unty, Tennessee.
Description: A certain tract of land containing 96 acres more or less lying and being in the county of Sullivan.
Witnesses: Willain Snodgrass, John Canfield, Samuel More.
Proven: State of Tennessee, Sullivan County, proven in open court by the oath of William Snodgrass.
Regst: January 22d, 1802. Test: Matw. Rhea, Cerlk of Sullivan County.

---

(413) JOSEPH CROCKET : DEED OF WARRANTY
to
JANE MOSS

Date: October 2d, 1800.
Consideration: $4.00 per acre.
Amt. of land: 80 acres.
Location: Sullivan County, Tennessee.
Description: A certain tract of land containing 80 acres lying and being in the county of Sullivan on a branch of Beaver Creek.
Witness: William Snodgrass.
Proven: State of Tennessee, Sullivan County, May Session 1801. Proven in open court by the oath of William Snodgrass.
Regst: Jan. 22d, 1801. Test: Mathew Rhea, Clerk of Sullivan County.

---

(414) JOSEPH YOUNG : DEED OF WARRANTY
to
KING & GOODSON,

Date: January 13th, 1802.
Consideration: $108.33.
Description, amt. of land, Location: A certain tract or parcel of land situate lying in Sullivan County aforesaid containing 6½acres be thr same more or less including the ore bank which James King purchased of James and Joseph Young and his part of the land whereon the said Jasper now lives.
Witness: Robert Cowan, Wm. Worsham, Joseph Punch.
Acknowledgement: State of Tennessee, Sullivan County, February Session 1802. Acknowledged in open court by Joseph- party thereto.
Regst: Feb. 17th, 1802. Matthew Rhea, Clerk of Sullivan County.

---

(415) JOHN SHRITE : DEED OF WARRANTY
to
HENRY STOPHEL

Date: September 5th, 1801.
Considerati n: $1920.65.
Amt. of land: 289 acres.
Location and Description: A certain tract or parcel of land containing 289 acres be the same more or less lying and being in Sullivan County aforesaid and on the waters of Steel Creek.
Witnesses: John Anderson, Geo. Vincent.
Sullivan County, February Session, 1802.
Proven: In open court by the oath of John Anderson. Test:
Matthew Rhea, Clk. of Sullivan County.
Registered: Feb. 18th, 1802.

(Page)

(416) MATTHIAS LITTLE : to : DEED OF WARRANTY GEORGE LITTLE :

Date: February 13th, 1802.
Consideration: $100.00.
Amt. of land: 100 acres.
Location: Sullivan County, Tennessde.
Description: A tract or parcel of land in the sd. County of Sullivan containing 100 acres.
Acknowledgement: Sullivan County, February Session 1802. Acknowledged in open court by Matthias Little.
Test: Mathw. Rhea Clk. of Sullivan County.
Regst: Feb. 18th, 1802.

JOHN GORSUCK : to : DEED OF WARRANTY GEORGE LITTLE :

Date: February 6th, 1802.
Consideration: $200.00.
Amt. of land: 100 acres.
Location: Sullivan County, Tennessee.
Description: A certain tract of land containing 100 acres situate lying and being in the State and county aforesaid on the south side of Holston River.
Witnesses: Thomas Rockhold, David Troxel.
Proven: State of Tennessee, Sullivan County, Febr. Session, 1802, proven in open court by the oath of Thomas Rockhold/
Regst: Feb. 18th, 1802. Test: Mattw. Rhea, Clerk of Sullivan County.

---

(417) JOHN ANDERSON, GEORGE RUTLEDGE, RICHARD GAMMON, COMMISSIONERS, : to : COMMISSIONERS' DEED WILLIAM DEARY :

Date: August 18th, 1801.
Consideration: $30.00.
Description: A certain lott of ground in the said town of Blountville known by Lott No. 2.
Acknowledged: State of Tennessee, Sullivan County, August Session, 1801, in open court by George Rutledge, and John Anderson, Senr.
Regst: Feb. 22d, 1802. Test: Mathew Rhea, Clerk of Sullivan County.

---

(418) JOHN ANDERSON, GEORGE RUTLEDGE, RICHARD GAMMON, COMMISSIONERS, : to : SOMMISSIONERS DEED WILLIAM DEARY :

Date: August 18th, 1801.
Consideration: $26.00.
Description: Two certain lotts in said town known by fromt lots Number 28 and 29, situated in the town of Blountville.
Acknowledged: State of Tennessee, Sullivan County August Session,

1801. George Rutledge and John Anderson at said session acknowledge the execution of the within deed to William Deery.
Regst: Feb. 22d,
Test: Matthew Rhea, Clerk of Sullivan County.

JOHN ANDERSON, GEORGE RUTLEDGE, :
RICHARD GAMMON, COMMISSIONERS, : COMMISSIONERS DEED
to :
WILLIAM DEERY :

Date: August 18th, 1801.
Consideration: $93.00.
Description: 2 certain lotts of ground in said town of Blountville known by front lots. Nos. 10 and 11 on the north side of street.
Acknowledgement: State of Tennessee, Sullivan County August Session, 1801. George Rutledge and John Andeerson acknowledged the within deed to William Deery. Test: Matw. Rhea, Clerk of Sullivan County.
Registered: Feb. 22d, 1802.

---

(419) WILLIAM BATY :
to : DEED OF WARRANTY
JAMES RHEA :

Date: July 6th, 1801.
Consideration: $1666.66.
Amt. of land: 250 acres.
Location: Sullivan County, Tennessee.
Description: One certain tract or parcel of land containing 250 acres lying and being in the county of Sullivan and on the north side of Holston River and on Bever creek.
Witnesses: John Rhea, James Baty.
Proven: State of Tennessee, Sullivan County, February Session, 1802, The Sullivan Sullivan County Feb. Session, Proven in open court by the oath of John Rhea, Test: Mathw. Rhea, Clerk of Sullivan County.
Regst: Feb. 22d, 1802.

---

(420) NATHANIEL BRITTON :
to :
ROBETH RHEA : DEED OF WARRANTY

Date: Sugust 31, 1801.
Consideration: A certain tract or parcel of land containing 222 acres be the same more or less lying and being in the County of Sullivan on the waters of fall creek.
Witnesses: Samuel Britton, Thomas Anderson.
Proven: State of Tennessee, Sullivan County, November Session 1801, proven in open court by the oath of Thomas Anderson.
Regst: Feb. 22d, 1802. Test: Mathew Rhea, Clerk of Sullivan County.

---

(421) JOHN SHRITE :
to : DEED OF WARRANTY
HENRY KINSERY :

Date: October 8th, 1801.
Consideration: $450.00.

Amt. of landand description: A certain tract or parcel of land lying and boing in Sullivan County andState afroesaid containing 107 acres.

Witnesses: Ephraim Smith, Jacob Susong.

Proven: Sullivan County, February Session, 1802, proven in open court by the oath of Ephraim Smith.

Regst: Feb. 22d, 1802, Test: Mathew Rhea, Clerk of Sullivan County.

---

(422) GEORGE BIRDWELL : to : DEED OF WARRANTY JOHN WALLER :

Date: Dec. 16th, 1800.

Consideration: 25 L.

Amt. of land: ;94 acres.

Location: Sullivan County, Tennossee.

Description: A certain tract or parcel of land containing 194 acres be the same more or less laying in the county aforesaid on Kendrick's Creek.

Witnesses: Daniel Allen, William Birdwell.

Proven: In open court Sullivan County, February Session, 1802, by the oath of William Birdwell.

Regst: Feb. 23d, 1802. Test: Mathew Rhea, Clerk of Sullivan County.

See Book 4

RECORDS OF SULLIVAN COUNTY

TENNESSEE

DEED BOOK RECORD VOL. 4 .

1803 - 1807.

COPYING HISTORICAL RECORDS PROJECT

WORKS PROGRESS ADMINISTRATION

Official Project No. 65-44-1498

MRS. JOHN TROTWOOD MOORE

STATE LIBRARIAN & ARCHIVIST, SPONSOR

MRS. ELIZABETH D. COPPEDGE

STATE DIRECTOR OF WOMEN'S & PROFESSIONAL PROJECTS

MRS. PENELOPE JOHNSON ALLEN

STATE SUPERVISOR

MRS. MARGARET HELMS RICHARDSON

SUPERVISOR FIRST DISTRICT

WORKERS:

MRS. BESSIE BRADSHAW

MISS HELEN CARTER

WORK COMPLETED

SEPT. 24, 1936.

The First Page in Deed Book 4 is Numbered 423.

Book 4

424 John Kellshaw, of Washington County, Va.

434 Lewis Schroyer of Washington County, Va.

435 Alexander Ford of Blount County, Tenn.

436 Jacob Yeast, of Bortetoit County, Va.

437 Robert Hensley, of Washington County, Va.

438 John Cox, of Coke County, Tenn.

440 John Cox, of Coke County, Tenn.

442 Thomas Bragg, Junr., of Green County, Tenn.

445 John Foust of Knox County, Tenn.

446 John Lindenbarger of Lancaster County, Penna.

449 James Campbell of Knox County, Tenn.

458 George Niceley of Washington County, Va.

464 Isaac Prewett, of Knox County, Tennessee to George Phillips, of Green County, Tenn.

470 William King, of Washington County, Va.

475 John Smith, of Washington County, Va.

476 John Smith of Washinggon County, Va.

482 Stockley Donelson of Knox County, Tenn.

490 Robert Gray of Washington County, Va.

492 Margaret Goad, of Hawkins County, Tenn.

494 Robert Preston, of Washington County, Va.

501 Francis Bird, of Hawkins County, Tenn.

502 Charles Ison of Hawkins County, Tenn.

508 Samuel McKinley of Knox County, Tenn.

511 John Sell, of Washington County, Va.

514 Benjamin Vanvactor, of Washington County, Va.

515 John Anderson of Washington County, Va.

521 Isaac Leabo, of Russell County, Va.

1795

Volume 4
Page 525 Thomas Capps, of Washington County, Va.

527 Jacob Seaver , of Hawkins County, Tenn.

540 John Davis, of Washington County, Va.

547 Richard March, of Washington County, Tenn.

561 Robert Craig, of Washington County, Va.

564 Richard Britton, of Smith County, Tenn.

565 John Houser, Jackson County, Tenn.

569 John Houser and David Vance of Jackson County, Tenn.

574 Peter Morgan, of Washington County, Va.

588 James Johnston, of Hawkins County, Tenn.

589 John Wadlow, of Washington County, Va.

594 James Davis, of Washington County, Va.

595 John Gifford of Washington County, Tenn. , to William Pallet of Hawkins County, Tenn.

616 Richard Condra, of Granger County, Tenn.

622 John Goodson of Washington County, Tenn.

628 Edmund Taylor, Executor of Edmund Pendleton, dec'd. & John Taylor, both of the county of Caroline.

632 John Funkhouser, of Buncum County, N. C.

636 John Newland, of With County, Va.

637 John Newland, to Joseph Newland, both of Wythe County, Va.

638 John Newland , to Joseph Newland, " " " " "

643 Nathaniel Grimms, of the County of Knoxville and Western Territory South of the River Ohio.

645 James Rowan, of Hawkins County, Tenn.

648 John Newland, of Wythe County, Va.

649 John Newland, of With County, Va.

663 John Funkhouser, Senr., of Buncomb County, N. C.

668 Lacey Bolling, of Hawkins County, Tenn.

umn 4

s 675 Joseph Everett, of Wythe County, Va.

679 Thomas Cox, Administrator of Greenbury Cox, deceased, of Davidson County, Tenn.

699 William Stacy, of Hawkins County, Tenn.

708 Jacob Work and Joseph Work, of Roan County, Tenn.- to Jenkins Whiteside of Knox County, Tenn.

711 Dallam Caswell, of Lenoir County, N. C.

712 Dallam Caswell, of Lenoir County, N. C.

722 John Baughman, Senr., son in law of Samuel Baughman, of Hawkins County, Tenn.

723 George Mortlock, of Hawkins County, Tenn.

728 William King, of Abingdon, Washington County, Va.

737 Jacob Bare, of Augusta County, Va.

740 David Ross, of Cumberland County, Va.

743 William King of Washington County, Va.

744 William King, of Abingdon, Washington County, Va.

749 John Fitzgerald, of Jackson County, Tenn.

750 John Tally, of Jackson County, Tenn.

765 Edmund Pendleton,& John Taylor, of Carline County, Virginia.

771 Nathaniel Davis, of Washington County,

777 Thomas Bragg, of North Carolina

779 Andrew Greer, Carter County, Tenn.

782 Andrew Russell, of Knoxville County, Tenn.

794 William Coper, Grainger County, Tenn.

798 Roger Browning of Green County, Tenn.

810 John Smith, late of the State of Va.

815 James Laughlin, of Washington County, Va.

821 Nicholas Wolf, of Hawkins County, Tenn. to Wm. Thomas

829 John Adams, Pendleton County, S. C.

(Page)

(423) ABRAHAM PALLET
to
THOMAS BEARD & JACOB HARTMAN : DEED OF WARRANTY

Date: Jan. 4th, 1802.
Consideration: 600 acres.
Amt. of land: 104 acres.
Location: Sullivan County, Tennessee.
Description: A certain tract of land situate lyingand being in the county aforesaid containing 104 acres.
Witness: Martin Roller, John Williams.
Proven: By the oath of Martin Roller Sullivan CountyFeb. Session 1802. Test: Mattw. Rhea, C. S. C.
Registered: Feb. 23d, 1802.

BATTICE ROLLER & HIS WIFE
ALICE,
to
JOHN KELSHAW : DEED OF WARRANTY

Date: Jan. 22d, 1802.
Amt. of land: 246 acres.
Consideration: $1000.00
Location? Sullivan County, Tennessee.
Descri ption: One tract containing 146 xacres being part of a Patent No. 571 dated July 29th, 1793. Another tract by another p patent No. 757 granted by Samuel Ashe dated Nov. 17th, 1797. Sd tracts being further described under quit claim deed of John Roller dated Feb. 18th, 1799.
Witnsses: John Thompson, John Anderson, Benj. Spezker.
Sullivan County, The execution of the within deed is proven in open court by the oath of John Anderson.
Regst; Feb. 23d, 1802.

----

(426) PETER MORRISON
to
GEORGE MORRISON, HIS SON : DEED OF WARRANTY

Date: Jan. 15th, 1802.
Consideration: Sd. land given to his son.
Location: Sullivan County, Tennessee.
Description: All that part of the tract of land I now live on South of the grate road leading down to Carters Valley. I except half the meadow and the priviledge of the pasture with all the other appurtenances thereunto belonging.
Witness: Acknowledgedd in open court by Peter Motrison, State of Tennessee, Sullivan County, Feb. Session, 1802.
Registered: March 1st, 1802.

(Page)

THOMAS FORGESON : DEED OF WARRANTY
to
CLABOURN DAVENPORT :

Date: Feb. 15th, 1802.
Consideration: $400.00.
Amt. of land: 140 acres.
Location: Sullivan County, Tennessee.
Description: A certain tract of parcel of lanf lying and being in the coutty and state aforesaid on the south side of Holston River the plantation the sd. Forgeson now lives on veing supposed to be 140 acres.
Acknowledged: In open court by Thomas Forgeson, party thereto, State of Tennessee, Sullivan County, Feb. Session, 1802.
Regst: March 1st, 1802. Test: Mattw. Rhea, C. S. C.

---

(427) ISAAC SHELBY, SHERIFF OF SULLIVAN COUNTY, : SHERIFF'S DEED
to
STEPHEN TAYLOR :

Date: August 29th, 1797.
Puppose: To settle a sute in the court of Sullivan County. Style of sute Joseph Cook against Hugh Duggan.
Amt. of land: 248 acres.
Description: A certain tract of land containing 248 acres lying and being in Sullivan County and including the plantation whereon the sd. Stephen Taylor now lives.
Executed: In open court by Isaac Shelby, Sullivan County, August Session, 1797. Test: Mattw. Rhea, C. S. C.
Registered: March 1st, 1802.

---

(428) ROBERT YANCE : DEED OF WARRANTY
to
JOHN WEAVER :

Date: Dec. 4th, 1801.
Consideration: $600.00.
Amt. of land: 151 acres.
Location: Sulivan County, Tennessee.
Description: A certain tract of land lying and being in the county aforesaid said tract containing 151 acres.
Witnesses: John Yance, Samuel Moor.
Proven: By the oath of John Yance in open court State of Tennessee, Sullivan County.
Registered: March 3d, 1802. Test: Mattw. Rhea, C. S. C.

---

(430) JOHN CURTIN : DEED OF WARRANTY
to
HENRY STAMMER :

Date: Nov. 16th, 1801.
Consideration: $243.00.
Amt. of land: 54 acres.
Location: Sullivan County, Tennessee.

Description: A certain tract or parcel of land containing 54 acres be the same more or less.
Witness: John Anderson.
Acknowledged: In open court by John Curtin.
Test: Mattw. Rhea, C. S. C.
Registered: March 3d, 1802.

---

(431) ROBERT WILLSON & WILLIAM WILLSON : to :DEED OF WARRANTY JOSEPH WILLSON :

Date: Feb. 15th, 1802.
Consideration: $100.00 current money.
Amt. of land: 180 acres.
Location: Sullivan County, Tennessee.
Desciption: One certain tract or parcel of land containing 180 acres being part of three surveys made in the name of Robert Willson and William Willson,
Witness: John Anderson.
Acknowledged: In open court by the oath of Robert Willson and William Willson, parties thereto. Test: Mattw. Rhea, C. S.C.
Registered: March 3d, 1802.

---

(432) SARAH SHOWN : to : DEED OF WARRANTY WILLIAM HATCHER :

Date: Dec. 7th, 1801.
Consideration: $200.00.
Amt. of land 98 acres.
Location; Sullivan County, Tennessee.
Description: A certain tract or parcel of land lying and being in Sullivan County containing 98 acres be the same more or less.
Witnesses: John Miller, Stpehen Walden, Thomas Morrell.
Proven: In open court by the oath of Thomas Morrell, State of Tennessee, Sullivan CountyFeb. Session,
Registered: March 30th, 1802. Test: Matw. Rhea, C. S. C.

---

(433) THEODORUS PRIGMORE : to : DEED OF WARRANTY JOHN THOMPSON :

Date: April 2d, 1798.
Consideration: 110 £ current money of Virginia.
Amt. of land: 200 acres.
Location: Sullivan County, State of Tennessee.
Description: A certain tract or parcel of land containing 200 acres lying and being in sd. county and state aforesaid on the North side of Holston River lying on a branch between Battice Hollers and the place that the sd. John Thompson now lives.on.
Witnesses: John Condary, Adam Stoke, Senr. .
Proven: In open court by Adam Stoke. Test: Matw. Rhea, C. S. C.
Registered: April 1st, 1802.

(Page)

(434) JOHN THOMPSON : to : DEED OF WARRANTY LEWIS SCHROGERS :

Date: Jan. 17th, 1802.
Consideration: $800.00.
Amt. of land: 250 acres.
Location: Sullivan County, State of Tennessee.
Description: The following messuage or tenements tract, piece or parcel of land situate lying and being int the county aforesaid containing 250 acres.
Witnesses: John Roller, James Igou.
Proven: In open court by John Thompson, State of Tennessee, Sullivan County Feb. Session, 1802. Test: Matw. Rhea, C. S. C.
Registered: April 2d, 1802.

----

(435) ALEXANDER FORD : to : DEED OF WARRANTY JACOB LAKE :

Date: Aug. 23d, 1800.
Consideration: $666.00.
Amt. of land: 200 acres.
Location: Sullivan County, Tennessee.
Description: A certain tract or parcel of land containing 200 acres be the same more or less lying and being in the county and state aforesaid.
Witnesses: John Anderson, Sanford Birdwell.
Proven: In open court by the oath of John Anderson State of Tennessee Sullivan County, May Session, 1802. Mattw. Rhea, C. S. C.
Registered: May 25th, 1802.

----

(436) JOHN ROLLER : to : DEED OF WARRANTY JACOB YEAST :

Date: March 19th, 1802.
Consideration: $1000.00.
Amt. of land: 254 acres.
Location: Sullivan County, Tennessee.
Description: A certain tract or parcel of land containing 254 acres lying on the waters of Reedy Creek including the plantation and improvements whreron the sd. John Roller now lives.
Witnesses: John Anderson, James Igou, Jas. Gains.
Proven: In open court by the oath of John Anderson, State of Tennessee, Sullivan County, Mat Session 1802. Test: Mattw. Rhea,C.S.C.
Registered: May 25th, 1802.

----

(437) ROBERT HENSLEY : to : DEED OF WARRANTY MICHAEL HICKMAN :

Date: April 3d, 1802.
Consideration: $250.00.
Amt. of land: 25 acres.

(Page) 5

Location: Sullivan County, State of Tennessee.
Description: A certain piece or parcel of land lying in the county and state aforesaid containing 25 acres, be the same more or less sd. lands joihing the lands of the sd. Michael Hickman.
Witnesses: Walter Preston, Peter Hiskman.
Proven: By the oath of Peter Hickman State of Tennessee, Sullivan County May Session, 1802.
Test: Mattw. Rhea, C. S. C.
Registered: May 25th, 1802.

----

(438) WILLIAM DENTON : to : DEED OF WARRANTY
JOHN COX :

Date: Aug. 27th, 1801.
Consideratinn: $483.00.
Amt. of land: 112 acres.
Location: Sullivan County, Tennessee.
Desctiption: All that tract or parcel of land situate in the county aforesaid containing 112 acres on a branch of Kendricks Creek.
Witness: Jacob Job, Zachariah Job.
Proven: In open court b y the oath of Zachariah Job.
State of Tennessee, Sullivan County.
Regst. May 25th, 1802.

----

(440) JAMES DENTON : to : DEED OF WARRANTY
JOHN COX :

Date: Aug. 25th, 1801.
Consideration: $683.00.
Amt. of land: 122 acres.
Location: Sullivan County, Tennessee.
Description: All that tract or parcel of land situate in the county of Sullivan on Kindrick Creek containing 122 acres be the same more or less.
Witnesses: Nathaniel Shipley, Samuel Job.
Proven: In open court State of Tennessee, Sullivan County May Session 1802, by the oath of Samuel Job.
Registered: May 25th, 1802.

(441)

ARTHUR HIGINS : to : DEED OF WARRANTY
WILLIAM MULLINUEX :

Date: Sept. 21st, 1801.
Consideration: $400.00.
Amt. of land: 140 acres.
Location: Sullivan County, State of Tennessee.
Description: A certain tract or ppercel of land containing 140 acres lying and being in the state and county aforesaid on the waters of the clear fork of Horse Creek.
Witnesses: John Charter, Luke Mellock.
Proven: In open court by the oath of John Chester, State of Tennessee, Sullivan County, May Session, 1802.
Registered: May 25th, 1802. Test: Mattw. Rhea, C. S.C.

(442) THOMAS BRAGG, JUNR. : to : DEED OF WARRANTY THOMAS BRAGG, SENR. :

Date: October 16th, 1801.
Consideration: $300.00.
Amt. of land: 50 acres.
Location: Sullivan County, Tennessee.
Description: A certain tract or parcel of land containing 50 acres lying and being in the county aforesaid on the walkers fork of Horse Creek.
Witness: Joseph White, Joseph White, Junr.
Proven: In open court, Sullivan County, Tennessee, by the oath of Thomas Bragg, Junr.
Registered: May 26th, 1802. Test: Matw. Rhea, C. S. C.

---

(443) MICHEL SNIDER : to : DEED OF WARRANTY BENJAMIN WHITE. :

Date: March 27th, 1802.
Consideration: $1333.33.
Amt. of land: 230 acres.
Location: Sullivan County, Tennessee.
Description: Two tratcts of land in Sullivan County aforesaid on the waters of Beaver Creek containing 150 acres and the other containing 80 acres which was granted to the sd. Snider by the State of North Carolina by patent bearing date Nov. 17th, 1797.
Witnesses: John Punch, Wm. Trigg, James King.
Proven: In open court, State of Tennessee, Sullivan County, May Session, by the oath of John Punch.
Registered: May 27th, 1802. Test: Mattw. Rhea, C. S. C.

---

(445) JOHN FOUST : to : DEED OF WARRANTY JOHN WILLIAMS :

Date: Jan. 17th, 1798.
Consideration: 50 £ current money of Virginia.
Amt. of land: 100 acres.
Location: Sullivan County, Tennessee.
Description: A certain tract or parcel of land containing 100 acres it being the land Jno. Foust obtained a patent for of the governor of Virginia bearing date 22d, July, 1793, lying in the county aforesaid on the waters of Reedy Creek a branch of the Holston River.
Witness: Alexander Campbell, John Weeks, Isaac Elliott.
Proven: In open court by the oath of John Weeks, State of Tennessee, Sullivan County, May Session, 1802.
Registered: May 28th, 1802. Test: Mattw. Rhea, C. S. C.

---

(446) JOHN LINDENBARGER : to : DEED OF WARRANTY DAVID WORLEY :

Date: Nov. 25th, 1801.

Consideration: $100.00.

Amt. of land: 74-1/2 acres.
Location: On Virginia boundary line.
Description: All that parcel of land containing 74-1/2 acres (bounds) be the same more or less.
Witness: William Gray, Peter Buckhoort, Michael Lindemude.
Proven: In open court by the oath of Michael Lindemude.
Registered: May 28th, 1802. Test: Mattw. Rhea, C. S. C.

---

(447) JOHN RILEY : to : DEED OF WARRANTY ANDREW RILEY :

Date: March 24th, 1800.
Consideration: $1000.00.
Amt. of land: 200 acres.
Location: Sullivan County, Tennessee.
Description: One certain tract or parcel of land in the sd. county aforesaid on the waters of Indian Creek on the South side of Holston River containing 200 acres.
Witnesses: Joseph Wallace, John Wallace.
Acknowledged: By John Riley, Sullivan County August Session, 1800.
Registered: June 10th, 1802. Test. Mattw. Rhea, C. S. C.

---

(448) SARAH SHOWN & HENRY SEGLER : to : DEED OF WARRANTY DOROTHY MILLER :

Date: Nov. 7th, 1801.
Consideration: $200.00.
Amt. of land: 50-more or less.
Location: Sullivan County, Tennessee.
Description: The first mentioned parties have bargained and sold unto the sd. Dorothy Miller a part of the south end of a tract of land containing 50 more or less. We the sd. Sarah Shown and Henry Segler this day received $200.00 in hand paid by the sd. Dorothy Miller for the above mentioned parcel or tract of land the receipt is hereby acknowledged by these presents.
Location: Sullivan County, Tennessee.
Witnesses: Thomas Morrell, William Hatcher, Stephen Walling.
Proven: In open court by the oath of Thomas Morrell, State of Tennessee, Sullivan County Feb. Session, 1802. Test: Matw. Rhea, C.S.C.
Registered: June 22d, 1802.

---

(449) JAMES CAMPBELL : to : DEED OF WARRANTY CATHERINE SHELBY :

Date: Dec. 8th, 1801.
Consideration: $200.00.
Amt. of land: 220 acres.
Location: State of Tennessee, Sullivan County.
Description: A certain tract or parcel of land containing 520 acres lying and being in the county and state aforesaid lying on both sides of Reedy Creek.
Witnesses: Samuel May, Isaac Shelby, John Shelby.
Proven: In open Court by the oath of Samuel May, State of Tennessee Sullivan County, August Session, 1802.

(Page)

(450) STATE OF NORTH CAROLINA :
SAMUEL ASHE, GOVERNOR, : LAND GRANT
to : NO. 775.
ISAAC LERO :

Date: Nov. 17th, 1797.
Consideration: 50 shillings for every 100 acres of land.
Amt. of land: 100 acres.
Location: Sullivan County, North Carolina.
Description: A tract of land containing 100 acres lying and being in the county aforesaid on the south side of Holston River.
Witness: Samuel Ashe, Gov. By his Excellys. Comd. J.Glasgow,Sec.
Registered: August 20th, 1802.

---

(451) GEORGE CRUMLEY :
to : DEED OF WARRANTY
JACOB TAYLOR :

Date: August 6th, 1802.
Consideration: 120 L.
Amt. of land: 74 acres.
Location? Sullivan County, Tennessee.
Description: A certain tract or parcel of land containing 7 4 acres lying and being in the said county aforesaid on the south side of Holston River.
Witnesses: William Carr, Ireson Longacre.
Proven: In open court by the oath of Wm. Carr, State of Tennessee, Sullivan County, Aug. Session, 1802.
Registered: Sept. 10th, 1802. Test: Matw. Rhea, C. S. C.

---

(453) JOHN BUCKLES :
to : DEED OF WARRANTY
ROBERT HOUSLEY :

Date: Dec. 25th, 1801.
Consideration: $450.00.
Amt. of land: By estimation 100 acres more or less.
Location: State of Tennessee, Sullivan County.
Description: A certain tract or parcel of land lying and being in said county and state aforesaid on the South side of Holston River containing by estimation 100 acres more or less.
Witnesses: Samuel Jones, John Clover.
Proven: In open court by the oath of Samuel Jones, State of Tennessee, Sullivan County, February Session, 1802.
Registered: Sept. 10th, 1802.

---

(455) DAVID BUSHONG :
to : DEED OF WARRANTY
HENRY BUSHONG :

Date: August 17th, 1802.
Consideration: $633.33.
Amt. of land: 148 acres be the same more or less.
Location: Sullivan County, State of Tennessee.
Description: A certain tract or parcel of land lying and being in

(Page)

the county and state aforesaid containing148 acres.
Witnesses: Honery Harkleroad, John Vance.
Proven: In open court by the oaths of John Vance.
State of Tennessee, Sullivan County, Aug. Session 1802.
Registered: Sept. 1[illegible]th, 1802. Test: Mattw. Rhea, C. S. C.

----

(455) JAMES CAMPBELL : to : DEED OF WARRANTY JOSHUA TAYLOR :

Date: Oct. 17th, 1795.
Consideration: 50 L.
Amt. of land: 100 acres.
Location: Sullivan County, Territory South of the Ohio.
Description: A certain tract of land containing 100 acres be the same more or less situate lying and being on the waters of Reedy Creek.
Witnesses: Joseph Cook, Alexander Campbell.
Proven: By the oath of Joseph Cook, Sullivan County, May Session 1796. Test: Mattw. Rhea, C. S. C.
Registered: Sept. 10th, 1802.

----

(456) JOHN LOWRY : to : DEED OF WARRANTY. SETH PORTERFIELD :

Date: July 24th, 1802.
Consideration: $250.00.
Amt. of land: 200 acres.
Location: Sullivan County.
Description: A certain tract or parcel of land containing 200 acres be the same more or less on the waters of fall creek.
Witness: John Anderson.
Proven: In open Court by the oath of John Anderson State of Tennessee, Sullivan County, Aug. Session, 1802.
Registered: Sept. 10th 1802. Test: Mattw. Rhea, C. S. C.

----

(457)

SETH POTERFIELD : to : DEED OF WARRANTY JOHN LOWRY :

Date: July 26th, 1802.
Consideration: $250.00.
Amt. of land: 220 acres be the same more or less.
Location: Sullivan County, Tennessee.
Description: A certain tract or parcel of land containing 220 acres be the same more or less said land lying and being in the county aforesaid on the waters of fall creek.
Witness: John Anderson.
Proven: In open court by the oath of John Anderson State of Tennessee Sullivan County August Session, 1802.
Registered: Sept. 11th, 1802. Test: Mattw. Rhea, C. S. C.

(Page)
(459) JOHN MAWRAS : to : DEED OF WARRANTY GEORGE NICELY :

Date: Aug. 17th, 1802.
Consideration: 200 £.
Amt. of land: 202 acres.
Location: Sullivan County, Tennessee.
Description: A certain tract or parcel of land lying and being in Sullivan County on Jarrats Branch on the South side of Holston River containing 20 acres.
Witness: Phillip King.
Acknowledged: In open court by Phillip King State of Tennessee, Sullivan County, August Session, 1802.
Registered: Sept. 11th, 1802. Test: Mattw. Rhea, C. S. C.

----

(460) EDMUND WARREN : to : DEED OF WARRANTY GEORGE MILLARD :

Date: August 14th, 1802.
Consideration: $200.00.
Amt. of land: 100 acres.
Location: Sullivan County, Tennessee.
Description: A certain tract or parcel of land containing 100 acres be the same more or less.
Witnesses: Thomas Majors, Samuel Carathers.
Acknowledged: In open court by Edmund Warren State of Tennessee, Sullivan County, August Session, 1802.
Registered: Sept.19th, 1802. Test: Mattw. Rhea, C. S. C.

----

(461) JOHN WERTMILLER : to : DEED OF WARRANTY DAVID HUGHS :

Date: Dec. 5th, 1801.
Consideration: $320.00.
Amt. of land: By estamation 150acres.
Location: Sullivan County, Tennessee.
Description: A certain tract or parcel of land whreon the sd. John Wertmiller formerly lived lying and being in the county aforesaid and adjoining the lands of the sd. David Hughes and George Emort, Senr. containing by estamation 150 acres.
Witnesses: Daniel Harkleroad, James Walker.
Proven: In open court by the oaths of Daniel Harklaroad State of Tennessee, Sullivan County, August Session, 1802.
Test: Matw. Rhea, C. S. C.
Registered: Sept. 11th, 1802.

----

(462) RICHARD SHIPLEY : to : DEED OF WARRANTY BENJAMIN SHIPLEY :

Date: Aug. 13th, 1802.
Consideration: $200.00.
Amt. of land: 122 acres be the same more or less.

Location: Sullivan County, Tennessee.
Description: A certain tract or parcel of land containing 122 acres lying and being in sd. county .
Witnesses: John Anderson, John Shipley.
Proven: In open court by the oath of John Shipley State of Tennessee Sullivan County August Session, 1802.
Registered: Sept. 12th, 1802. Test. Matw. Rhea. C. S. C.

---

(463) JOHN SPURGIN : to : DEED OF WARRANTY JOHN MANMELTON :

Date: Aug. 18th, 1702.
Consideration: $300.00.
Amt. of land: 100 acres more or less.
Location: Sullivan County, Tennessee.
Description: A certain tract or parcel of land containing 100 acres more or less lying and being in the sd. county aforesaid on the Wrst Fork of Muddy Creek.
Witness: John Spurgin.
Acknowledged: In open court by John Spurgin, State of Tennesese, Sullivan County, August Sessions, 1802.
Registered: Sept. 12th, 1802. Test: Matw. Rhea, C. S. C.

---

(464) ISAAC PRUETT : to : DEED OF WARRANTY GEORGE PHILLIPS :

Date: Nov. 12th, 1800.
Consideration: $200.00.
Amt. of land: 400 acres.
Location: Sullivan County, Tennesee.
Description: A certain tract or parcel of land containing 400 acres lying and being in the county aforesaid on the West fork of Horse Creek.
Witnesses: Daniel Slaven, William S;aven, William Phillips.
PRoven: In open court by the oath of William Phillips, State of Tennessee, Sullivan County, August Session 1802.
Registered: Sept. 12th, 1802. Test: Mattw. Rhea, C. S. C.

---

(465) JOHN SHIPLEY : to : DEED OF WARRANTY RICHARD SHIPLEY :

Date: May 17th, 1802.
Consideration: $200.00.
Amt. of land: 71 acres more or less.
Location: Sullivan County, Tennessee.
De scription: A certain tract of land containing 71 acres in the co unty of Sullivan on the waters of fall creek.
Wi tnesses: John Jennings, James Hogan.
Acknowledged: In open court by John Shipley, State of Tennessee, Sullivan County, August Sessions, 1802. Test: Matw. Rhea, C. S C.
Registered: Sept. 13th, 1802.

(Page)

(466) FRANCIS H. GAINES, Sheriff : to :SHERIFF'S DEED JOHN FEGAN :

Date: Nov. 13th, 1801.
Purpose: To settle the suit of Fireas Facies issued from the court of pleas and quatter Session for the county afoResaid at the suit of David W. Benazel and other writ of Fire Facias issued as aforesaid ath the suit of John Fegan both against John Riley and directed to the Sheriff of Sullivan County commanding the sd. Sheriff that of the goods and chattels, lands and tenements of the sd. John Riley he should cause to be made the sum of $8.725 being the amount of fire facias at the suit of DavidW. Benazel and of the fire facias at the suit of John Fegan the sum of $114.31 being the amount which was recovered against the said John Riley which James Ware recovered in sd. court against John Riley. By virtue of which write a certain tract of land containing 200 acres be the same more or less was sold at public auction.
Description: A certain tract of land containing 200 acres be the same more or less the land lying on Indian Creek.
Said land was sold by sd. Sheriff for the sum of $21.00.
Acknowledged: In open court by Francis H. Gaines, State of Tennessee, Sullivan County, August Session, 1802. Test: Matw. Rhea, C. S. C.
Registered: Oct. 19th, 1802.

----

(467) JEREMIAH TAYLOR, SENR.
to
ROBERT PALLET

Date: Feb. 12th, 1802.
Consideration: $500.00.
Amt. of land: 100 acres.
Location: Sullivan County, Tennessee.
Description: A certain piece or parcel of land situate lying and being in the county and state aforesaid and containing 100 acres which sd. piece or parcel of land is to include the piece or parcel of land whereon Jeremiah Taylor, Junr. formerly dwelt. If upon an actual survey to be hereafter made by several agreed upon by the sd. Jeremiah Taylor, Senr. and Robert Pallet it shall appear that there are more than 100 acres contaimined within within sd. lines then the sd. Robert shall pay to the sd. Jeremiah for the overplus at the same rate per acre he was to pay for the sd. 100 acres and if any deficiency should appear the sd. Jeremiah to allow the sd. Robert at the same rate per acre for such deficiency, and the said Robert doth hereby for him his heirs and assigns relinquish all right and claim to 1/2 acre of said land allowed by Jeremiah Senr. and now made use of as a place of religious worship.
Acknowledged: In open court by Jeremiah Taylor, State of Tennessee, Sullivan County, February Session, 1802. Test: Mattw. Rhea, C. S.C.
Registered: October 19th, 1802.

----

468 — ? 6

(Page)

(469) STATE OF TENNESSEE: :
ROBERT CHRISTIAN :
to : DEED OF WARRANTY
WILLIAM KING, SON OF :
JAMES KING :

Date: Nov. 11th, 1802.
Amt. of land: 1 acrex more or less.
Location: Sul ivan Countr, Tennessee.
Description: A certain <u>lott</u> or parcel of land lying and being in the county aforesaid containing 1 acre more or less being <u>lott</u> number 2 beginning at William King's of Abingdon upper corner.
Witnesses: Thos Shelby, John Goodson.
Proven: In open court by the oath of Thomas Shelby State of Tennessee, County of Shelby, Nov. Session 1802.
Registered: Dec. 1st, 1802. Test: Mattw. Rhea, C. S. C.

----

(470) ROBERT CHRISTIAN :
to : DEED OF WARRANTY
WILLIAM KING : (Original deed to the town of Kingsport)

Date: Nov. 11th, 1802.
Consideration: $60.00.
Amt. of land: 3-1/4 acres be the same more or less.
Location: Sullivan County, Tennessee.
Description: Two certain* or parceld of land lying and being in the county aforesaid, one containing 2-1/4 acres(of land) more or less, ~~the other tract containing 1 acre more or less the other being No. 1 on the hill adjoining the above heenly being separated by a road and commons with the right of commons to spring water on sd. Christian plantation~~ together with <u>priviledge</u> of landing for boats also the <u>priviledge</u> of a road or roads out to the great Road leading from Roses Furnace to Hawkins Courthouse the most <u>conveneant</u> and best road also the right of commons up the road to the River Bottom and of the front of the lots laid off and intended to be laid off and the <u>presant</u> road up to Reedy creek fording or the best way into the road leading from Roses furnace to Abingdon with the <u>Previledge</u> of boats laying along the River Bank also the rights of commons to cross streets and <u>allays</u> and to a street 90 feet wide laid off to the lots and paraleld with the river sd. Street, Commons the Road and <u>way</u>(?) aforesaid leading from River Bottom to Hawking Courthouse at the back of the second Row of <u>Lotts</u> from the river and running east <u>parel</u> with the River until it intersect with the Bottom road.
Witnesses: A Wilds, Thomas Shelby, John Goodson.
State of Tennessee, Sullivan County, Nov. Session, 1802:
Proven: In open court by the oath of Thomas Shelby, Matw. Rhea, C.S.C.
Registered: Dec. 2d, 1802.

This deed corrected Page 13 B

----

(472) JOSHUA TAYLOR :
to : DEED OF WARRANTY
BARNALEY WAGONER :

Date: Oct. 8th, 1802.
Consideration: $1000.00.
Amt. of land: 100 acres.
Location: Sullivan County, Tennessee.
Description: A certain tract or parcel of land containing 100

(Page)
(470) ROBERT CHRISTIAN : DEED OF WARRANTY
to
WILLIAM KING

Date: Nov. 11th, 1802.
Consideration: $60.00.
Amt. of land: 3 1/4 acres be the same more or less.
Location: Sullivan County, Tennessee.
Description: Two certain * or parcels of land lying and being in the county aforesaid, one containing 2 1/4 acres more or less beginning at the sd. Christian's survey and a corner of David Ross line on the bank of Holston River thence with sd. Christian and Ross line, East with a road and commons thence with the road and Commons on River Bottom to a large bank on the River Holston West to the beginning. The other tract containing 1 acre more or less being No. 1 on the hill adjoining the above nearly being seperated by a road and commons with the right of Commons to spring water on said Christian plantation, together with priviledge of landing for boats also the priviledge of a road or roads out to the great road leading from Rosses Furnace to Hawkins Courthouse the most conveneant and best road also the right of Commons to the Road up the River Bottom and of the front of the lots laid off and intended to be laid off and the preseant road up to Reedy Creek fording or the best way into the road leading from Rosses Furnace to Abingdon with the priviledge of boats laying along the River Bank also the rights of Commons to Cross streets and allays and to a street 90 feet wide laid off to the lots and paraleled with the River sd. Streets, Commons, the Road and way (?) aforesaid leading from River Bottom to Hawkins Courthouse at the back of the second Row of Lotts from the river and runningeast parel with the River until it intersects with the Bottom road.
Witnesses: A. Wilds, Thomas Shelby, John Goodson.
Proven: In open court by the oath of Thomas Shelby, State of Tennessee, Sullivan County, Nov. Session, 1802. Matw. Rhea, C. S. C.
Registered: Dec. 2d, 1802.

The above is abstract to the deed for the town of Kingsport.

acres be the dame more or less sd. land lying and being in the county of Sullivan and on the waters of Reedy Creek.
Witness: John Droke,
State of Tennessee, Sullivan County, November Session, 1802, the within deed was proven in open court by the oath of John Droke.
Registered: Dec. 2d, 1802. Test: Matw. Rhea, C. S. C.

---

(473) JOHN SMITH : to : DEED OF WARRANTY CONRAD MILLER :

Date: April 2d, 1802.
Consideration: 25 L Virginia money.
Amt. of land: 50 acres.
Location: Washington County, State of Virginia.
Description: A certain tract or parcel of land containing 50 acres lying and being in the county aforesaid on the waters of Reedy Creek Igon Spring Branch Granted to the sd. Commonwealth of Virginia by patent bearing date 25th of February, 1880, & Surveyed 14th of May, 1796.
Witnesses: John Anderson, James Igou, John Wall.
State of Tennessee, Sullivan Counyt, November Session, 1802.
Proven: In open court by oath of James Igou. Mathew Rhea, C.S.C.
Registered: Dec. 2d, 1802.

---

(474) DANIEL AGEE : to :: DEED OF WARRANTY JOHN SPURGIN :

Date: Oct. 26th, 1802.
Consideration: $250.00.
Amt. of land: 100 acres.
Location: Sullivan County, Tennessee.
Description: All that tract or parcel of land containing 100 acres more or less lying and being in sd. county aforedaid on the south side of Holston River being part of a 300 acres tract patten No. 268 o of 300 acres from the Secretary's office and attested by his Excellys. Alexander Martin, Esquire.
Witnesses: William Nash, John Hamelton,
Proven: State of Tennessee, Sullivan County, proven in open court by the oath of John Hamelton. Test: Matw. Rhea, C. S. C.
Registered: Dec. 2d, 1802.

---

(475) FREDRICK DECK : to : DEED OF WARRANTY JACOB DECK ::

Date: Oct. 1st, 1802.
Consideration: $270.00.
Amt. of land: 59 acres.
Location: Sullivan County, Tennessee.
Description: A certain tract or parcel of land lying and being in the county aforesaid on the waters of Reedy Creek beign part of a

tract of land that was granted to the Frederick Deck by deed of Phillip Lsly bearing date the 16th of February, 1801.
Witnesses: Peter Minick, Peter Shelby.
Proven: State of Tennessee, Sullivan County, Nov. Session, 1802 in open court by the oath of Peter Winsick . Test: Mathw. Rhea, C.S.C.
Registered: Dec. 2d, 1802.

---

(476) JOHN SMITH : to : DEED OF WARRANTY JOHN HALL :

Date: April 2dn 1802.
Consideration: 40 £ Virginia money.
Amt. of land: 50 acres.
Location: Washington County, Commonwelth of Virginia.
Description: A certain tract or parcel of land containing 50 acres lying and being in the county aforesaid on the waters of Timber tree branch granted to the sd. John Smith Commonwelth of Virginia by patent bearing date 28th of February, 1800, surveyed May 5th, 1795.
Witnesses: John Anderson, James Igou.
Proven: In open court by the oath of John Anderson, State of Tennessee, Sullivan County, Nov. Session, 1802.
Regst: Dec. 2d, 1802. Test: Matw. Rhea, C. S. C.

---

(477) JEREMIAH HARRIS : to : DEED OF WARRANTY SAMUEL VANCE :

Date: Sept. 14th, 1802.
Consideration: $1241.66 2/3.
Amt. of land: 200 acres.
Location: Sullivan County, Tennessee.
Description: A certain plantation or tract of land whereon the sd. Samuel now lives situate lying and being in Sullivan County, containing 200 acres.
Witneses: Elkanah R. Dulaney, Laurance Snapp.
Proven: In open court by the oath of Elkanah R. Dulaney, State of Tennessee, Sullivan County, November Session, 1802.
Registered: Dec. 2d, 1802. Test: Mattw. Rhea, C. S. C.

---

(478) JOHN YANCE, SENR. : to : DEED OF WARRANTY JOHN YANCE, JUNR :

Date: March 26th, 1802.
Consideration: $1000.00.
Amt. of land: 360 acres.
Location: Sullivan County, Tennessee.
Description: One certain tract or parcel of land containing 360 acres more or less, beginning on Henry Borrowgets line.
Witnesses: John Jenmings, James Kain, Willaim Anderson.
Proven:InState of Tennessee, Sullivan County, May Session, 1802, by the oath of Wm. Anderson, Test: Mattw. Rhea, C. S. C.
Registered: Dec. 2d, 1802.

(Page)
(479) JOSEPH SMITH :
to : DEED OF WARRANTY
HENRY RUBY

Date: Jan. 9th, 1798.
Consideration: $40,00.
Amt. of land : 30 acres.
Location: Sullivan County, State of Tennessee.
Description: A certain tract of land lying and being in the county and state aforesaid containing 30 acres on the Big Ridge between John Crawfords land and John Waldrops.
Witnesses: John Chester, Richard Matheny.
Prove: In State of Tennessee, Sullivan County, May Session, 1802, by the oath of John Chester. Test: Matw. Rhea, C. S. C.
Registered: Dec. 4th, 1802.

---

(480) MARTIN MOYERS :
to : DEED OF WARRANTY
DAVID WORLEY :

Date: Sept, 20th, 1802.
Consideration: $400.00.
Amt. of land: 103 acres.
Location: Sullivan County, Tennessee.
Description: Whereas the sd. Martin Moyers claims 103 acres of land on the waters of Bever Creek lying between lines run by Walker and Henderson the sd. land being part of 386 acres granted to the sd. Martin Moyers by the State of North Carolina Pattent bearing date 26th of November, 1789 and part of a tract of land which was conveyed to the Martin Moyers by the State of North Carolina Pattent Baring date the 26th of November, 1789, and part of a tract of land which was conveyed to the sd. Moyers by Daniel Bealor Pattent bearing date the 26th of October 1797. The Sd. Worley also claims a part of the 103 acres the sd. Moyers in order to quit the claim of himself & Worley to the sd. in consideration of the sum of $400 to him in hand paid by the sd. Worley conveys the same to sd. Worley.
Proven: In open court by the oath of James King, State of Tennessee Sullivan CountyNov. Session, 1802. Test: Matw. Rhea, C. S. C.
Registered: Dec. 4th, 1802.

---

(482) STOKELY DONNELSON :
to : DEED OF WARRANTY
MICHAEL MONTGOMERY :

Date: Dec. 29th, 1800.
Consideration: $2000.00.
Amt. of land: 300 acres.
Location: Sullivan County, Tennessee.
Description: A certain tract of land containing 300 acres lying in Sullivan Ccounty, joining lines with Julius Hacker and Henry Harkleroad.
Witnesses: Richard Reseygrant, Hugh Stewart,State of Tennessee, Knoxville.
Affadavit: Richard Rosey Grant appeared before Andrew Jackson one of the Judges of the Superior Courts of Lard and Equity and made oat that he Richard Rosey Grant was present when sd. Stockley Donnelson signed the foregoing deed.

Andrew Jackson orfered the same to be registered.
(signed) Robert Rosey Grant.
Registered: Feb. 8th, 1803.

---

(483) EDWARD WARREN : to : DEED OF WARRANTY
JOHN WASHAM :

Date: Nov. 16th, 1801.
Consideration: $1500.00.
Amt. of land: 300 acres.
Location: Sullivan County, Tennessee.
Description: Whereas by Pattent under the Sale of North Carolina Baring date 9th of Juby, 1793, the sd. Edmond Warren bedemo seized and possesed of a certain tract of land in Sullivan County said Waren hath sold unto George Millard 100 acres of sd. tract of land, and for the aforementioned sum paid by the said John Washam hath bargained and sold unto the sd. John Washam all the remainder of sd. tract of land being 300 acres, as by the sd. grant may more fully appear.
Witnessex: Francis H. Gaines.
Proven : In open court by the oath of Francis H. Gains, State of Tennessee, Sullivan County, November Session, 1801.
Registered: Feb. 17th, 1803. Test: Mattw. Rhea, C. S. C.

(485-489) JOHN GOODSON : to : DEED OF WARRANTY
WILLIAM KING, JAMES KING, :
SAMUEL GOODSON :

Date: Feb. 17th, 1803.
Consideration: Natural love and affecetion and the sum of $150.00.
Amt. of land: 1213 acres.
Location; Sullivan County, Tennessee.
Description: Several tracts or parcels of land hereinafter mentioned containing 1213-$\frac{1}{2}$ acres lying and being in Sullivan County.(There are 5 tracts of land mentioned in the deed containing 763$\frac{1}{2}$ acres of land). Ont tact of land containing 200 acres which was conveyed by Henry Harlekroad to James King and Company by indenture bearing date January 4th, 1796. One tract or parcol of land situate lying and being in Sullivan County aforesaid containing 190 acres which was conveyeed by Julius Hacker to James King and Company by indenture bearing date Jan. 10th, 1796. One tract of land containing 200 acres situatet lying and being in aforesaid county adjoining the last mentioned tract which was conveyed to James King by John Bealor by indenture bearing date Match 10th, 1798.
One tract containing 73$\frac{1}{2}$ acres lying and being in the county aforesaud which was conveyed to James King by John Holloway by indenture bearing date october 17th, 1798.
One tract containing 100 acres including the Oer Bank known by the name of Harrises Oer Bank lying and being in the county aforesaid which was conveyed to James King by James Harris by indenture bearing date May 28th, 1799.
Witnesses: John Bredin, John Punch.
Proven: In open court by the oath of John Punch, State of Tennessee,

(489) BENJAMIN ROYSTON : REVOKING OF DEED ON PAGE 290, DEED BOOK NO.3.

Date: Feb. 23d, 1803.
Prupose: To revoked annul & manke void the above insturment so that I amy hereafter give the wholr of said lands and negroes in whatever tracts that I may desire to any of my children at ahy time diring my life.
Signed: Benjamin Royston.
Acknowledged: In open court stste of Tennessee, Sullivan County Feb. Session, 1803, by Benjamin Royston. Test: Mattw. Rhea, C.S.C.
Registered: Feb. 26th, 1803.

PETER GOAD : to : DEED OF WARRANTY MICHAEL STEAR :

Date: March 20th, 1802.
Consideration: $350.00. current money.
Amt. of land: 200 acres.
Location: Sullivan County, Tennessee.
Description: A tract of land containing 200 acres lying and being in the county aforesaid on the south side of Bay Mountain including the first bottom below the Gap of the sd. Mountain and bounded by Bays Mountain on one part and John Goad's old line on the other side.
Witnesses: Patrick Smiley, John Smiley.
Prove: In open c urt, State of Tennessee, Sullivan County, Feby. Session, 1802. Test: Mattw. Rhea, C. S. C.
Registered: Feb. 24th, 1803.

---

(490) FRANCIS H. GAINES, DEPUTY SHERIIF OF SULLIVAN COUNTY : to : DEPUTY SHERIFF'S DEED ROBERT CRAIG :

Date: March 29th, 1800.
Purpose: To enforce writ of fire faces ih a judgment claimed in the court of Sullivan County by Robert Craig against John Musgrove including 208 acres of land sd. land being sold for the sum of $10.00.
Amt. of land, one tract containing 176 acres and the other tract containing 23/ 3/4 acres.
Description: The aforesaid land lying in Sullivan County aforesaid on the waters of Bever Creek on the main road from Abington to Jonesborough .
Witness: Francis H. Gaines, Joseph Cocke.
Acknowledged: In open court Sullivan County, May Session, 1801, by Francis H. Gaines. Test: Mattw. Rhea, C. S. C.
Registered: Feb. 24th, 1803.

(Page)
(492) MARGARET GOAD : to : DEED OF WARRANTY
MICHAEL STERN :

Date: May 15th, 1802.
Consideration: $240.00.
Amt. of land: 100 acres more or less.
Location: Sullivan County, Tennessee.
Description: A certain tract or parcel of land containing 100 acres lying and being in the county aforesaid on little horse Creek.
Witnesses: Patrick Smiley, Timothy Dallon.
Proven: State of Tennessee, Sullivan County, Feb. Session, 1803, in open court by the oath of Patrick Smiley. Test: Mattw. Rhea, C.S.C.
Registered: Feb. 26th, 1803.

---

(493) JOHN ROLLER :
JOHN HAWK :
MARTIN ROLLER, DAVID ROLLER, :
GEORGE ROLLER, JACOB ISLEY, :
to :
DAVID ROLLER :

Date: Dec. 13th, 1802.
Consideration: $2000.00.
Amt. of land: 5/9 of sd. tractof land (acreage not stated).
Description: A certain tract or parcel of land lying and being in the sd. county of Sullivan and State aforesaid on the waters of fall creek on the north side of Holston River it being the plantation lately occupied by Martin Roller, deceased, adjoining Wm. Anderson, Jacob Isley, Martin Roller, Junr., Erwins Orphants and Sarah Patterson.
Witnesses: John Jennings, James Erwin,
Proven: In open Court Sullivan County, Tennessee, Feb. Session, 1803, by the oath of John Jennings. Test: Mattw. Rhea, C. S. C.
Registered: Feb. 26th, 1803.

---

(494) ROBERT CHRISTIAN : to : DEED OF WARRANTY
ROBERT PRESTON :

Date: Nov. 11th, 18o2.
Consideration: $50.00.
Amt. of land: 1 acre more or less.
Location: Sullivan County, Tennessee.
Description: A certain lot or parcel of land lying and being in the county aforesaid containing 1 acre more or less. being Lott No. 4 beginning on the sd. Robert Christian's upper line.
Witnesses: A. Wilds, Thomas Shelby, John Goodson.
Prpven : In open court by the oath of Thomas Shelby, State of Tennessee, Shelby County, Nov. Session, 1802. Test: Matw. Rhea, C. S.C.
Registered: Feb. 27th, 1803.

(Page)

(495) JOHN HICKMAN : DEED OF WARRANTY
to
JAMES ENGLISH :

Date: Dec. 7th, 1802.
Consideration: $300.00.
Amt. of land: 40 acres.
Location: Sullivan County, TENNESSEE..
Description: A certain tract or parvel of land situatel lying and being on Sullivan County aforesaid on Cedar Creek a brnach of Bever Creek being the same whereon the sd. John Hickman now resides containing 40 acres be the same more or less.
Witnesses: John Goodson, John Breden; John Punch.
Proven: In open Court, Sullivan C.untym State of Tennessee, Feb. Session, 1802, by the oath of John Punch.
Regst: Feb. 28th, 1803. Test: Matw. Rhea, C. S. C.

---

(496) TARRANCE SWINEY : DEED OF WARRANTY
to
FREDERICK WHITMAN :

Date: Feb. 15th, 1803.
Consideration: $666.67.
Amt lof land: 288 acres.
Location: Sullivan County, State of Tennessee.
Description: One certain tract or parcel of land containing 288 acreslying in the county and state aforesaid on Reedy Creek including land on both sides of the creek.
Acknowledged: In open court by Tarrance Swinney, State of Tennessee, Sullivan County, Feb. Session, 1803. Test: Mattw. Rhea, C. S. C.
Registered: Feb. 28th, 1803.

---

(497) JOHN CRAWFORD : DEED OF WARRANTY
to
DAVID ROLLER :

Date: Dec. 11th, 1802.
Consideration: $400.00.
Amt. of land: 1/9 part of a tract of land (acreage not stated)
Location: Sullivan County, State of Tennessee.
Description: One-ninth part of a tract of land lying and being in the county and state aforesaid on the North side of Holston River on the waters of fall creek and including the plantation whereon the- David Roller now lives.
Witnesses: John Jinings , James Erwin.
Proven: In open court by the oath of John Jinings Sullivan County State of Tennessee, Feb. session 1803. Test: Mattw. Rhea, C.S.C.
Registered: Feb. 28th, 1803.

---

(498) JOHN ANDERSON, SHERIFF : SHERIFF'S DEED.
to
ARCHABALD TAYLOR :

Date: Feb. 20th, 1801.
Purpose: Whereas a writ of fire faces bearing date the 6th of March 1799, at the suit of Archabald Taylor against Wm. Tatham from the county court of pleas and quarter Session for Sullivan County----- directed to John Anderson, High Sheriff of said county commanding

sd. Sheriff to make of the goods and chattiles, lands and tenements of William Chatham the sum of $106.75 also the sum of $26.67. Land sold Nov. 18th, 1799. Said Archabald Taylor having bid $50.00 for this tract of land was deeded same.
Description: Being part of a tract of land numbered in the office book 404 the land lying and being in the counnty of Sullivan and State of Tennessee lying on the North side of Holston River on the waters of Reedy Creek and on the bald hill branch.
Acknowledged: In open court by John Anderson, State of Tennessee, Sullivan County, Feb. Session, 1801, Test: Matw. Rhea, C. S. C.
Registered: March 1st, 1803.

---

(499) JACOB HARTMAN : to : DEED OF WARRANTY MARTIN ROLLER :

Date: Dec. 27th, 1802.
Consideration: $600.00.
Amt. of land: 104 acres.
Location: Sullivan County, Tennessee.
Description: A certain tract or parcel of land situate lying and being in Sullivan County aforesaid containing 104 acres.
Witnesses: John Jenings, John Queenor.
Proven: In open Courtx by the oath of John Queener, State of Tennessee, Sullivan County, Feb. Session, 1803. Test: Matw. Rhea, C. S. C.
Registered: March 1st, 1803.

---

(501) WILLIAM TREDWAY : to : DEED OF WARRANTY FRANCIS BIRD :

Date: Feb. 20th, 1796.
Consideration: 50 L Virginia currency.
Amt. of land: 150 acres more or less.
Description: A certain tract or parcel of land lying on the North side of Holston River containing 150 acres.
Witnesses: John W. Crunk, John Woolf.
Deposition: State of Tennessee, Washington County on the 14th day of March, 1803, personally came John Woolf a witness to the within indenture before me David Campbell one of the Judges of the Superior Courts of law and Equity in and for the State of Tennessee who being first duly sowrn Deposith and soueth that he was present and saw William Tredway the within named signs seal and deliver as his act and deed the within indenture for the purpose therein.(Signed) John Woolf, David Campbell.
Registered: April 16th, 1803.

---

(502) WILLIAM TREDWAY : to : DEED OF WARRANTY CHARLES ISON :

Date: March 14th, 1796.
Consideration: 50 L.
Amt. of land: 150 less or more.

Location: Hawking Couhnty, Tennessee.
Description: A certain tract or parcel of land lying and being in the county of Hawkins on the North side of the North fork of Holston River containing 150 more or less.
Witnesses: John W. Crunk, John Woolf.
Acknowledged: State of Tennessee, WashingtonCounty on the 14th of March 1805, before David Campbell one of the Judges of the Superior Court of Law and Equity in and for the State of Tennessee, personally appeared before me John Woolf who first being duly sworn deposith and saieth that he was present and saw William Tredway sign the foregoing deed for the use and purpose therein expressed.
(signed) John Woolf, David Campbell.
Registered: April 16th, 1803.

---

(503) JONATHAN BRADLEY : to : DEED OF WARRANTY JOHN GRAHAM :

Date: April 8th, 1800.
Consideration: $200.00.
Amt. of land: 59¼ acres.
Location: Sullivan County, Tennessee.
Description: A certain tract of pand containing 59¼ acres situate lying and being intoh county of Sullivan.
Witnesses: John Scott, John Scott, Junr.
Proven: In open court by John Scott, State of Tennessee, Sullivan County, May Session, 1803, Test: Matw. Rhea, C. S. C.
Registered: May 24th, 1803.

***

(504) JOHN GRAHAM : to : DEED OF WARRANTY JAMES KING :

Date: Feb. 15th, 1803.
Consideration: $233.00.
Amt. of land: 59 ¼ acres.
Location: Sullivan County, Tennessee.
Description: A certain tract or parcel of land containing 59 acres and 1/4 situate lying and being in the state and county aforesaid.
Proven: In open court by the oath of John Scott, State of Tennessee, Sullivan County, May Session, 1803, Test: Matw. Rhea, C. S. C.
Registered: May 24th, 1803.

*****

(505) CONRAD ISLEY : to : DEED OF WARRANTY JACOB LADY :

Date: April 26th, 1803.
Consideration: $1166.67.
Amt. of land: 238 acres.
Location: Sullivan County, Tennessee.
Description: A certain tract or parcel of land containing 238 acres be the same more or less.
Witnesses: John Jening, John Roller, John Quecner.

Proven: State of Tennessee, Sullivan County, May Session, 1803, proven in open court by the oath of John Quesener.
Registered: May 24th, 1803. Test: Matw. Rhea, C. S. C.

(506) ROBERT WILLSON : to : DEED OF WARRANTY WILLIAM WILLSON :

Date: May 15th, 1803.
Consideration: $300.00.
Amt. of land: 152 acres.
Location: Sullivan County, Tennessee.
Description: A certain tract or parcel of land containing 152 acres be the same more or less said land lying and being in the county and State aforesaid and on the waters of Reedy Creek.
Witnesses: John Anderson, James Cooke.
Acknowledged: In open court by Robert Willson, State of Tennessee, Sullivan County, May Session 1803. Test: Mathw. Rhea, C S. C.
Registered: May 24th, 1803.

SAMUEL MCKINLEY : to : DEED OF WARRANTY ISAAC MCKINLEY :

Date: Feb. 23d, 1803.
Conisderation: $333.33 1/3.
Amt. of land: By estimation 150 acres.
Desdription: A certain tract or parcel of land containing by estimation 150 acres situate lying and being in the county aforesaid joining Christian Weaver from survey.
Wtinesses: John Scott, Joseph Scott.
Acknowledged: In open court by the oath of Joseph Scott, State of Tennessee, Sullivan County, May Session, 1803.
Registered: May 24th, 1803.

(507) FRANCIS H. GAINES : to : DEED OF WARRANTY JAMES KAIN :

Date: June 21st, 1802.
Consideration: $2000.00.
Amt. of land: 262 acres.
Location: Sullivan County, Tennessee.
Description: One certain tract or parcel of land lying on Tennessee River above the mouth of Clinch which tract of land granted by the State of North Carolina to William Cloud, Isaac Cloud, Jason Cloud, and James Gaines sd. grant beraing date the 27th of November, 1799, doth full7 set forth b ounded as follows to wit Beginning at the lower point of the first large Island in Tennessee River above the mouth of Clinch.
Witness: John Jennings.
Proven:InState of Tennessee, Sullivan County, Feb. Session, 1803, open court by the oath of John Jenings. Test: Matw. Rhea, C. S.C.
Registered: May 25th, 1803.

(Page)

(508) MARY POPE AND GEORGE MOODY : to : DEED OF WARRANTY JOHN SHIPLEY :

Date: May 14th, 1803.
Consideration: $100.00.
Amt. of land: 300 acres.
Location: Sullivan County, Tennessee.
Description: All that tract or parcel of landsituate lyingandd being in the county aforesaid on the North side of Holston River containing 100 acres be the same more or less its being part of a tract of land by the state of North Carolina to Valentine Pope containing 300 acres No. 531 Feb. 13th, 1798.
Witnesses: PeterEAsley, Adam Stoke.
Proven: In open court by the oath of Robert Easley, State of Tennessee, Sullivan County, May Sessions, 1803.
Registered: May 25th, 1803. Test: Matw. Rhea, C. S. C.

---

(510) MARY POPE & GEORGE MOODY : to : DEED OF WARRANTY ELI SHELBY :

Date: May 14th, 1803.
Consideration: $100.00.
Amt. of land: 300 acres.
Location: Sullivan County, Tennessee.
Description: A;; that tract or parcel of land situate lying and being in the affresaid county on the North side of Holston River containing 100 acres be the same more or less it being part of a tract of land granted by the state of North Carolina to Valentine Pope containing 300 acres No. 531 dated Feb. 13th, 1791.
Witnesses: Robert Easley, Adam Stoke.
Proven: In open court by the oath of Robert Easley, State of Tennessee, Sullivan County, May Session, 1803. Test: Matw.Rhea, C.S.C.
Registered: May 25th, 1803.

---

(511) JOHN SMITH : to : DEED OF WARRANTY NATHAN PEOPLES :

Date: May 14th, 1803.
Consideration: $100.00.
Amt. of land: 31 acres.
Location: Sullivan County, State of Tennessee.
Description: A certain tract or parcel of land containing 31 acres lying and being in the state and county aforesaid on the waters of Horse Creek it being a piece of land out of the tract belonging to said Smith.
Acknowledged: In open court by John Smith, State of Tennessee, Sullivan County, May Session, 1803. Test: Matw. Rhea, C. S. C.
Registered: May 26th, 1803.

---

(512) JOSEPH SMITH : to : DEED OF WARRANTY JAMES MITHINIA :

Date: May 16th, 1803.

(Page)

(512) Consideration: $450.00.
Amt. of land: 180 acres.
Location: Sullivan County, State of Tennessee.
Description: A certain tract or parcel of land containing 180 acres be the same more or less lying and being in the county and state aforesaid on the waters of horde creek including the plantation where James Mithinia now lives.
Witnesses: John Chester, Mary Chester.
Proven: In open court, State of Tennessee, Sullivan County, May Session 1803, by the oath of John Chester.
Registered: May 26th, 1803.

---

(513) JOHN SELL : to : DEED OF WARRANTY MARTIN MICKLY :

Date: April 14th, 1803.
Consideration: $50.00.
Amt. of land: 14 acres being part of a 204 acres tract.
Location: Sullivan County, Tennessee.
Description: One certain tract or parcel of land in the county aforesaid containing 14 acres being part of a 204 acres tract of land granted sd. Sells by indenture of bargain and sale and from John Solomon Sells lying on the waters of Bever Creek.
Witnesses: Henry Harkleroad, John Shoe.
Proven: State of Tennessee, Sullivan County, May Session 1803, proven in open court by the oath of Henry Harkleroad.
Test: Matw. Rhea, C. S. C.
Registered: August 10th, 1803.

---

(514) JOHN BROOKS : to : DEED OF WARRANTY BENJAMIN VANVACTOR :

Date: Nov. 8th, 1796.
Consideration: 130 £ Virginia money.
Amt. of land: 120 acres.
Location: Sullivan County, Tennessee.
Description: All that tract or parcel of land lying and being in the county of Sullivan and on the south side of Holston River containing 120 acres.
Witnesses: John Billingsby, Charles Porter.
Proven: In open court by the oath of John Billingsby, Sullivan County, Tennessee, May Session, 1796.
Registered: Aug. 18th, 1803. Test: Matw. Rhea, C. S. C.

---

(515) JOHN RICHARDSON : to : DEED OF MORTGAGE :: JOHN ANDERSON :

Date: August 11th, 1803.
Consideration: $200.00 good and lawful money of the State of Tennessee.
Condition: The above sum is to be paid on or before Aug. 11, 1804, otherwise this deed to become null and void.

AMT. of land: 380 acres.
Location: Sullivan County, Tennessee.
Description: A certain tract or parcel of land containing by estimation 380 acres ly ing and being in the county of Sullivan and State of Tennessee.
Witnesses: Samuel Powel, John Anderson.
Proven: In State of Tennessee, Sullivan County, August Sessions, 1803, mortgage of land from John Richardson to John Ander son is proven by the oath of Samuel Powell. Test: Matw. Rhea, C. S. C.
Registered: Aug. 18th, 1803.

---

(518) THOMAS SHELBY, SHERIFF, to WALLACE WILLOUGHBY : SHERIFF'S DEED

Date: Aug. 15th, 1803.
Purpose: To satisfy 12 writes of Venditone Exponas dated May 12, 1803 at the suit of Francis Berry and others against Joseph Friend, the amount to be made as follows:

Francis Berry	$40.00
Conrad Sharrats	5.00
Thomas Saddler	12.00
John McCrob	13.18
Wm. Carmack	9.25
Andrew Bear	3.00
John Bookers	8.00
Stanton Pemberton 0000	12.00
Robert Preston	14.19
Jonathan Ebbler	16.00
James Graham	
Peter Brickbill	51.00

Executed: By Sheriff'ssale at public auction to the highest bidder agreeable to law the lot lying in the town of Greenfield said lott lying and being in the county of Sullivan, State of Tennessee being part of Lott No. 1 agrreable to the plat of said town said lot being sold at the price of $132.00.
Acknowledged: State of Tennessee, Sullivan County, August Sessions, 1803. The execution of the within deed is acknowledged in open court by Thomas Shelby. Test: Mattw. Rhea, C. S. C.
Registered: Aug. 18th, 1803.

---

(519) JOSEPH YOUNG and JOHN SHARP IN BEHALF OF IRESON LONGACRE : AGREEMENT

Date: March 23d, 1803.
James Young , now deceased, was possessed in fee simple in partnership with Joseph Young a certain undivided moiety of land containing 250 acres and a half more or less of good land exclusive of the knobs. Whereas James young had mortgaged sd. undivided moiety of land to John Sharp and afterward said land was sold by a judgment obtained in Sullivan County Court against James Young by sd. sheriff of sd. county and Ireson Longacre become purchaser and a deed in fee simple was executed by him to sd. Longacre. A petition was presented to sd. County Court by sd.

Ireson Longacre praying a pertition of sd. individual moiety of land and Joseph Yuungand John Sharp for himself and Ireson Longacre have mutuatlly agreed to make a pertition themselves. Joseph Young in the first place and John Sharp for himself and Ireson Longacre are to have half of the sd. undivided moiety of land as soon as Capt. Shyker can lay it off which shall be between this and the 26th of the month, and the knobs land is to be equally divided.
Witnesses: Benjamin Shyker, Thomas Machesney, James George, John Holland.
Proven: State of Tennessee, Sullivan County, August Session, 1803, the Execution of this indenture of writing is proven in open court by the oath of Thomas Machesney ans James George.
Registered: August 27th, 1803, Test: Mathw. Rhea, C. S. C.

---

(520) ROBERT PALLET to ABRAHAM PALLET : DEED OF WARRANTY

Date: Feb. 22d, 1803.
Consideration: $800.00 .
Amt. of land: 100 acres.
Location: Sullivan County, Tennessee.
Description: A certain piece or parcel of land situate lying and being in the county aforesaid and sd. land to contain 100 acres.
Witness: State of Tennessee, Sullivan County, Feb. Session, 1803.
Acknowledged: Execution of the deed is acknowledged in open court by Robert Pallet. Mattw. Rhea, C. S. C.
Registered: August 27th, 1803.

---

(521) ISAAC LEABO to JOHN SPURGIN : DEED OF WARRANTY

Date: March 17th, 1803.
Consideration: $166.66.
Amt. of land: By estimation, $100.00res.
Location: Sullivan County, Tennessee.
Description: All that tract or parcel of land lying and being in the county aforesaid on the south side of Holston River,containing by estimation 100 acres.
Witness: James Gregg, John Sanders.
Proven: In open court, State of Tennessee, Sullivan County, May Session, 1803. by the oath of James Gregg. Test: Matw. Rhea,C.S.C.
Registered: Aug. 27th, 1803.

---

(522) JOHN ROLLER to JACOB LADY : DEED OF WARRANTY

Date: June 18th, 1803.

Consideration: $410.00.
Amt. of land: 82 acres.
Location: Sullivan County, Tennessee.
Description: A certain tract or parcel of- containing 82 acres be the same more or less sd. land lying and being in sd. county aforesaid .
Witnesses: Elianor Fagan, John Anderson.
Acknowledged: State of Tennessee, Sullivan County, August Sessions, 1803, in open court by John Roller. Test: Matw. Rhea, C. S.C.
Registered: Aug. 27th, 1803.

---

(523) JOHN PHILLIPS to JONATHAN PHILLIPS : DEED OF WARRANTY

Date: March 12th, 1803.
Consideration: $200.00.
Amt. of land: 100 acres.
Location: Sullivan County, State of Tennessee.
Description: A certain tract or parcel of land situate lying and being in state and county aforesaid on the south dide of Holston River.
Witnesses: William Thomas, John Allen.
Proven: State of Tennessee, Sullivan County, August Session, 1803, execution of the within deed proven in open court by the oath of John Allen. Test: Mathw. Rhea, C. S. C.
Registered: August 27th, 1803.

---

(524) ROBERT HENSLEY to FREDERICK LEONARD : DEED OF WARRANTY

Date: August 31, 1802.
Consideration: $1000.00.
Amt. of land: 75 ¼ acres.
Location: Sullivan County, State of Tennessee.
Description: A certain tract or parcel of land containing 75 ¼ acres of land be the same more or less lying and being int the county and state aforesaid on the waters of Beber Creek.
Witnesses: Ephraim Smith, Ephraim Johnston, Isaac Stoffle.
Proven: State of Tennessee, Sullivan County, August Session, 1803, execution of the within deed proven in open court by the oath of Isaac Stoffle. Test: Mattw. Rhea, . C .S. C.

---

(525) JOHN FEGAN to THOMAS CAPPS : DEED OF WARRANTY

Date: October 4th, 1800.
Consideration: $1000.00.
Amt. of land: 261 acres.
Description: A certain tract ot parcel of land containing 261 acres be the same more or less granted to the sd. Fegan by a deed of conveyance from the Sheriff of Sullivan County, Sd. deed bearing date Sept. 1789.

Witnesses: John Anderson, David Dyer.
Acknowledged: In open court by John Fegan, Sullivan County, February Session, 1803. Test: Matw. Rhea, C. S. C.
Registered: Sept. 10th, 1803.

---

(526) HENRY MAUK : to : DEED OF WARRANTY JOHN MAUK :

Date: Aug. 15th, 1803.
Consideration: Natural love and affection, which the said Henry Mauk hath and bareth to this son John Mauk also for the better maintenance and support livelihood and preferment of him the said John Mauk.
Description: A certain tract or parcel of land containing 127 acres lying and being on the north side of Holston River.
Witnesses: John Anderson.
Acknowledged: In open court State of Tennessee, Sullivan County, Aug. Session, 1803, by Henry Mauk. Test: Matw. Rhea, C. S. C.
Registered: Sept. 10th, 1803.

---

(527) WILLIAM NASH : to : DEED OF WARRANTY JACOB SEAVER :

Date: Aug. 15th, 1803.
Consideration: $180.00.
Amt. of land: 180 acres.
Location: Sullivan County, Tennessee.
Description: A certain tract or parcel of land containing 180 acres be the same more or less lying in the county aforesaid on the waters of Reedy Creek.
Witness: John Jennings.
Acknowledged: In open court State of Tennessee, Sullivan County, August Session, 1803. by William Nash. Test: Matw. Rhea, C. S. C.
Registered: Sept. 10th, 1803.

---

(528) HENRY MAUK : to : DEED OFR WARRANTY GEORGE WILYARD :

Date: August 15th, 1803.
Consideration: Natural love and affection which the sd. Henry Mauk hath and beareth to the sd. George Wilyard, as also for the better maintenance, support livelihood and preferment.
Amt. of land: 122 acres.
Description: One certain tract or parcel of land containSng 122 acres be the same more or less situate lying and being onthe North side of the Holston River.
Witness: Jihn Anderson.
Acknowledged: In open court State of Tennessee, Sullivan County, August Session, 1803, by Henry Mauk. Test: Matw. Rhea, C.S.C.
Registered: Sept. 12th, 1803.

---

(530) THOMAS TOVERA : to : DEED OF WARRANTY THOMAS CAPPS :

Date: March 28th, 1802.
Consideration: $960.68.
Amt. of land: 275 acres.
Location: Sullivan County, Tennessee.
Desdription: A certain tract or parcel of land lying and being in sd. County containing 275 acres be the same moreor less.
Witness, John Andersonl
Proven: In open court by the John Anderson, State of Tennessee, Sullivan County, May Session, 1803. Test: Matw. Rhea, C. S. C.
Registereed: Sept. 20th, 1803.

---

(531) GEORGE BEALOR : to : DEED OF WARRANTY FREDERICK NICODEMUS :

Date: Dec. 4th, 1802.
Consideration: 650 L.
Amt. of land: 267 acres.
Location: Sullivan County, State of Tennessee.
Description: A certain tract or parcel of land containing 267 acres lying and being in the connty and state aforesaid.
Witnesses: John Vance, Conrad Sharretz.
Proven: In open Court, State of Tennessee, Sullivan county, May Session, 1803, by the oath of Conrad Sharretz.
Registered: Sept. 28th, 1803. Test. Matw. Rhea, C. S. C.

---

(532) STATE OF NORTH CAROLINA : SAMUEL ASHE, GOV. : LAND GRANT to : NO. 702. THOMAS TONEY :

Date: July 20th, 1796.
Consideration: 5o shillings for every 100 acres of land.
Amt. of land: 117 acres.
Location: Sullivan County, North Carolina.
Descriptikn: A tract of land conatining 117 acres lying add being in our County aforesaid, surveyed the 30th day of August, 1795.
Witness: Samuel Ashe, Gov. By Comd. J. Glasgow, Sec.
Registered: Nov. 21, 1803.

---

(533) STATE OF NORTH CAROLINA : RICHARD DOBBS SPAIGHT, GOV. : LAND GRANT to : NO. 571 ROBERT JACKSON :

Date: June 27th, 1793.

(Page)
Consideration: 50 shillings for every 100 acres of land.
Amt. of land: 50 acres.
Location: Sullivan County, Tennessee.
Description: A tract of land containing 50 acres lying and being in our county and state aforesaid.
Witness: Richard Dobbs Spaight, Gov. By Command J. Glasgow, Sec.
Registered: Nov. 22d, 1803.

---

(534) WALLACE WILLOUGHBY : to : DEED OF WARRANTY
WILLIAM N. GALE :

Date: Nov. 21st, 1803.
Consideration: $130.00
Amt. of land: A certin lot.
Description: A certin house and lot in the town of Greenfield int eh county and state aforesaid its being at this time in possession of Joseph Fiend and has been taken by the sheriff of sd. County and executed and sold as the p roperty of the sd. Friend wherein the aforesaid Wallace Willoughby became the purchaser by virtue whereof the sd. Sheriff aforesaid hath executed a conveyance.
Witnesses: William King, Jacob Booher.
Stateof tTennessee, Sullivan County November Sessions, 1803, acknowledged in open court by William N. Gale. Test: Matw. Rhea, C.SC
Registered: Nov. 23d, 1803.

---

(535) WALLACE WILLOUGHBY : to : DEED OF WARRANTY
JACOB BOCHER :

Date: Nov. 21st, 1803.
Consideration: $40.00
Description: A certain lot or piece of land now in his actual possession in the town of Greenfield.
Amt. of land: 1 acrex and 59 poles.
Location: In the town of Greenfield, near Sinking Creek.
Witnesses: Willism King, Hannah Friend, William N. Gale.
Proven: In open court, State of Tennessee, Sullivan County, Nov. Session, 1803, by William King. Test: Matw. Rhea, C. S. C.
Registered: Nov. 23d, 1803.

---

(535) WILLIAM N. GALE : to : DEED OF WARRANTY
CONRAD SHARRATZ :

Date: Nov. 21st, 1803.
Consideration: $140022
Amt. of land: 75 acres.
Location: Sullivan County, State of Tennessee.

Description: A certain tract or parcel of land lying and being in the county and state aforesaid containing 75 acres West of Sinking Creek.
Witness: State of Tennessee, Sullivan County, November Session, 1803, proven in open court by William N. Gale.
Registered: Nov. 23d, 1803.

---

(536) WALLACE WILLOUGHBY : to : DEED OF WARRANTY CONRAD SHARRATZ :

Date: Nov. 21st, 1803.
Consideration: $100.00.
Amt. of land: 15 acres and 58 poles.
Description: A certain piece or parcel of land containing 15 acres and 58 poles near the mill road. (Sullivan County, Tennessee)
Witnesses: William N. Gale, William King. Test: Matw. Rhea, CSC.
Registered: Nov. 23d, 1803.

---

(537) WILLIAM ELLIOTT : to : DEED OF WARRANTY ADAM MILLER :

Date: Aug. 13th, 1803.
Consideration: $2666.66.
Amt. of land: 300 acres.
Location: Sullivan County, State of Tennessee.
Description: A certain tract or parcel of land lying and being in the county and state aforesaid containing 300 acres, one of the boundaries being Reedy Creek.
Proven: State of Tennessee, Sullivan County, Aug. Session, 1803, proven in open court by the oath of Isaac Elliott.
Witnesses: David Tullis, Isaac Elliott.
Registered: Nov. 23d, 1803.

---

(538) RICHARD SHIPLEY : to : DEED OF WARRANTY MARSHAL GALLOWAY :

Date: Nov. 25th, 1803.
Consideration: $300.00.
Amt. of land: 71 acres.
Location: Sullivan County, Tennessee.
Description: A certain tract of land containing 71 acres more or less lying in the county aforesaid on the waters of Fall Creek.
Witnesses: John Jennings, George Gifford, David Roller.
Proven: State of Tennessee, Sullivan County, Nov. Session, 1803, in open court by the oath of Richard Shipley.
Registered: Nov. 23d, 1803. Test: Matw. Rhea, C. S. C.

---

(539) WILLIAM NASH, SENR. : to : DEED OF WARRANTY
WILLIAM NASH, JUNR. :

Date: Oct. 6th, 1803.
Consideration: $2000.00 good and lawful money of Tennessee.
Amt. of land: By estimation 434 acres.
Location: Sullivan County, State of Tennessee.
Description: A certain tract of land containing by estimation 434 acres be the same more or less lying and being in the county and state aforesaid.
Witness: Willaim Nash, Junr.
State of Tennessee, Sullivan County, Nov. Session, 1803½
Proven and acknowledged in open court by William Nash, Senr.
Registered: Nov. 23d, 1803. Test: Matw. Rhea, C. S. C.

---

(540) JOHN DAVIS : to : DEED OF WARRANTY
JACOB DECK :

Date: June 21st, 1803.
Consideration: $600.00.
Amt. of land: 143 acres.
Description: One certain tract or parcel of land containing 143 acres lying on the waters of Beech and Reedy Creek it being a part of a survey granted to John Davis by patent bearing date August 21st, 1794.
Witness: Michael Deck.
Proven: In open Court, State of Tennesse, Sullivan County, Nov. Session, 1803, by Michael Deck. Test: Matw. Rhea, C.S.C.
Registered: Nov. 23d, 1803.

---

(541) PETER FOUTS : to : DEED OF WARRANTY
JACOB DROKE :

Date: Sept. 28th, 1803.
Consideration: $300.00.
Amt. of land: 80 acres.
Location: Sullivan County, Tennessee.
Description: A certain tract or parcel of land lying and being in the county and state aforesaid containing 80 acres be the same more or less.
Witnesses: John Anderson, Peter Droke.
Proven: State of Tennessee, Sullivan County, Nov. Session, 1803, in open court by the oath of Peter Droke.
Registered: Nov. 23d, 1803. Test: Matw. Rhea, C. S. C.

---

(542) BARANEY WAGONER : to : DEED OF WARRANTY
JACOB SINK :

Date: Nov. 21st, 1803.

CONSIDERATION: $1000.00.
Amt. of land: 100 acres.
Location: Sullivan County, Tennessee.
Description: A certain tract or parcel of land wontaning 100 acres be the same more or less said land lying and being in the county aforesaid on the waters of Reedy Creek.
Acknowledged: State of Tennessee, Sullivan County, Nov. Session, 1803, in opne court by the oath of Barnaby Wagoner.
Registered: Nov. 23d, 1803. Test: Matw. Rhea, C. S. C.

---

(543) WILLIAM TOWSON : to : DEED OF WARRANTY JACOB HARTMAN :

Date: Feb. 23d, 1803.
Consideration: $140.00.
Amt. of land: 25 acres.
Location: Sullivan County, Tennessee.
Description: A certain tract of land containing 25 acres be the same more or less lying and being in Sullivan County aforesaid, beginning at a poplar on a branch of Muddy Creek.
Witnesses: William Snodgrass.
Proven: In open court by William Towson, State of Tennessee, Sullivan County, Feb. Session, 1803. Test: Matw. Rhea, C. S. C.
Registered: Nov. 23dm 1803.

STEWARY ANDERSON : to : DEED OF WARRANTY HENRY DECK :

Date: Nov. 12th, 1803.
Consideration: $250.00.
Amt. of land: 50 acres.
Location: Sullivan County, Tennessee.
Description: A certain tract or parcel of land containing 50 acres be the same more or less saif land lying and being in sd. county aforesaid and on the waters of Reedy Creek.
Witnesses: John Anderson, Josiah Whitnel.
Proven: In open court by the oath of John Anderson, State of Tennessee, Sulliwan County, Nov. Session, 1803.
Registered: Nov. 24th, 1803. Test: Matw. Rhea, C. S. C.

---

(545) JOHN PHILLIPS : to : DEED OF WARRANTY HENRY MOCK :

Date: Oct. 29th, 1803.
Consideration: $1000.00.
Amt. of land: 100 acres.
Location: Sullivan County, Tennessee.
Description: A certain tract or parcel of land lying and being in the county aforesaid it being a tract of land granted to Alexander Cavitt by the state of North Carolina containing 100 acres more/or less.

Witnesses; George Vincent, George Wilyard.
Proven: In open Court State of Tennessee, Sullivan County, Nov. Session, 1803, by the oath of George Wilyard.
Registered: Nov. 24th, 1803. Test: Matw. Rhea, C.S.C.

---

(545) JOHN PHILLIPS : to : DEED OF WARRANTY HENRY MAUCK :

Date: Oct. 29th, 1803.
Consideration: $1000.00.
Amt. of land: 148 acres.
Description: A certain tract of land lying and being on the south side of Holston River it being the plantation where Jonathan Phillips now lives on.
Proven: In open court by the oath of George Wilyard, State of Tennessee, Sullivan County, Nov. Session, 1803.
Registered: Nov. 24th, 1803. Test: Matw. Rhea, C. S. C.

---

(547) PETER MCINTOSH : to : DEED OF WARRANTY RICHARD BARCH :

Date: Oct. 22d, 1803.
Consideration: $1000.00.
Amt. of land: 156 acres.
Location: Sullivan County, State of Tennessee.
Description: A certain tract or parcel of land containing by estimation 156 acres be the same more or less situate lying and being in the county and state aforesaid south side of Holston River on the waters of Kindrick Creek.
Witnesses: Alex Droke, Robert Deak.
Proven: In open court, State of Tennessee, Sullivan County, Nov. Session, 1803, by the oath of Peter McIntosh.
Registered: Nov. 24th, 1803. Test: Matw. Rhea, C.S.C.

NICHOLAS GENTRY : to : DEED OF WARRANTY JACOB DROKE :

Date: July 22d, 1803.
Consideration: $341.66.
Amt. of land: 138 acres.
Location: Sullivan County, Tennessee.
Description: A certain tract or parcel of land containing 138 acres lying and being in the county aforesaid on the waters of Reedy Creek.
Witnesses: John Anderson, Peter Droke.
Proven: In open court, State of Tennessee, Sullivan County, Aug. Session, 1803.,b y the oath of Peter Droak.
Registered: Nov. 25th, 1803. Test: Matw. Rhea, C. S. C.

(Page)

(548) RICHARD SHIPLEY, SENR. : DEED OF WARRANTY
to
MARTIN ROLLER

Date: August 20th, 1803.
Consideration: $100.00.
Amt. of land: 32 acres.
Location: Sullivan County, Tennessee.
Description: A certain tract or parcel of land containing 32 acres lying and being in the county of Sullivan aforesaid.
Witnesses: John Jenings, John Quencer.
Proven: State of Tennessee, Sullivan County, Nov. Session, 1803, in open court by John Jening. Test: Matw. Rhea, C. S. C.
Registered: Nov. 25th, 1803.

---

(549) GEORGE CROMLEY, SENR. : DEED OF WARRANTY
to
GEORGE CROMLEY, JUNR.

Date: Oct. 8th, 1803.
Consideration: $300.00.
Amt. of land: 90 acres.
Location: Sullivan County, Tennessee.
Description: A certain part of land in sd. county of Sullivan lying on the south side of Holston River on the middle part of a tract whereon sd. George Cromley, Senr. Now lives, containing 90 acres more or less sd. land was conveyed to sd. Cromley Senr. by Frederick Kaler the 10th of March, 1783.
Witnesses: Abraham Vandevanter, Daniel Cromley.
Proven: In open court State of Tennessee, Sullivan County, Nov. Session, 1803, by the oath of Abraham Vandevanter.
Registered: Nov. 25th, 1803. Test: Matw. Rhea, C. S..C.

---

(550) JACOB ISLEY : DEED OF WARRANTY
to
DAVID ROLLER

Date: Nov. 12th, 1803.
Consideration: $800.00.
Amt. of land: 142 ½ acres.
Location, Sullivan County, Tennessee.
Description: A certain tract of land lying and being in the county aforesaid on both sides of fall Creek containing 142 ½ acres.
Witnesses: John Jinings, Wm. Anderson.
Proven: In open court, State of Tennessee, Sullivan County, Nov. Session, 1803, by the oath of John Jening.
Registered: Nov. 26th, 1803. Test: Matw. Rhea, C.S.C.

(Page)
(551) SAMUEL PATTERSON : to : DEED OF WARRANTY ARCHABALD TAYLOR :

Date: Oct. 25th, 1803.
Consideration: $1000.00.
Amt. of land: 262 acres.
Location: State of Tennessee, Sullivan County.
Description: A certain tract or parcel of land containing 262 acres be the same more or less lying and being in sd. County of Sullivan and state aforesaid its being part of a grant of 265 acres of land granted by the state of North Carolina to James Patterson bearing date the 23d of October in the year 1812 and No. 17 the sd. land lying on the waters of fall creek on the north side of Holston River.
Witnesses: James Erwin, Junr, William Erwin.
Proven: In open court by the oath of William Erwin, State of Tennessee, Sullivan County, Nov. Session, 1803.
Registered: Nov. 26th, 1803. Test: Matw. Rhea, C. S. C.

---

(552) JOHN TIPTON : to : DEED OF WARRANTY WILLIAM DEARY :

Date: Nov. 23d, 1803.
Consideration: $48.00.
Amt. of land: 2 acres, a quarter and half quarter and 1617 sq. ft.
Location: Sullivan County, Tehnessee.
Description: A certain tract or parcel of land containing 2 acres, a quarter and half quarter and 1617 square feet land lying and being in sd. county and joining the town of Blountville.
Witness: John Anderson.
Acknowledged: In open court by John Tipton, State of Tennessee, Sullivan County, Nov. Session, 1803. Test: Matw. Rhea, C.S.C.
Registered: Dec, 10th, 1803.

---

(553) JOHN TIPTON : to : DEED OF WRITING WILLIAM DEARY :

Date: Nov. 23d, 1803.
Consideration: $36.00.
Amt. of land: 3/4 of an acre and 4950 square feet.
Location : Sullivan County, Tennessee.
Description: A certain tract or parcel of land containing 3/4 of an acre and 4950 square feet, sd. land lying and being in sd. county and joining the town of Blountville.
Witness: John Anderson.
Ackjowledged: In open court by the oath of John Tipton, State of Tennessee, Sullivan County, Nov. Session, 1803.
Registered: Dec. 10th, 1803. Test: Matw. Rhea, C. S. C.

---

(554)

(Page)
(554) SAMUEL VANCE : to : DEED OF WARRANTY SAMUEL EVANS :

Date: May 17th, 1803.
Consideration: $744.00.
Amt. of land: 720 acres.
Location: Sullivan County, Tennessee.
Description: A certain tract or parcel of land containing 720 acres be the same more or less lying and being in sd. county.
Witnesses: Philip Snapp, John Vance.
Acknowledged: By Samule Vance, State of Tennessee, Sullivan County, May Session, 1803. Test: Matw. Rhea, C. S.C.
Registered: Dec. 10th, 1803.

---

(555) WILLIAM N. GALE : to : DEED OF WARRANTY WILLIAM KING, SENR. :

Date: Nov. 21st, 1803.
Consideration: $130.00.
Amt. of land: A certin house and lot in the town of Greenfield.
Description: Sell all the right, title, interest and claim of him the sd. Gale in to a certain house and lott in the town of Greenfield and being occupied at this time by Joseph Friend and the lodt containing 30 poles, 3poles in front containing 10 poles back being part of lot No. 1 agreeabel to a plan of sd. town.
Acknowledged: State of Tennessee, Sullivan County, Nov. Session, 1803, in open court by sd. Willism N. GAle.
Registered: Dec. 14th, 1803. Test: Matw. Rhea, C. S. C.

FRANCES BERRY : to : DEED OF WARRANTY WILLIAM KING :

Date: Feb. 24th, 1800.
Consideration: $1500.00.
Amt. of land: 148 acres.
Location: Sullivan County, Tennessee.
Description: A certain tract or parcel of land containing 148 acres of land more or less lying and being in sd. county of Sullivan on both sides of Sinking Creek including the plantation that the sd. Berry now lives on.
Acknowledged: In open court by Frances Berry, Sullivan County, Feb. Session, 1801. Test: Matw. Rhea, C. S. C.
Registered: Dec. 14th, 1803.

JACOB SNAPP : to : DEED OF WARRANTY NICHOLAS KRESSELL :

Date: Feb. 24th, 1803.
Consideration: $616.00.
Amt. of land: 137 acres.
Location: Sullivan County, Tennessee.
Description: A certain tract or parcel of land lying and being in the county aforesaid containing 137 acres be the same more or less. ~~Witnesses~~
Witnesses: Elkanah R. Dulaney, William Owen.
Proven: State of Tennessee, Sullivan County, in open court by the oath of Elkanah Dulaney. Test: Matw. Rhea, C. S. C.
Registered: Feb. 23d, 1804. T est: Matw. Rhea, C.S.C.

---

(557) JOHN SMITH : to : DEED OF WARRANTY JONATHAN BAUGHMAN :

Date: May 16th, 1803.
Consideration: $800.00.
Amt. of land: 500 acres.
Location& description: A certain tract of land containing 500 acres be the same more or less 31 acres that the sd. Smith sold and deeded to Nathan Peoples, Senr. the ballance of sd. tract of land conveyed to sd. Baughman.
Proven: State of Tennessee, Sullivan County, May Session, 1803, in open court by the oath of John Smith.
Registered: Feb. 23d, 1804. Test: Mathew. Rhea, C. S. C.

ALEXANDER MOORE : (558) to : DEED OF WARRANTY JOHN TAYLOR :

Date: Dec. 3d, 1803.
Consideration: $595.00.
Amt. of land: 150 acres.
Location: Sullivan County, State of Tennessee.
Description: A certain tract or parcel of land containing 150 acres lying in the county and State aforesaid on the South bank of Holston River.
Witnesses: William Grimsley, Samuel Strickler.
Proven: In open court. State of Tennessee, Sullivan County, Febb. Session, 1804, by the oath of William Grimsley.
Registered: Feb. 24th, 1804. Test: Matw. Rhea, C.S.C.

---

(559) GEORGE FLIN : to : DEED OF WARRANTY JAMES PROFIT :

Date: March 6th, 1801.

Consideration: 98 £
Amt. of land: 95 acres.
Location: Sullivan County, Tennessee.
Description: All that tract or parcel of land situate lying and being in the county aforesaid containing 95 acres.
Witnesses: John Billingsby, John Proffit.
Proven: State of Tennessee, Sullivan County, Feb. Session, 1804, by the oath of John Proffitt. Test: Matw. Rhea, C.S.C.
Registered: Feb. 24th, 1804.

---

(560) JOHN HEDERICK to PETER MORGAN : DEED OF WARRANTY

Date: June 8th, 1803.
Consideration: $80.00.
Amt. of land: 30 acres.
Location: Sullivan County, Tennessee.
Description: A certain tract or parcel of land lying and being in Sullivan County containing 30 acres more or less.
Witnesses: William Stevenson, Gabriel Morgan, Isaac Wheeler.
Registered: Feb. 24th, 1804. Test: Matw. Rhea, C.S.C.

---

(561) JOHN ANDERSON, LATE SHERIFF OF SULLIVAN COUNTY to ROBERT CRAIG : SHERIFF'S DEED

Date: Aug. 12th, 1803.
Purpose: Whereas at the court of pleas and quarter Session held in the court house at Blountville August 21st, 1798, it was considered by the sd. court that Robert Craig should recover against John Musgrove $600.00 damages. The sheriff was direceted by a writ that of the possessions of the sd. John Musgrove to be made the sum of $615.085 besides other endorsed fees. Writ made returnable at the court house of the sd. townBlountville, 3d Monday in Feb. 1799. Writ returned by Francis H. Gaines deputy Sheriff with the following words nothing found an antmotion an alias fire faces issued on behalf of the sd. Robert Craig the following endorsed thereon Levied on John Musgrove right to a tract of land that sd. Musgrove now lives on and sold to Robert Craig for $10.00. Deed made by Francis H. Gaines was found defecient. To correct this, deed made by the sd. John Anderson to Robert Craig,
Description: The aforesaid tract or parcel of land lying in Sullivan County on the waters of Bever Creek on the main road from Abingdon to Jonesborough joining Woolery Bealor, Isaac Bealor, Jasper Bealor and Edward Richards the same being in containing 2 tracts, the first tract containing by estimation 176 acres the other containing 24 acres.
Witnesses: John Thomas, George Thomas,
Proven: In open court by the oath of John Thomas, State of Tennessee Sullivan County, Nov. Sessions, 1803.
Registered: Feb. 24th, 1804. Test: Mathw. Rhea, C.S.C.

(564) RICHARD BRITTON : to : DEED OR WARRANTY ROBERT RHEA :

Date: Sept. 1st, 1803.
Consideration: 244 L.
Amt. of land: 133 acres.
Location: Sullivan County, Tennessee.
Description: One certain tract or parcel of land containing 133 acres lying and being in Sullivan County, on the waters of Fall Creek.
Witnesses: Joseph Cox, William Rhea, Junr. Mathw. Rhea.
Proven: State of Tennessee, Sullivan County, in open court by the oath of Wm. Rhea, Test. Matw. Rhea, C.S.C.
Registered: Feb. 24th, 1804.

----

(565) JOHN HOUSER : to : DEED OF WARRANTY JAMES PROFIT :

Date: Sept. 9th, 1803.
Consideration: 15 L.
Amt. of land: 53 acres.
Location: Sullivan County, Tennessee.
Description: All that tract or parcel of land situate lying and being in Sullivan County on the waters of Sinking Creek.
Witnesses: Endr. Baker, William Denton.
Proven: State of Tennessee, Sullivan County, Febr. Session, 1804, by the oath of Endr. Baker. Registered: March 1st, 1804.
Test: Matw. Rhea, C. S. C.

----

(566) JEREMIAH HICKS : to : QUIT CLAIM DEED THOMAS HICKS :

Date: Feb. 28th, 1803.
Description: I do hereby give up and relinquish deliver and make over to Thomas Hicks during his lifetime a part of my land called the River field where the graveyard is also the sd. Thomas is to have half the profits of my orchard during his life time.
Witnesses: Isaac Hicks, William Morgan.
Proven: Teh execution of the above is proven in open court by the oath of Wm. Morgan, State of Tennessee, Sullivan County, Feb. Session, 1804.
Registered: March 1st, 1804. Test: Matw. Rhea, C. S. C.

JOHN ALLEN : to : DEED OF WARRANTY WILLIAM ALLEN :

Date: Sept. 9th, 1803.

Consideration: $300.00.
Amt. of land: 48 acres.
Description: A parcel of land part of a tract originially granted to Henry Goucher from the State of North Carolina bearing date 1782 No. 51, containing 48 acres more or less.
Witnesses: John Mauck, John Phillips.
Proven: State of Tennessee, Sullivan County, Feb. Session, 1804, proven in open court by the oath of John Mauck.
Registered: March 1st, 1804. Test: Matw. Rhea, C.S.C.

---

(567) JEREMIAH TAYLOR : to : DEED OF WARRANTY ROBERT PALLET :

Date: Feb. 3d, 1804.
Consideration: $1333 1/3.
Amt. of land: 165 acres.
Location: Sullivan County, State of Tennessee.
Description: A certain tract or parcel of land lying and being in sd. County of Sullivan and State aforesaid and including the plantation where the sd. Jeremiah Taylor now lives containing 165 acres/
Witnesses: Joseph Taylor, John Jenings.
Proven: In open court by the oath of John Jenings, State of Tennessee Sullivan County, Feb. Session, 1804.
Registered: March 1st, 1804. Test: Matw. Rhea, C.S.C.

---

(568) JOHN ALLEN : to : DEED OF WARRANTY WILLIAM ALLEN :

Date: Sept. 9th, 1803.
Consideration: $33.00.
Amt. of land: 25 acres.
Location+ description: A certain tract or parcel of land containing 25 acres be the same more or less situate lying and being in Sullivan County, Tennessee, on the south side of Holston River.
Witnesses: John Mauck, John Phillips.
Proven: State of Tennessee, Sullivan County, proven in open court by the oath of John Mauck, Feb. Session, 1804/
Registered: March 1st, 1804. Test: Matw. Rhea, C.S.C.

JOHN HOUSER : to : DEED OF WARRANTY DAVID VANCE :

Date: Sept. 16th, 1802.
Consideration: 200-L.
Amt. of land: 200 acres.
Location: Sullivan County, State of Tennessee.
Description: A certain tract or parcel of land situate lying and being in the county and state aforesaid containing 200 acres it being the same land granted to Jacob Goucher.
Witnesses: Jacob Slaughter, James Proffitt.
Proven: In open court, State of Tennessee, Sullivan County, Feb. Session, 1804, by the oath of James Proffitt.
Registered: March 2d, 1804. Test: Mattw. Rhea, C.S.C.

(Page)

(570) JOHN TAYLOR : to : DEED OF WARRANTY WILLIAM GRIMSLEY :

Date: Feb. 16th, 1804.
Consideration: $543.33.
Amt. of land: 120 acres.and 1/2
Location: Sullivan County, Tennessee.
Description: All that tract and parcel of land situate lying and being in the county and state aforesaid containing 120 acres and 1/2 be the same more or less.
Witnesses: Jacob Slaughter, Sarah Slaughter.
Proven: In open court by the oath of John Taylor, State of Tennessee Sullivan County, Feb. Session, 1804. Test: Matw. Rhea, C.S.C.
Registered: March 2d, 1804.

---

(571) MORRIS BAKER : to : DEED OF WARRANTY SAMUEL STRICKLER :

Date: Oct. 12th, 1800.
Consideration: $400.00.
Amt. of land: 116 acres.
Location: Sullivan County, Tennessee.
Description: Every part and parcel of a certain pace of land lying and being in Sullivan County aforesaid containing 116 acres.
Witnesses: Daniel Allen, John Day, John Hunt.
Proven: State of Tennessee. Sullivan County, May Session, 1802, Proven in open court by the oath of John Hunt.
Registered: March 2d, 1804. Test: Matw. Rhea, C.S.C.

---

(572) PETER MORGAN : to : DEED OF WARRANTY GABRIEL MORGAN :

Date: Feb. 18th, 1804.
Consideration: $800.00.
Amt. of land: 100 acres.
Location: Sullivan County, Tennessee.
Description: All that tract or parcel of land situate lying and being in sd. county of Sullivan on a fork of Horse Creek it being part of the land William Holland formerly lived on and also where where Gabriel Morgan now lives on.
Witnesses: Wm. Stevenson, Abraham Galeymore, Thomas Bragg.
Proven: State of Tennessee, Sullivan County, Feb. Session, 1804, in open court by the oath of Thomas Bragg. Test: Matw. Rhea? S.S.C.
Registered: March 10th, 1804.

(Page)

(574) PETER MORGAN : to : DEED OF WARRANTY
WILLIAM HOLLAND :

Date: Aug. 31st, 1802.
Consideration: $1200.00.
Amt. of land: 300 acres.
Location: Sullivan County, State of Tennessee.
Description: A certain tract or parcel of land containing 300 acres be the same more or less lying and being in the county and state aforesaid on the fall branch of Horse Creek.
Witnesses: Abraham Moore, Daniel Duff, John Bride,
Proven: State of Tennessee, Sullivan County, Feb. Session, 1803, by the oath of John Duff. Test: Mattw. Rhea, C.S.C.
Registered: March 10th, 1804.

---

(575) ALEXANDER MOORE : to : DEED OF WARRANTY
JOHN TAYLOR :

Date: Dec. 3d, 1803.
Consideration: $312.00.
Amt. of land: 81 acres.
Location: Sullivan County, State of Tennessee.
Description: A certain or parcel of land containing 81 acres situate lying and being in the county and state aforesaid on the south bank of Holston River.
Witnesses: William Grimsley, Samuel Strickler.
Proven: State of Tennessee, Sullivan County, Feb. 1804, in open court by the oath of William Grimsley.
Registered: March 10th, 1804. Test: Matw. Rhea, C. S. C.

---

(576) HENRY MAUCK : to : DEED OF WARRANTY
JACOB COOK :

Date: Jan. 2d, 1804.
Consideration: $566.66.
Amt. of land: 125 acres.
Location: Sullivan County, Tennessee.
Description: A certain tract or parcel of land containing 125 acres same more or less.
Witnessxx John Yancey.
Proven: State of Tennessee, Sullivan County, Feb. Session, 1804, Proven in open court by the oath of John Yancey.
Registered: March 10th, 1804. Test: Matw. Rhea, C. S. C.

STATE OF NORTH CAROLINA :
ALEXANDER MARTIN, GOV. : LAND GRANT
to : NO. 306.
DAVID HUGHS :

Date: June 17th, 1803.

Consideration: 50 shillings for every 100 acres of land.
Amt. of land: 200 acres.
Location: County of Washington.
Description: A tract of land containing 200 acres lying and being in the county of Washington on Coopers Creek.
Witness: Alexander Martin, Gov. By Comd. J. Glasgow, Sec.
Registered: June 17th, 1803, at Ragkle. William White, Sec.

---

(578) SAMUEL MCCORKLE : to : DEED OF WARRANTY JACOB GITT :

Date: Feb. 20th, 1804.
Consideration: $100.00 current money.
Amt. of land: 1 house and lott 1/4 of an acre.
Location: Sullivan County,
Description: 1 house and lott in the county aforesaid in Middletown No. 28 1/4 of an acrex being part of the tract of land sd. Miller now lives on.
Witnesses: John Anderson, William Scott.
Acknowledged: In open court by Samule McCorkle, State of Tennessee, Sullivan County, Feb. Session, 1804.
Registered: March 26th, 1804. Test: Matw. Rhea, C.S.C.

SAMUEL MCCORKLE : to : DEED OF WARRANTY JACOB GITT :

Date: Feb. 20th, 1804.
Consideration: $100.00. current money.
Amt. of land: 1 house and lott 1/4 of an acre.
Location: Sullivan County, Tennessee.
Description: 1 house and lott 1/4 of an acre in Middle Town No. 12 being part of the tract of land McCorkle now lives on.
Witnesses: John Richardson, William Scott.
Acknowledged: In open court, State of Tennessee, Sullivan County, Feb. Session, 1804, by Samuel McCorkle.
Registered: March 26th, 1804. Test: Matw. Rhea, C.S.C.

---

(579) STEPHEN MAJORS : to : DEED OF GIFT THOMAS MAJOR :

Date: Feb. 7th, 1804.
Consideration: Natural love and affection for my son Thomas Major and for other good causes.
Nature of gift: One negro man the name of Top to the property of my son Thomas Major during the life of sd. negro. I, Stephen Major, reserved this negor to myself and wife during our life time and after our death sd. negor Top to be the property of my son Thomas Major.
Witness: William Blevins.
Acknowledged: In open court by Stephen Major, State of Tennessee, Sullivan County, Feb. Session, 1804.
Test: Matw. Rhea, C. S. C. Registered: March 26th, 1804.

(Page)

(580) MICHAEL MONTGOMERY : DEED OF WARRANTY
to
JAMES ROWAN

Date: Oct. 1st, 1801.
Consideration: 100 L.
Amt. of land: 200 acres.
Location: Sullivan County, State of Tennessee.
Description: A certain tract or parcel of land containing 200 aces lying and being in the county and state aforesaid on the waters of Reedy Creek.
Witnesses: George Jacksoh. Anny Jackson.
Acknowledgement: State of Tennessee, this 4th of April, 1804, George Jackson appeared before me Hugh L. White one of the Judges of the Superior Court of law ams Equity in and for sd. state and made oath that he saw Michael Montgomery sign seal and deliver the within conveyance for the use therein expressed that he subscribed his mark as a witness and that he saw Anny Jackson make her mark as a witness thereot let it be registered. Hugh L. White.
Registered: April 9th, 1804.

---

(581) JOHN HOUSER : DEED OF WARRANTY
to
JOHN JONES

Date: March 18th, 1800.
Consideration: $333.00.
Amt. of land: 97 acres.
Location: Sullivan County, Tennessee.
Desctiption: To inslude the Double Spring and Capt. Charles muster ground situate lying and being in Tennessee, Sullivan County containing 97 acres more or less.
Witnesses: Charles Jones, Arthur Hagin.
Proven: State of Tennesse, Sullivan County, May Session, 1804, in open court by the oath of Charles Jones.
Registered: May 23d, 1904. Test: Matw. Rhea, C. S. C.

---

(583) JOHN HOUSER : DEED OF WARRANTY
to
CHARLES JONES

Date: March 18th, 1800.
Consideration: $300.00.
Amt. of land: 100 acres.
Description: Two tracts of land containing 100 acres more or less; a part being thereof being sold to Charles Jones.
Witnesses: John Jones, John Willingford.
Proven: State of Tennessee, Sullivan County, May Session, 1804, proven in open court by the oath of John Jones.
Registered: May 23d, 1804. Test: Matw. Rhea, C. S. C.

(Page)
(584) WILLIAM GOAD : to : DEED OF WARRANTY JOHN CRAWFORD :

Date: May 17th, 1804.
Consideration: 100 $.
Amt. of land: 200 acres.
Location: Sullivan County, State of Tennessee.
Descroption: A certain tract or parcel of land containing 200 acres lying and being in Sullivan County, and state aforesaid on Walkers Fork of Horse Creek.
Witnesses: Peter Easley, Thomas Easley.
Proven: In open court by the oath of Robert Easley.
Registered: May 23d, 1804. Test: Matw. Rhea, C.S.C .

---

(585) JOSEPH ROSE, EXECUTOR OF " " DECEASED & LEGATEES OF SD. DECEASED : to : THOMAS TITWORTH : DEED OF WARRANTY

Date: Dec. 9th, 1803.
Consideration: $560.00.
Amt. of land: 140 acres.
Location: Sullivan County, Tennessee.
Description: A certain tract or parcel of land containing 140 acres be the same more or less lying and being in the county of Sullivan joining Edmond Pendleton patent line so as to be so much of that tract of land conveyed Alex Berry to the sd. execution of Joseph Ross, deceased, to be the same land whereon the sd. executor now lives be the same more or less aforesaid.
Witnesses: John Pryor, Nathan Alsworth, Phillip King.
Proven: State of Tennessee, Sullivan County, May Session, 1804, in open court by Phillip King.
Registered: May 23d, 1804. Test: Matw. Rhea, C. S. C.

BENJAMIN ROYSTON : to : MY CHILDREN : : DEED OF GIFTS JOSHUA ROYSTON, BENJAMIN ROYSTON, : SARAH ROYSTON, SUSANAH ROYSTON :

TO
JOSHUAR ROYSTON: 100 acres of the sd. tract of land next to and joining Jacob Boys land and also give to my sd. son Joshua a negro boy cauled Nicholas, during the life time of the sd. Nicholas.
BENJAMIN ROYSTON : 200 acres part of the sd. tract of land being that part whereon he now resides and to certain the dwelling house out buildings orchard and spring and I give unto sd. Benjamin a negro wemana cauled Fan during the natural life of themsd . Fan
Sarah Royston: I give unto my daughter Sarah Royston 50 acre part of the sd. tract of land next adjoining my son Benjamins part.lower down on the river.
Susannah Royston: I give unto my daughter Susannah Royston 50 acres

part of the sd. tract next a joining sd. Sarahs tract lower on the river.
Reservations: Reserving nevertheless to myself the power of giving the whole or any part of sd. lands or negroes to my children and also reserving the power of laying off the above mentioned tracts in any manner I please.
Consideration: Natural love and affection which I have for my children hereinafter named and for other good cuases.
Cetertificate of annulament: The same Benjamin Royston who made the foregoing deed of gifts hereby declares and voids these gifts so that the sd. Benjamin Royston may give the sd. negores and sd. land in his lifetime as he sees fit.
Acknowledged: State of Tennessee, Sullivan County, Feb. Sessions, 1803, acknowledged in open court by Benjamin Roysdon.
Registered: Feb. 26th, 1803. Test: Matw. Rhea, C. S. C.

---

(588) JAMES JOHNSTON : to :: DEED OF WARRANTY ABRAHAM HUDSON :

Date: March 27th, 1804.
Consideration: $166.00.
Amt. of land: 83 acres.
Location: Sullivan County, Tennessee.
Description: A certain tract or parcel of land containing 83 acres be the same more or less sd. land lying and being in the aforesaid county of Sullivan.
Witnesses: John Anderson, John F. G. Johnston.
Proven: State of Tennessee, Sullivan County, May Session, 1804, inopen court by John Anderson.
Registered: May 26th, 1804. Test: Matw. Rhea, C. S. C.

---

(589) JOHN WADLOW : to : DEED OF WARRANTY JOHN SHEER :

Date: April 17th, 1804.
Consideration: $100.00.
Amt. of land: 50 acres.
Location: County of Washington and Commonwealth of Virginia.
Description: A certain tract or parcel of land granted to the sd. Waldow by the Commonwealth of Virginia on the waters of Reedy Creek.
Witnesses: John Anderson, Samuel Rose.
Proven: State of Tennessee, Sullivan County, May Session, 1804, in open court by the oath of John Anderson.
Registered: May 26th, 1804. Test: Mate. Rhea, C. S. C.

TIMOTHY ACUFF : to : DEED OF WARRANTY NATHANIEL MUNSEY :

Date: Feb. 21st, 1804.
Consideration: $400.00.

Amt. of land: 126 acres.
Location: Sullivan County, Tennessee.
Description: All that tract or parcel of land situate lying and being in the county aforesaid including the place whereon sd. Munsey now lives on containing 126 acres be the same more or less.
Acknowledged: State of Tennessee, Sullivan County, Feb. Session 1804, in open court by Timothy Acuff.
Registered: May 27th, 1804. Test: MAtw. Rhea, C. S. C.

---

(591) CONRADE GOODNER : to : DEED OF WARRANTY BENJAMIN LEE :

Date: Nov. 2d, 1803.
Consideration: $500.00.
Amt. of land: 150 acres.
Location: Sullivan County, Tennessee.
Description: A certain tract or parele of land containing 150 acres be the same more or less lying and being in Sullivan County on the waters fo Reedy Creek.
Witnesses: John Anderson, Rachel Anderson.
Proven: State of Tennessee. Sullivan County, Nov. Session, 1803, by the oath of John Anderson.
Registered: May 24th, 1804. Test: Matw. Rhea, C. S. C.

---

(592) WILLIAM OWEN : to : DEED OF WARRANTY WILLIAM KING :

Date: May 10th, 1804.
Consideration: $850.00 lawful money.
Amt. of land: 200 acres.
Location: Sullivan County.
Description: A certain tract of land containing 200 acres lying and being in the county of Sullivan between land of William King, John Sharp, David King William Lock.
Witnesses: Isaac King, Benjamin King.
Acknowledged: In open court by William Owen, State of Tennessee, Sullivan County, May Session, 1804.
Registered: May 27th, 1804. Tesy: Matw. Rhea, C. S. C.

---

(593) WILLIAM GIFFORD : to : DEED OF WARRANTY JOHN GIFFORD :

Date: Feb. 7th, 1804.
Consideration: $333.00.
Amt. of land: 174 acres.
Location: Sullivan County, State of Tennessee.
Description: A certain tract or parcel of land containing 174 acres be the same more or less lying and being in the county and state aforesaid including the plantation whereon the sd. William Gifford now lives.

Witnesses: John Jenings, Alexander Gitgood.
Proven: In open court by John Hennings, State of Tennessee, Sullivan County, May Session, 1804.
Registered: Aug. 21st, 1804. Test: Matw. Rhea, C. S. C.

---

(594) JAMES DAVIS :
to : DEED OF WARRANTY
JOHN CHESTER :

Date: May 16th, 1803.
Consideration: $500.00.
Amt. of land: 150 acres.
Location: Sullivan County, State of Tennessee.
Description: A certain tract or parcel of land containing 150 acres more or less lying and being in the county and State aforesaid on the waters of the Clear Fork of Horse Creek.
Witnesses: James Pickins, Thomas Allen, James Allen.
Proven: State of Tennessee, Sullivan County, August Session, 1804, in open court by the oath of James Pickins. Test: Matw. Rhea, C.S.C.
Registered: Aug. 24th, 1804.

---

(595) JOHN GIFFORD :
to : DEED OF WARRANTY
WILLIAM PALLET :

Date: March 16th, 1804.
Consideration: $1333.00.
Amt. of land: 174 acres.
Location: Sullivan County, State of Tennessee.
Description: A certain tract or parcel of land contahing 174 acres be the same more or less lying and being in the county of Sullivan and state afwresaid and including the plantation wherson William Gifford, Senr, William Giffordm Junr. now lives.
Witnesswn: John Jenings, Abraham Pallet, Isaac Acuff.
Proven: In opne court by the oath of Abraham Pallet, State of Tennessee, Sullivan County, August Session, 1804.
Registered: Aug. 24th, 1804. Test: Matw. Rhea, C. S. C.

---

(596) JOHN TORBETT :
to : DEED OF WARRANTY
JOSEPH TORBETT :

Date: Aug. 20th, 1804.
Consideration: $100.00.
Amt. of land: By estimation 115 acres.
Location: Sullivan County, State of Tennessee.
Description: All that tract or parcel of land whereon the Joseph Torbet now lives lying and being in Sullivan County.
Acknowledged: In open court by John Torbett, State of Tennessee, Sullivan County, Aug. Session, 1804.
Registered: Aug. 24th, 1804. Test : Matw. Rhea, C. S. C.

(Page)

WALTER JAMES : to : DEED OF WARRANTY
FREDERICK BRONSTOTTER :

Date: Aug. 20th, 1804.
Consideration: $1590.00.
Amt. of land: 300 acres.
Location: Sullivan County, Tennessee.
Description: All that plantation ot tract of land whereon the sd. Walter James now lives situated lyihg and being in sd. county of Sullivan.
Witnesses: John Ashby, Robert Easley.
Proven: State of Tennessee, Sullivan County, August Session, 1804 in open court by the oath of Robert Easley.
Registered: Aug. 28th, 1804. Test: Matw. Rhea, C. S. C.

---

(598) ROBERT CHRISTIAN : to : DEED OF WARRANTY
THOMAS HOPKINS :

Date: Aug. 20th, 1804.
Consideration: $50.00.
Amt. of land: Lott containing 1 acres.
Location: Sullivan County, S tate of Tennessee.
Description: All that tract or let situate lying and being in the county and state aforesaid on Holston River including in bounds of a town laid outand cauled Christian Ville sd. lott containing 1 acres be the same more or less.
Acknowledged: State of Tennessee, Sullivan County, August Session, 1804, in open court by Robert Christian.
Registered: Aug. 28th, 1804. Test: Matw. Rhea, C. S. C.

SAMUEL MCORKLE : to : DEED OF WARRANTY
JOSHUA RICHARDS :

Date: Feb. 20th, 1804.
Consideration: $20.00.
Amt. of land: 2 lotts 1/4 of an acre.
Location: Sullivan County, Tennessee.
Description: 2 lotts in the county aforesaid in Middletown No.5 and No. 6, 1/4 of an acre in each lot.
Acknowledged: In open court by Samuel McOrkle, State of Tennessee, Sullivan County, Aug. Session, 1804.
Registered: Nov. 13th, 1804. Test: Matw. Rhea, C. S. C.

JOHN MILLER : to : DEED OF WARRANTY
JOSHUA RICHARDS :

Date: Aug. 18th, 1804.
Consideration: $1000.00.
Amt. of land: 248 acres.
Location: Sullivan County, Tennessee.
Description: A certain tract or parcel of land containing 248 acres

be the seem more or less lying and being in the county aforesaid.
Witnesses: John Anderson, Henry Harkleroad.
Proven: State of Tennessee, Sullivan County, Aug. Session, 1804, in open court by the oath of John Naderson.
Registered: Nov. 13th, 1804. Test: Matw. Rhea, C.S.C.

---

(601) MARTIN WADDLE to HONORABLE CHURCH OF LUTHERINES OR PRESBETERIANS : DEED OF WARRANTY

Date: Nov. 19th, 1804.
Consideration: $50.00.
Amt. of land: 1 acres.
Description: A certain tract or parcel of land containing 1 acre be the same more or less to the aforesaid Church Sucksession that the sd. church built the meeting hiuse for the use of the sd. church or for the use of the sd. tract of land lying and being on the south side of Eaton's Ridge.
Acknowledged: State of Tennessee, Sullivan County, Nov. Session 1804, in open court by John Waddle.
Registered: Nov. 25th, 1804. Test: Matw. Rhea, C. S. C.

---

(602) JOSHUA RICHARDS to EDWARD RICHARDS : DEED OF WARRANTY

Date: Sept. 17th, 1804.
Consideration: $108.00.
Amt. of land: 27 acres.
Location: Sullivan County, Tennessee.
Description: A certain tract or parcel of land containing 27r acres be the same more or less sd. land lying and being in sd. county.
Witness: John Vance.
Proven: In open court by the oath of John Vance, State of Tennessee Sullivan County, Nov. Session, 1804. Test: Matw. Rhea, C.S.C.
Registered: Nov. 25th, 1804.

---

(603) JACOB GITT to GEORGE GITT : DEED OF WARRANTY

Date: March 13th, 1804.
Consideration: $160 .00
Amt. of land: One house and lott 1/4 of an acre.
Location: Sullivan County, Tennessee.
Description: One house and lott in Middletown in the county afore said No. 28 one quarter of an acre being part of the tract of land Samuel Mcorkle now lives on.
Witness: Richard Meredith,
Acknowledged: State of Tennessee, Sullivan County, May Session, 1804, in open court by Jacob Gitt.
Registered: Nov. 25th, 1804. Test: Matw. Rhea, C. S. C.

ZEKIEL JONES
to : DEED OF WARRANTY
JOHN JONES

Date: Nov. 16th, 1804.
Consideration: $600.00.
Amt. of land: Suposed to be 80 acres.
Location: Sullivan County, State of Tennessee.
Desdription: A certain tract or parcel of land lying and being in the county and state afowesaid suposed to be 80 acres be the same more or less lying on a branch known by the name of the Jarrats branch.
Witness: William Fulsem Charles Jones.
Proven: State of Tennessee, Sullivan County, Nov. Session 1804, in open court by Charles Jones. Test: Matw. Rhea. C.S. C.
Registered: Nov. 25th, 1804.

---

(604) ELIZABETH HARRIS & WILLIAM HARRIS, EXECUTORS OF JAMES HARRIS, DECEASED
to : DEED OF WARRANTY
JACOB MILLER

Date: Oct. 10th, 1803.
Consideration: $100.00.
Amt. of land: 50 acres.
Location: A certain tract or parcel of land now his actual possession situate lying and being in the county aforesaid containing 50 acres.
Witnesses: William N. Gale, John Booker.
Acknowledged: State of Tennessee, Sullivan County, by Elizabeth and William Harris, Exetrs. of James Harris, deceased.
Registered: Nov. 25th, 1804. Test: Matw. Rhea, C. S. C.

---

(605) MARY POPE & GEORGE MOODY
to : DEED OF WARRANTY
JAMES JETT

Date: March 13th, 1804.
Consideration: $133.00.
Amt. of land: 33 acres.
Location: Sullivan County, Tennessee.
Description: All that tract or parcel of land situate lying and being in the county of Sullivan aforesaid on fall creek.
Witness: Robert Easley.
Proven: In open court by Robert Easley, State of Tennessee, Sullivan County, Nov. Session, 1804. Test: Matw. Rhea, C. S. C.
Registered: Nov. 25th, 1804.

(Page)
(606) JOHN TORBETT to JOHN HUNTER : DEED OF WARRANTY

Date: Nov. 19th, 1804.
Consideration: $500.00.
Amt. of land: By estimation 100 acres.
Location: Sullivan County, Syate of Tennessee.
Description: A certain tract or parcel of land whereon the sd. John Hunter now lives lying and being in the county and state aforesaid.
Acknowledged: State of Tennessee, Sullivan County, Nov. Session, 1804, in open court by John Torbet.
Registered: Nov. 27th, 1804. Test: Matw. Rhea, C. S. C.

---

(607) STEPHEN TAYLOR to THOMAS JOHNSTON & JOSHUA JOHNSTON : DEED OF WARRANTY

Date: Oct. 24th, 1804.
Consideration: $1000.00.
Amt. of land: 248 acres.
Location: Sullivan County, Stare of Tennessee.
Description: A certain tract or parcel of land containing 248 acres be the same more or less lying and being in the county and State aforesaid.
Witnesses: Abraham Looney, John Jenings.
Acknowledged: State of Tennessee, Sullivan County, Nov. Session, 1804, in open court by Stephen Taylor. Test: Matw. Rhea, C.S.C.
Registered: Nov. 27th, 1804.

---

(608) JEREMIAH TAYLOR to THOMAS & JOSHUA JOHNSTON : DEED OF WARRANTY

Date: Oct. 23d, 1804.
Consideration: $105.00.
Amt. of land: 22 acres.
Location: Sullivan County, Tennessee.
Description: A certain tract or parcel of land containing 22 acres be the same more or less lying and being in the county of Sullivan and State aforesaid.
Witnesses: John Jening, Joseph Taylor.
Proven: In open court by John Jening, State of Tennessee, Sullivan County, Nov. session, 1804.
Registered: Nov. 27th, 1804. Test: Matw. Rhea, C. S. C.

---

(609) FREDERICK WHITEMAN to JACOB BOCHER : DEED OF WARRANTY

Date: Nov. 22d, 1804.

Consideration: $400.00.
Amt. of land: 51 acres.
Location: Sullivan County, Tennessee.
Description: A certain tract or parcel of land containing 51 acres be the same more or less lying and being in the county aforesaid on Reedy Creek.
Acknowledged: State of Tennessee, Sullivan County Nov. Session, 1804, in open court by Frederick Whitman.
Registered: Nov. 29th, 1804. Test: Matw. Rhea, C. S. C.

----

(610) JOHN FORD OF WM. : to : DEED OF WARRANTY FREDERICK T.C.D. FORD :

Date: Nov. 19th, 1804.
Consideration: $200.00.
Amt. of land: 640 acres.
Location: Sullivan County, Tennessee.
Description: A certain tract or parcel of land lying in Sullivan County on the waters of Holston River it being part of an ols survey of 640 acres of land that Fitzgeral purchased of Charles Roberts,Senr.
Witnesses: Jacob Slaughter, William Grimsby.
Proven: State of Tennessee, Sullivan County, Nov. Session, 1804, in open court by the aoth of Jacob Slaughter. Test: Matw/ Rhea,CSC.
Registered: Nov. 29th, 1804.

ISAAC SHELBY :2 to : DEED OF WARRANTY ROBERT ALLISON :

Date: August 21st, 1804.
Consideration: $200.00.
Akt. of land: 87 acres.
Location: Sullivan County, State of Tennessee.
Description: A certain tract or parcel of land lying and being in the county and state aforesaid and containing 87 acres more or less.
Acknowledged: State of Tennessee, Sullivan County, August Session, 1804, in open court by Isaac Shelby. Test: Matw. Rhea, C.S.C.
Registered: Jan. 2d, 1805.

----

(611) CHRISTIAN WEAEER : to : DEED OF WARRANTY JOHN FUNKHOUSER :

Date: Feb. 11th, 1805.
Consideration: Amt. not stated.
Amt. of land: 38 acres.
Location: Sullivan County, Tennessee.
Description: One certain tract of landit being part of L of the tract of land sd. Weaver sold to John Funkhouser the 12th of November 1790, and left out of this deed of conveyance by mistake, 38 acres its lying and being in sd. county on the south side of Holston river, including a bottom field beginning at three white oaks on the bank of Jacob Weavers Spring branch.

Witness: Jacob Gitt, Solomon Smith.
Proven: State of Tennessee, Sullivan County, Feb. Session, 1805, in open court by the oath of Solomon Smith. Test: Matw. Rhea, C.S.C.
Registered: Feb. 19th, 1805.

---

(613) SAMUEL DUNSMORE : to : DEED OF WARRANTY JOHN TORBET :

Date: Feb. 15th, 1803.
Consideration: 180 L.
Amt. of land: By estimation 153 acres.
Location: Sullivan County, State of Tennessee.
Description: A certain tract or parcel of land situate lying and being in the county and state aforesaid on the north side of Wataugha joining John Torbet, Senr. William Fraim and George Emit.
Acknowledged: State of Tennessee, Sullivan County, Feb. Session, 1805, execution of the within deed was acknowledged in open court by Samuel Dunsmore.
Registered: Feb. 19th, 1805. Test: Matw. Rhea, C. S. C.

---

(614) JOHN ALLISON : to : DEED OF WARRANTY PETER HARRINGTON :

Date: Aug. 22d, 1800.
Consideration: $50.00.
Amt. of land: 75 acres.
Location: Sullivan County, Tennessee.
Description: A certain tract or parcel of land lying and being in the county aforesaid adjoining the plantation whereon the sd. Peter now lives and the lands of John Torbet and the lands of sd. John Allison being part of a tract originally granted to William Hughes.
Witness: John Torbet, Joseph Torbet.
Proven: State of Tennessee, Sullivan County, Feb. session, 1805. in open court by the oath of Joseph Torbet. Test: Matw. Rhea, C.S.C.
Registered: Feb. 20th, 1805.

---

(615) SAMUEL KING : to : DEED OF WARRANTY ISAAC KING & : JOSEPH TORBET :

Date: Feb. 16th, 1805.
Consideration: $300.00.
Amt. of land: By estimation 59 1/4 acres.
Location: Sullivan County, State of Tennessee.
Description: All that tract or parcel of land whereon the sd. Samuel King now lives, lying and being in the county and state

aforesaid containing 59 1/4 acres be the same more or less.
Acknowledged: State of Tennessee, Sullivan County, Feb. Session, 1805, in open court by Samuel King.
Registered: Feb. 20th, 1805. Test: Matw. Rhea, C. S. C.

---

(616) RICHARD CANDRA : to : DEED OF WARRANTY HENRY CLICK :

Date: Sept. 22d, 1804.
Consideration: $300.00.
Amt. of land: 200 acres.
Location: Sullivan County, Tennessee.
Description: A certain tract or parcel of land containing 200 acres lying and being in the county of Sullivan on the waters of Reedy Creek on the north side of Sd. Creek.
Witnesses: George Wilcox, Matthias Click.
Proven: State of Tennessee, Sullivan County, Feb. Session, 1805, in open court by the oath of George Wilcox.
Registered: Feb. 20th, 1805. Test: Matw. Rhea, C. S. C.

---

(617) PETER MORISON : to : DEED OF WARRANTY MATHIAS CLICK :

Date: Jan. 17th, 1805.
Consideration: $10.00.
Amt. of land: 160 sq. poles.
Location: Part in Tennessee and part in Virginia.
Description: A certain tract or parcel of land containing 160 square poles lying and being part in Tennessee and part in Virginia being part of a survey granted to the sd. Peter Morrison by the state of North Carolina No. 526.
Witnesses: Henry Click, Peter Click, George Morrison, Sullivan County Feb. Session, 1805.
Registered: Feb. 20th, 1805. Test: Matw. Rhea, C. S. C.

JOHN HUNTER : to : DEED OF WARRANTY JOSEPH TORBET :

Date: Feb. 16th, 1805.
Consideration: $533.00.
Amt. of land: 100 acres.
Location: State of Tennessee, Sullivan County,
Description: A certain tract or parcel of land lying and being in the county and state aforesaid containing 100 acres be the same more or less.
Witnesses: Samule King, Peter Harrington.
Registered: Feb. 27th, 1805. Test: Matw. Rhea, C. S. C.

WILLIAM GODDARD :
(619) to : DEED OF WARRANTY
SAMUEL MCDAVID :

Date: Nov. 20th, 1804.
Consideration: $190.00.
Amt. of land: 66 acres.
Location: Sullivan County.
Description: A certain tract or parcel of land containing 66 acres be the same more or less sd. land lying and being in sd. county and on the waters of Reedy Creek.
Acknowledged: In open court by William Goddard, State of Tennessee, Sullivan County, Nov. Session, 1804. Test: Matw. Rhea, C. S. C.
Registered: Feb. 27th, 1805.

---

(620) JOHN TEVERA :
to : DEED OF WARRANTY
WILLIAM GODDARD :

Date: Feb. 26th, 1803.
Consideration: $165.00.
Amt. of land: 66 acres.
Location: Sullivan County, Tennessee.
Description: A certain tract or parcel of land containing 66 acres be the same more or less sd. land lying and being in sd. county on the waters of Reedy Creek.
Witnesses: Thomas Capps, John Anderson.
Acknowledged: In open court by John Tevera, State of Tennessee, Sullivan County, May Session, 1803.
Registered: Feb. 27th, 1805. Test: Matw. Rhea, C. S. C.

THOMAS TOVERA :
to : DEED OF WARRANTY
JOHN TOVERA :

Date: Aug. 19th, 1801.
Consideration: $100.00.
Amt. of land: 66 acres.
Description: A certain tract or parcel of land containing 66 acres be the same more or less sd. land lying and being on the waters of Reedy Cr eek.
Witness: John Anderson.
Acknowledged: State of Tennessee, Sullivan County, August Session, 1801, in open court by Thomas Tonevra. Test: Matw. Rhea, C. S.C.
Registered: Feb. 27th, 1805.

---

(621) JOSEPH COOK :
to : DEED OF WARRANTY
GEORGE LOWE :

Date: May 19th, 1801.

Consideration: $200.00.
Amt. of land: 100 acres.
Location: Sullivan County, Tennessee.
Description: A certain tract or parcel of land containing 100 acres be the same more or less lying and being in the county aforesaid and on the waters of Reedy Creek.
Witnesses: John Anderson, Thomas Vincent.
Acknowledged: In open court by Joseph Cook, State of Tennessee, Sullivan County,. Test: Matw. Rhea, C. S. C.
Registered: Feb. 27th, 1805.

---

(622) JAMES ENGLISH : to : DEED OF WARRANTY JOHN GOODSON :

Date: Feb. 19th, 1805.
Consideration: $250.00.
Amt. of land: 40 acres.
Location: Sullivan County, Tennessee.
Description: A certain tract of land situate lying and being in Sullivan County and state aforesaid on Cedar Creek a branch of Beaver Creek which was conveyed to the sd. James English by John Hickman by indenture bearing date the 17th of Dec. 1802, containing 40 acres.
Acknowledged: State of Tennessee, Sullivan County, Feb. session, 1805, in open court by James English. Test: Mathw. Rhea, C. S.C.
Registered: March 12th, 1805.

---

(623) STATE OF NORTH CAROLINA : SAMUEL ASHE, GOV. : DEED OF WARRANTY to : PETER HICKMAN :

Date: Nov. 10th, 1796.
Consideration: 50 shillings for every 100 acres of land.
Amt. of land: 60 acres.
Location: Sullivan County, Tennessee.
Description: Sixty acres lying and being in our county pf Sullivan as by the plat hereunto annexed doth appear.
Witness: Samuel Ashe, Gov. By Command J. Glasgow, Sec.
Registered: April 17th, 1805.

---

(624) LEWIS FOUST & CATHERINE FOUSE : EXECUTORS OF PHILLIP FOUST, DECD. : DEED OF WARRANTY to : ROBERT RHEA :

Date: Jan. 31st, 1805.
Consideration: $315.00.

Amt. of land: 63 acres.
Location: Sullivan County, Tennessee.
Description: A certain tract or parcel of land containing 63 acres lying and being in the county of Sullivan and on the waters of Fall Creek.
Witnesses: Philip Foust, Mattw. Rhea.
Registered: May 21st, 1805. Mattw. Rhea, Clerk of Sullivan County.

---

(625) HENRY MAUK : to : DEED OF WARRANTY JOHN MAUK :

Date: May 18th, 1805.
Consideration: $500.00.
Amt. of land: 114 acres.
Location: Sulliven County, Tennessee.
Description: A certain tract or parcel of land lying and being situated in the aforesadi state and county containing 114 acres more or less.
Witnesses: John Yancey, Peter Bronstotter.
Proven: State of Tennessee, Sullivan County, May Session, 1805, in open court by the oath of Peter Bronstotter.
Registered: May 27th, 1805. Test: Matw. Rhea, C. S. C.

---

(626) DAVID ROBERTS : to : DEED OF WARRANTY JACOB TROKE :

Date: March 13th, 18o5.
Consideration: $40.00.
Amt. of land: 183 akres .
Location: Sullivan County, Tennessee.
Description: Two certain tracts or parcels of land containing 183 acres be the same more or less said land lying and being in the county aforesaid and on the waters of Reedy Creek, one tract containing 124 acres the other containing 60 acres.
Witnesses: John Anderson, Rachel Anderson.
Acknowledged: In open court by David Roberts, State of Tennessee, Sullivan County May Session, 1805.
Registered: May 27th, 1805. Test: Matw. Rhea, C. S. C.

---

(627) ABRAHAM HAMBLETON : to : DEED OF WARRANTY WM. NASH, JUNR. :

Date: Jan. 5th, 1805.
Consideration: $450.00.
Amt. of land: 131 acres.
Location: Sullivan County, State of Tennessee.
Description: A certain tract or parcel of land containing by estimation 131 acres be the same more or less lying and being in the county and state aforesaid, together with all houses etc. thereunto belonging.
Witnesses: Joshua Hambleton, William Nash, Senr.
Acknowledged: In open court by Abraham Hambleton, State of Tennessee Sullivan County, Feb. Session, 1805. Test: Matw. Rhea, C. S. C.
Registered: May 27th, 1805.

(Page)
(628)

EDMUND PENDLETON, EXECUTOR :
of EDMUND PENDLETON, DECEASED :
AND JOHN TAYLOR : DEED OF WARRANTY
to :
THOMAS AND JAMES GAINES :

Date: Sept. 25th, 1804.
Consideration: 596 L 18 s. to be paid to the sd. Edmond Pendleton deceased- 746 L 8 shillings to be paid to the sd. John Taylor.
Amt. of land: 3000 acres.
Note: The quantity is understood to be more than 3000 acres, but 500 acres given by the sd. Edmond Pendleton, deceased to his nephew Phillip Pendleton before the said agreement.
Description: Sd. Edmond Pendleton, deceased, in his life time and the said John Taylor did by article of agreement dated the 25th of January, 1790 agree to sell unto the sd. Thomas and James Gaines a tract of land lying on Reedy Creek near Holston rivermostly in the state of Tennessee, but part in the state of Virginia granted to the sd. Edward Pendleton deceased by patent dated the 16th of August, 1756, containing by patent 3000 acres but grand for more or less as the quantity understood to be greater except 500 acres given by the sd. Edmond Pendleton deceased to his nephew Phillip Pendleton beffore the said agreemant but since laid off or conveyed Except also certain tracts or parcel of land being parts of the sd. patented tract agreed to be sold which the sd. Thomas and James Gaines have since the sd. contract disposed of or sold to David Ross and others and which the sd. Edmond Pendleton, deceased, and John Taylor and the sd. Edmond Pendleton party hereton and the said John Taylor have by their desire conveyed for the above mentioned sums and where as the sd. Edmund Pendleton, deceased by his last will and testament of record in the county court of Caroline did devise unto the sd. John Taylor all his title to the sd. lands so sold in trust to convey the same whenever the purchaser should comply with the agreement on their parts of the sd. will and the sd. Edmund Pendleton is the only acting executor, residuary legatee and administrator. For and in consideration of these premises and for the further sum of 5 shillings by the sd. Thomas and James Gaines to them paid, th ey have granted, bargained, sold and conveyed the above described parcel of land. In case of eviction of any part or parts of the lands sold so much of the purchase money is to be restored.
Witnesses: John Gray, Thomas Miller, Rockham Keener, Daniel Turner, At. to Col Taylor, John Pendleton, At. to Col. Taylor, Rubin Turner, At. to Col. Taylor.

At a court held for Caroline County at the court house of the sd. County in the State of Virginia.

: Received on the day of the date of this deed the Administrator's money of 5 shillings therein expressd to paid to us.
: Edmund Pendleton, John Taylor.
: Test: John Gray.

Acknowledged: By the sd. Edmund Pendleton and John Taylor to be their act and deed ordered to be cretified, in testimony whereof I William Nelson Clerk of the sd. court have hereunto signed my name and affixed the seal of the county this 3th day of April, 1805. Wm. Nelson, Clk.
I, Anthony, now presideing magistrate in the county of Caroline in the State of Virginia do certify that Wm. Nelson whose name is subscribed to the above is clerk of the county and that the attestation is in due form. Given under my hand this the 9th day of April, 1805. Antony new Tenn. Sullivan County May Session, 1805, the within deed is admitted by virtue of the above certificate of Wm. Nelson Clerk, Carlin County aforesaid and Anthony New, presiding.magisterate ordered to be Regst. Test: Mattw. Rhea, Clerk of Sullivan County.
Registered: May 28th, 1805.

---

(631) JAMES GAINES & THOMAS GAINES to JOHN RHEA : DEED OF WARRANTY

Date: May 20th, 1805.
Consideration: $500.00.
Amt. of land: 353 acres.
Location: Sullivan County, Tennessee.
Description: One certain tract or parcel of land containing 353 acres lying and being in the county of Sullivan on the north side of Holston River on both sides of Reedy Creek.
Witnesses: James H. Gaines, Robert Christian, Laurence Snapp.
Proven: State of Tennessee, Sullivan County, May Session, 1805, in open court by the oath of James H. Gaines.
Registered: May 29th, 1805. Test: Matw. Rhea, C. S. C.

---

(632) JOHN FUNKHOUSER to WILLIAM ROCKHOLD : DEED OF WARRANTY

Date: Feb. 19th, 1805.
Consideration: $900.00.
Amt. of land: 80 acres.
Location: Sullivan County, Tennessee.
Description: A certain plantation or tract of land whereon sd. Samuel Evans now lives situate lying and being in Sullivan County on the south side of Holston River.
Witnesses: Jas. Carathers, Elkhanah R. Dulaney.
Registered: May 29th, 1805. Test: Matw. Rhea, C. S. C.

---

(635) JOHN TIPTON to ROBERT BENHAM : DEED OF WARRANTY

Date: Aug. 18th, 1803.

Consideration: $100.00.
Amt. of land: Half an acre Lott
Location: Sullivan County, Tennessee.
Description: A certain lott or parcel of land containing half an acre be the same more or less situate lying and being the county aforesaid and near joining the town of Blountville and on the west side of the branch and on the north side of the street and known by the lot number 3.
Witness: John Anderson.
Acknowledged: State of Tennessee, Sullivan County, August Session, 1802, in open court by John Tipton. Test: Mstw. Rhea, C. S. C.
Registered: May 29th, 1805.

---

(636) JOHN NEWLAND : to : DEED OF WARRANTY JOSEPH NEWLAND :

Date: March 5th, 1804.
Consideration: $50.00.
Amt. of land: 87 acres.
Location: Sullivan County, State of Tennessee.
Description: A certain tract or parcel of land containing 87 acres be the same more or less lying and being in the county and state aforesaid.
Witnesses: James Gaines, Ambrose Gaines.
Proven: State of Tennessee, Sullivan County, August Session, 1804, in open court by the oath of Ambrose Gaines. Test: Matw. RheamCS.C.
Registered: May 29th, 1805.

---

(637) JOHN NEWLAND : to : DEED OF WARRANTY JOSEPH NEWLAND :

Date: March 5th, 1804.
Consideration: $350.00.
Amt. of land: 100 acres.
Location: Wythe County, Virginia.
Description: One certain tract of land containing 100 acres be the same more or less lying and being in the county and state afore said on the North Side of Holston River on a branch of Reedy Creek.
Witnesses: James Gaines, Ambrose Gaines, Phillisnon Bonhamon.
Proven: State of Tennessee, Sullivan County, August Sessionsm 1804, in open court by the oath of Ambrose Gaines.
Registered: May 29th, 1805. Test: Matw. Rhea, C. S. C.

---

(638) JOHN NEWLAND :2 to : DEED OF WARRANTY JOSEPH NEWLAND :

Date: March 5th, 1804.
Consideration: $100.00.
Amt. of land: 90 acres.
Description: Two certain tracts or parcels of land one of 60 acres and the other of 3 acres be the same more or less the first mention ed tract of 60 acres begins at Saml. Brashers corner , the 30 acres

begins at hickory and dogwood on sd. Branch (timber tree branch)
Witnesses: James Gaines, Ambrose Gaines.
Proven: In open court by the oath of Ambrose Gaines, State of Tennessee, Sullivan County, August Session, 1804.
Registered: May 29th, 1805. Test: Matw. Rhea, C. S. C.

---

(639) JOHN MAUK : to : DEED OF WARRANTY JOHN HOWLARD :

Date: Nov. 17th, 1804.
Consideration: $100.00.
Amt. of land: 127 acres.
Location: Sullivan County, State of Tennessee.
Description: A certain tract or parcel of land situate lying and being in sd. county and state aforesaid containing 127 acres.
Witnesses: Henry Mauk, Elisha Harbour.
Proven: State of Tennessee, Sullivan County, Nov. Session, 1804, in open court by Elisha Harbour.
Registered: June 3d, 1805. Test: Matw. Rhwa, C. S. C.

---

(640) THOMAS SHELBY, late sheriff of Sullivan County, : to : SHERIFF'S DEED ISAAC SHELBY :

Date: Aug. 21st, 1804.
Consideration: $300.00.
Purpose: A Writ of fires facias directed from Superior Court of Law and Equity Washington District to carry into effect judgment obtained in the court by Francis Allison against Samuel May confirmed unto Isaac Shelby in fair and open market he being by his agent Alexander McNabb the highest bidder at Publick sale being first advertised according to law the said sale at Public Vandue being made on the 29th of August for the sum of $30.00.
Description: One tract of land of the property of Samule May lying and being in the county of Sullivan, beginning at a beach on Watauga River containing 87 acres.
Acknowledged: State of Tennessee, Sullivan County, August Session, 1804, in open court by Thomas Shelby.
Registered: June 3d, 1805. Test: Mattw. Rhea, C' S. C.

---

(641) ARCHAPALD TAYLOR : AGAINST : SUIT PHILLIP HORN :

JOHN ANDERSON? SHERIFF : to : SHERIFF'S DEED. PHILLIP HORN :

Date: May 20th, 1805.

(Page)

A writ of Fire faces bearing date the 3rd Monday of August, 1799, at the above styled suit Isued form the County Court of Pleas and Quarter Session of Sullivan County directed to John Anderson High Sheriff Commanding the sd. Sheriff to make of the goods and chattels of Phillip Horn the sum of $28.52 besides other endorsed fees in the same court recovered agianst him.
Execution of writ: By virtue of whish writ a certain part of an entry of land of 200 acres with the improvement thereon was duly executed by the sd. Sheriff Advertised and Exposed to Sale at public auction to the highest bidder agreeable to law.the sd. entry being No. 1 in the office book 713.
Description: The land lying in the county of Sullivan and state of Tennessee lying on the North side of Holston River and on the North side of Eaton's Ridge and Arch Taylor appeared at the auction and bids $21.00 for the part of the entry of land with the improvement.
Consideration: The above mentioned sum of $21.00 being part of the sum mentioned in the firie faces sd. Arch Taylor recovered against him the sd. Phillip Horn.
Acknowledged: In open court by John Anderson, State of Tennessee, Sullivan County, May Session, 1805. Test: Matw. Rhea, C. S. C.
Registered: June 3d, 1805.

---

(642) JOHN CAVATT : to : DEED OF WARRANTY HENRY MAUK :

Date: Aug. 4th, 1804.
Consideration: $400.00.
Amt. of land: 136 acres.
Location: Sullivan County, State of Tennessee.
Description: A certain tract or parcel of land lying and being in the county and state aforesaid containing 136 acres.
Witnesses: John Yancy, John Mauk.
Proven: State of Tennessee, Sullivan County, Aug. Session, 1804, proven in open court by the oath of John Yancey.
Registered: June 4th, 1805. Test: Matw Rhea, C. S. C.

---

(643) NATHANIEL GRIMES : to : DEED OF WARRANTY SETH PORTERFIELD :

Date: Jan. 16th, 1794.
Consideration: 100 L.
Amt. of land: 400 acres.
Location: Sullivan County, Tennessee.
Description: A certain tract or parcel of land containing 400 acres be the same more or less lying and being in the county of Sullivan and on the waters of fall creek.
Witnesses: John Naderson, John Lowery, Andrew Anderson.
Proven: Sulllivan County , March Session, 1794, by the oath of John Anderson. Test: Matw. Rhea, C. S. C.
Registered: June 28th, 1805. Test: Matw. Rhea, C. S. C.

(Page)

(645) JAMES ROWAN : to : DEED OF WARRANTY THOMAS HOPKINS :

Date: Jan. 31st, 1805.
Consideration: $100.00.
Amt. of land: 200 acres.
Location: Sullivan County, Tennessee.
Description: A certain tract pr parcel of land containing 200 acres lying and being in the county and state aforesaid on the waters of Reedy Creek.
Witnesses: John Lynn, Robert Christian.
Proven: State of Tennessee, Sullivan County, Feb. Session, 1805, in open court by the oath of Robert Christian.
Registered: Aug. 7th, 1805. Test: Matw. Rhea, C. S. C.

----

(646) STATE OF NORTH CAROLINA : RICHARD DOBBS SPAIGHT, GOVERNOR, : LAND GRANT to : NO. 572. ALEXANDER OUTLAW :

Date: July 27th, 1793.
Consideration: 50 shillings for every 100 acres of land.
Amt. of land: 24 3/4 acres.
Location: Sullivan County, North Carolina.
Description: A tract of land containinf 24 3/4 acres of land lying and being in our county of Sullivan on the North side of Holston River.
Witness: Richard Dobbs. Spaight, Gov. By his Exceys. Comd. J. Glasgow, Secretary.
Registered: Aug. 24th, A. D. 1805. By Stephen Major Register for Sullivan County and Co.

----

(647) MICHAEL JOHNSTON : to : DEED OF WARRANTY JOHN NEWLAND :

Date: Nov. 1st, 1803.
Consideration: $100.00.
Amt. of land: 90 acres.
Description: Two certain tracts or parcels of land one of 60 acres and the other of 30 acres be the same more or less the first mentioned tract of 60 acres beginning at Samuel Brashers corner popler and timber tree branch. The other tract of 30 acres begins at a hickory and dogwood on sd. branch.
Witnesses: Ambrose Gaines, Samuel Brashers, Henry Maggitt.
Registered: Aug. 28th, 1805. Test: Matw. Rhea, C. S. C.

----

(648) MICHAEL JOHNSTON : to : DEED OF WARRANTY JOHN NEWLAND :

Date: Nov. 1st, 1803.
Consideration: $350.00

Amt. of land: 100 acres.
Location: Sullivan County, Tennessee.
Description: One certain tract or parcel of land containing 100 acres be the same more or less lying and being in the County and State aforesaid on the North side of Holston River on a branch of Reedy Creek.
Witnesses: Ambrose Gaines, Samuel Brashares, Henry Maggitt.
Proven: State of Tennessee, Sullivan County, Nov. Sessions, 1803, in open court by the oath of Ambrase Gaines, Henry Maggitt.
Registered: Aug. 28th, 1805. Test: Matw. Rhea, C. S. C.

---

(649) MICHAEL JOHNSTON : to : DEED OF WARRANTY JOHN NEWLAND :

Date: Nov. 1st, 1803.
Consideration: $50.00.
Amt. of land: 87 acres.
Location: Sullivan County, State of Tennessee.
Description: A certain tract or parcel of land containing 87 acres be the same more or less lying in sd. county aforesaid.
Witnesses: Samuel Brashares, Henry Maggist.
Proven: State of Tennessee, Sullivan County, Nov. Session, 1803, in open court by the oath of Ambrose Gaines and Henry Maggist.
Registered: Aug. 28th, 1805. Test: Matw. Rhea, C. S. C.

---

(650) THOMAS ROCKHOLD, SHERIFF, : to : SHERIFF'S DEED DAVID MARTIN :

Date: Aug. 22d, 1805.
Cause of sale: At a Rit of Fira Faces diected from the county court of Carter to carry into effect a judgment obtinined in sd. court Thomas Stewart and Montgomery Stewart &C against Armstead Blevins, Sd. David Martin being the highest bidder in fare and open market he being the highest bidder at publick sale hereof the same first being advertised according to law the sd. sale being made on the day of May in the year aforesaid, and for the sum of $5.00.
Description: Thomas Rockhold acknowledged the sale of one tract of land the property of Armstead Blevins lying and being in the county of Sullivan aforesaid and known by the name of Shugar Hollow containing 200 acres be the same more or less.
Acknowledged: State of Tennessee, Sullivan County, Aug. Session, 1805 in open court by Thomas Rockhold, Sheriff of Sullivan County.
Registered: Aug. 28th, 1805. Test: Matw. Rhea, C. S. C.

DAVID MARTIN : to : DEED OF WARRANTY ISAAC SHELBY :

Date: May 23d, 1805.
Consideration: $5.00.
Amt. of land: 200 acres.

(Page)

(651) Location: Sullivan County, Tennessee.
Description: A certain tract or parcel of land lying and being in the county and state aforesaid and known by the name of the Shugar hollow containing 200 acres be the same more or less.
Acknowledged: In open court by David Martin, State of Tennessee, Sullivan County, August Session, 1805.
Registered: Aug. 29th, 1805. Test: Mathw. Rhea, C. S. C.

---

(652) JACOB SINK : DEED OF WARRNAYY
to :
Oscar Shelby :

Date: March 15th, 1805.
Consideration: $2000.00.
Amt. of land: 100 acres.
Description: A certain tract of land cojtaining 60 acres be the same more or less sd. land lying on the waters of Reedy Creek.
Witnesses: Frederick Witnesses: John Cartain, Michael Davenatt.
Proven: In open court by the oath of John Cartain, State of Tennessee. Sullivan County, August Sessioh, 1805.
Registered: Aug. 29th, 1805. Test: Matw. Rhea, C. S. C.

---

(653) DAVID TULLIS : DEED OF WARRANTY
to :
WILLIAM N. GALE :

Date: Oct. 5th, 1804.
Consideration: $1000.00.
Amt. of land: 60 acres.
Description: A certain tract or parceo of land containing 60 acres be the same more or less said land lying on the waters of Reedy Creek.
Witnesses: Frederick Widamany, John Steer.
Proven: State of Tennessee, Sullivan CountyNovember Session, 1804. In open court by the oath of Frederick Widamany.
Registered: Aug. 29th, 1805. Aug. 29th

---

(654) ROBERT ALLISON : DEED OF WARRANTY
to :
JOHN SHIART :

Date: Aug. 19th, 1805.
Consideration: $150.00.
Amt. ofland: 35 acres and 30 poles.
Location: Sullivan County, Tennessee.
Description: 35 acres and 30 poles of land situate lying and being in the county and state aforesaid joining John King, Robert Allison and Frances Hodge the same being part of the tract of land whereon the sd. Robert Alison now lives.
Witnesses: None.
Proven : State of Tennessee, Sullivan County, August Session, 1805, in open court by Robert Alison. Test: Matw. Rheam C. S. C.
Registered: Aug. 29th, 1805.

(655) HENRY MAUK : to : DEED OF WARRANTY BOLDEN HOWARD :

Date: May 18th, 1805.
Consideration: $500.00.
Amt. of land: 135 acres.
Location: Sullivan County, Tennessee.
Description: BAacertain tract or parcel of land situate lying and being in SULLIVAN COUNTY aforesaid cojtaining 135 acres be the same more or less.
Witnesses: John Yancey, Peter Bronstotter.
Acknowledged: In open court by Henry Mauk, State of Tennessee, Sullivan County, August Session, 1805. Test: Matw. Rhea, C. S. C.
Registered: Aug. 29th, 1805.

---

(656) JOSIAH WHITNER : to : DEED OF WARRANTY WILLIAM W. GALE :

Date: Aug. 19th, 1805.
Consideration: $730.00.
Amt. of land: 182 acres.
Location: Sullivan County, Tennessee.
Description: A certain tract or parcelof land containing 182 acres be the same more or less land lying and being in the county and state aforesaid and on the waters of Reedy creek.
Witnesses: John Anderson, George Morrison.
Acknowledged: In open court by Josiah Whitnak, State of Tennessee, Sullivan County, August Session, 1805. Test: Matw. Rhea, C. S. C.
Registered: Aug. 29th, 1805.

---

(657) JAMES MATHANY : to : DEED OF WARRANTY JONATHAN BACHMAN :

Date: April 3d, 1805.
Consisderation: $1250.001
Amt. of land: 180 acres.
Location: Sullivan County, State of Tennessee.
Description: A certain trat or parcel of land containing 180 acres of land be the same more or less lying and being in the county and state aforesaid and on the waters of Horse Creek and including the plantation whereon James Matheny now lives.
Witnesses: Robert Easly, Ceswg Vincent.
Proven: In open court by Rober Easley State of Tennessee, Sullivan County, May Session, 1805.
Registered: Sept. 4th, 1805. Test: Matw. Rhea, C. S. C.

(Page)

(659) THOMAS ROCKHOLD, SHERIFF : to : SHERIFF'S DEED ROBERT ALLISON :

Date: Feb. 9th, 1805.
Object: Robert Allison obtainied an judgment against William Hughes and John Smith Borden in the Superior*of the District of Washington in the State of Tennessee, Sd. judgment plureas Writ of Fire Faces issued from the sd. Superior court Sept. term 1804, directed to the Sheriff of Sullivan County and by virtue of sd. writ and by virtue of the power in law of the sd. sheriff Thomas Rockhold did levy upon the property of sd. William Hughes.
Description: A certain tract or parcel of land situate lying and being in the county of Sullivan and state of Tennessee on the north side of Watauga River within about a mile of sd. river being the same tract of land where John Alison formerly lived supposed to contain 100 acres.
Sale: According to law 9th of Feb. 1805, did expose the dd. tract of land to public sale to the highest and best bidder and at the sd. sale Robert Alison was the highest and best bidder in consideration of the sum of $100.00. ($100.00).
Witness: James White.
Acknowledged: State of Tennessee, Sullivan County, May Session 1805, in open court by Thomas Rockhold. Test: Mayw. Rhea, C. S. C.
Registered: Sept. 4th, 1805.

---

(660) WALLACE WILLOUGHBY : to : DEED OF WARRANTY JACOB BEALOR & JOHN VANCE, ESQ. :

Date: Aug. 15th, 1805.
Consideration: $15.00.
Amt. of land: A lote of land containing 40 poles.
Location: Town of Greenfield.
Description: A lote of land containing 40 poles and situated in the town of Greenfield and designated by the number 15 in the plett of that town.
Acknowledged: State of Tennessee, Sullivan County, August Session, 1805, in open court by Wallace Willoughby. Test: Matw. Rhea, C.S.Cc
Registered: Sept. 4th, 1805.

---

(661) ROBERT CHRISTIAN : to : DEED OF WARRANTY THOMAS HOPKINS :

Date: Sept. 4th, 1805.
Consideration: $25.00.
Amt. of land: 1/2 acres including a house.
Location: Sullivan County, Tennessee.
Description: A certain tract or parcel of land containing 1/2 acre including a house built lying and being in the county of Sullivan and town of Christiansville.
Witnesses: James English, John Tredway.
State of Tennessee, Sept. 6th, 1805, John Tredway appeared before me Hugh L. White one of the judges of the Suprior Court af law and equity in and for the sd. state made oath that he saw Robert Christian seign seal and acknowledge the within instrument of writing to be his act

and deedfoe the use therein expressed and that he saw James English subscribe his name as witness.
Registered: Sept. 4th, 1805. Test: Matw. Rhea, C. S. C.

---

(662) AGATHA CAWOOD & William DULANEY EXECUTORS FOR JOHN CAWOOD, DEC'D. to STEPHEN MAJORS : DEED OF BARGAIN AND SALE

Date: Aug. 22d, 1803.
Consideration: $426.00.
Property sold: One negro man caled Top about 28 years of age for and in consideration of the sum of $426.00.
Witnesses: Peter Brackbill, William Blevins.
Proven: State of Tennessee, Sullivan County, Nov. Session, 1803, ordered to be recorded in off. volume 2 and page 211. Test: Matw. Rhea, C.SC.
Registered: Sept, 4th, 1805.

---

(663) JOHN FUNKHOUSER to WILLIAM MORREL : DEED OF WARRANTY

Date: Feb. 29th, 1805.
Consideration: $600.00.
Amt. of land: 104 ____.
Locati n: Sullivan County, Tennessee.
Description: A certain tract or parcel of land containing 104*be the same more or less land lying and being in county aforesaid to wit Sullivan on the south side of Holston River.
Witnesses: John McLain, John Shell.
Proven: In open court by John Shell, State of Tennessee, Sullivan County, May Session, 1805. Test: Matw. Rhea, C. S. C.
Registered: Sept. 4th, 1805.

*---

(664) JAMES BLEVINS, WALTER BLEVINS, SALLY BLEVINS, MILLY O. BLEVINS, CLARY BLEVINS, to JOHN BLEVINS : DEED OF RELEASE

Date: October 18th, 1805.
Agreement: These aforesaid agreedto bargain sell and relinquish to the sd. John Blevins son of William aforesaid the land belonging to the estate now in possession of Ann Blevins widow of the sd. William Blevins, deceased.
Consideration: $300.00 that is to say $50.00 to each and every one of them in hand paid.
Witnesses: John Morrell, Jonathan Morrel.
Proven: In open court by John Morrel and Jonathan Morrel, Sullivan County, Nov. Session, 1805. Test: Mayw. Rhea, C. S. C.
Registered: Nov. 21st, 1805.

---

(665) GILBERT KERR : to : DEED OF WARRANTY RHODE WELCH :

Date: Nov. 18th, 1805.
Consideration: Natural love and affection and the better maintenance and preferment of sd. Rhode Welch.
Amt. of land: 155 acres.
Location: Sullivan County, Tennessee.
Description: A certain tract or parcel of land containing 155 acres be the same more or less lying and being in the vounty aforesaid and on the waters of Back Creek.
Witness: John Anderson.
Acknowledged: Sullivan County, Nov. Session, 1805, by Gilber Kerr.
Registewed: Nov. 22d, 1805. Test: Matw. Rhea, C. S. C.

---

(666) WALTER JAMES : to : DEED OF WARRNATY JACOB STORM :

Date: May 21st, 1805.
Consideration: A valuable consideration.
Amt. of land: 92 acres.
Location: Sullivan County, Tennessee.
Description: A certain tract or parcel of land containing 92 acres said land lying and being in the county aforesaid.
Witnesses: John Anderson, William Derry.
Acknowledged: State of Tennessee, Sullivan County, May Session, 1805. in open court by Walter James.
Registered: Nov. 22d, 1805. Test: Matw. Rhea, C. S. C.

---

(667) THOMAS GAINES & : JAMES GAINES : to : DEED OF WARRANTY JOSEPH NEWLAND :

Date: May 22d, 1805.
Consideration: $1629.00.
Amt. of land: 543 acres.
Location: Sullivan County, State of Tennessee.
Desctiption: A certain tract or parcel of land containing 543 acres be the same more or less lying and being in the county and state aforesaid on both sides of Reedy Creek.
Witnesses: James Gaines, Elizabeth Bohannon, Ambrose Gaines, James T. Gaines.
STATE OF TENNESSEE? Seulivan County, August Session, 1805., proven in open court by the oath of Ambrose Gaines, Test: Matw. Rhea, C.SC.
Registered: Nov. 22d, 1805.

---

(668) LACY BOLLING : to :BILL OF SALE WILLIAM BLEVINS :

Date: March 22d, 1802.

Consideration: $333.33.
Prpperty sold: A negro man the name of Sam for the valuable sum of $333.33. Luch Bolling do warrant and forever defend the said negro Sam to William Blevins and his heirs.
Witnesses: Stpehen Majors, John Cawood, Peter Brickbill.
Proven: May Session, 1804, Recorded Vol. 2, Page 288.
Registered: Dec. 2d, 1805.

---

(668) SIMON HOLT : to : DEED OF WARRANTY HUGH CHRISTY :

Date: Nov. 5th, 1805.
Consideration: $90.00.
Amt. of land: 100 acres.
Description: A certain tract or parcel of land containing 100 acres be the same more or less.
Witnesses: Ireson Longacre, Robert Rutledge.
Proven: State of Tennessee, Sullivan County, Nov. Session, 1805, in open court by the oath of Ireson Longacre. Test: Matw. Reha, C.S.C.
Registered: Dec. 23d, 1805.

---

(669) WILLIAM SNODGRASS : to : DEED OF WARRANTY PETER HICKMAN :

Date: May 19th, 1800.
Consideration: $30.00.
Amt. of land: 158 acres.
Description: A certain tract or parcel of land containing 158 acres be the same more or less,
Witnesses: John Anderson.
Acknowledged: In open court by William Snodgrass, Sullivan County, May Session, 1800. Test: Matw. Rhea, C. S. C.
Registered: Mah. 4th, 1806.

---

(670) CLAYBOURN DAVENPORT : to : DEED OF WARRANTY JOHN GARLAND :

Date: July 28th, 1805.
Consideration: $400.00.
Amt.of land: 140 acres.
Location: Sullivan County, Tennessee.
Description: A certain tract or parcel of land containing 140 acres be the same more or less lying and being in the county aforesaid and on the south side of Holston River the plantation whereon the sd. Davenport now lives suposed to be 140 acres of land be the same more or-less. [illegible]
Witnesses: James Young, John Cawood.
Proven: State of Tennessee, Sullivan County, May Session, 1805, in open court by James Young. Test: Matw. Rhea, C. S. C.
Registered: Feb. 1st, 1806.

(Page)
(671) HENRY MAGGERT :
to : DEED OF WARRANTY
RICHARD HASSELRIG :

Date: July 25th, 1805.
Consideration: $1300.00.
Amt. of land: 284 acres.
Location: Sullivan County, Tennessee.
Description: A certain tract or parcel of land containing 284 acres be the same more or less said land lying and being in the county aforesaid and on both sides of Reedy Creek.
Witness: John Anderson,.
Acknowledged: State of Tennessee, Sullivan County, Nov. Session, 1805. in open court by Henry Maggert. Test: Matw. Rhea, C. S. C.
Registered: Feb. 18th, 1806.

---

(673) WILLIAM WADLOW :
to : DEED OF WARRANTY
THOMAS WADLOW, JOHN :
WADLOW, SAMUEL WADLOW. :

Date: March 20th, 1804.
Consideration: 24 £ lawful money.
Amt. of land: 20 acres.
Location: Sullivan County, Tennessee.
Description: One certain tract or parcel of land containing 20 acres being the said tract conveyed from Joseph Cole, Senr. to the heirs of William Wadlow deceased and the sd. William Wadlow do hereby convey my part of sd. land to the sd. Thomas, John and Samuel Wadlow and their heirs.
Witnesses: James Harly, George Wallace.
Proven: In open court by the oath of James Harley and George Wallace Sullivan County, Nov. Session, 1805.
Registered: Feb. 1st, 1806. Test: Matw. Rhea, C. S. C.

THOMAS WADLOW, DANIEL WADLOW, :
DANIEL WADLOW, SAMUEL WADLOW : DEED OF WARRANTY
to :
JOSEPH RHEA :

Date: Nov. 22d, 1805.
Consideration: $450.00.
Amt. of land: 100 acres.
Location: Sullivan County, Tennessee.
Description: A certain tract of land sithate in the county aforesaid containing 100 acres which sd. tract of land was granted by Joseph Cole to Thomas Wadlow, Samuel Wadlow, heirs of William Wadlow, deceased, unto Thomas Wadlow, Daniel Wadlow, John Wadlow, Samuel Wadlow.
Executed: In open Court by Thomas Wadlow, Daniel Wadlow, John Wadlow, Samuel Wadlow, State of Tennessee, Sullivan County, Nov. Session, 1805.
Registered: Deb. 2nd, 1806. Stepehn Major, Regst.

(Page)

(675) JAMES GAINES & THOMAS GAINES : to : DEED OF WARRANTY JOSEPH EVERETT :

Date: May 24th, 1805.
Consideration: $1456.33.
Amt. of land: 145 3/4 acres.
Location: Sullivan County, Tennessee.
Description: A certain tract or parcel of land containing 145 3/4 acres of land be the same more or less lying and being in the county aforesaid and on the North side of Reedy Creek.
Witness: James Gaines. Proven: State of Tennessee, Sullivan County August Session, 1805, in open court by James Gaines.
Registered: Feb. 11th, 1806. Test: Matw. Rhea, C. S. C.

---

(676) WALLACE WILLOUGHBY : to : DEED OF WARRANTY JACOB BOOHER :

Date: May 21st, 1805.
Consideration: $15.00.
Amt. of land: 40 poles, being a lot laid off for a town lot.
Location: State of Tennessee & Sullivan County.
Description: A certain lot of landlying and being in the county and state aforesaid on Sinking Creek adjoining the lot that the said Booher now lives on being a lot laid off for a town lot No. 37, agreeable to a plan of thw town of Greenfield.
Acknowledged: State of Tennessee, Sullivan County, May Session, 1805, in open court by Wallace Willoughby. Test: Matw. Rhea, C. S. C.
Registered: Feb. 12th, 1806.

---

(677) JOHN EVERET, JOHN TIPTON, SAMUEL PRESTON, ROBERT PRESTON, JACOB WLEAN, BENJAMIN VENAMBER : vs. : SUIT ARMSTEAD BLEVINS :

THOMAS ROCKHOLD : to : SHERIFF'S DEED. JOHN TIPTON, JUNR. :

Date: June 25th, 1804.
Consideration: $20.00.
Sale: Pleases Write of Fire Faces Isued by said court of Sullivan County at their session in May, 1804, direced to the Sheriff of said County on the 25th, of June, 1804, did levy the aforesaid writs of fire faces upon a negro man called Harry as the proprty of the said Armstead Blevins and according to law did advertise the aforesaid negro man for publick sale at the house of said Armstead Blevins in the county aforesaid Aug. 16th, 1804. The sd. Thomas Rockhold did sell the said negro man at publick sale to John Tipton, Junr. he being the highest bidder, for the sum of $20.00.
Witnesses: George Rutledge, Frances Rockhold.
Acknowledged: In open court by Thomas Rockhold, State of Tennessee, Sullivan County, Nov. Session, 1805.
Registered: Feb. 20th, 1806. Test: Matw. Rhea, C.S.C.

(Page)

(678) ABRAHAM HUDSON : to : DEED OF WARRANTY NICHOLAS BERGER :

Date: Feb. 19th, 1806.
Consideration: $563.00.
Amt. of land: 169 acres.
Location: Sullivan County, Tennessee.
Description: A certain tract or parcel of land containing 169 acres be the same more or less land lying and being in the county aforesaid.
Witness: John Anderson.
Acknowledged: State of Tennessee, Sullivan County, in open court by Abraham Hudson. Test: Matw. Rhea, C. S. C.
Registered: Feb. 20th, 1806.

---

(679) THOMAS COX, ADMINISTRATOR : to : DEED OF CONVEYANCE EDWARD GOSSAGE :

Date: Jan. 25th, 1806.
Consideration: In consequence of a bond given by Greenberry, Cox deceased, for whom Thomas Cox is Administrator,
Location: Sullivan County, Tennessee.
Description: A certain tract of land containing 100 acres situate lying on Muddy Creek in Sullivan County.
State of Tennessee, Mero District., Jan. 25th, 1806. Thomas Cox came before me John Overton, esquire, one of the Judges of the Supreme Court of Law and Equity for the state aforesaid acknowledged the Execution of the within deed of conveyance to be his as Admininstrator of Greenberry Cox.
Registered: Feb. 20th, 1806. Test: John Overton.

---

(681) ANTHONY SHARP & SAMUEL GAMBLE : to : DEED OF WARRANTY JOHN KING :

Date: Jan. 23d, 1806.
Consideration: $200.00.
Amt. of land: 17 acres and 34* be the same more or less.
Location: Sullivan County, State of Tennessee.
Description: A certain tract or parcel of land lying and being in the county and state aforesaid on the North side of Watauga near the mouth of Sand River being part of the tract whereon Samuel Gamble now lives.
Witnesses: James Gregg, Nathaniel T. Call.
Proven: In open court by James Gregg, Sullivan County, Feb. Session, 1806. Test: Matw. Rhea, C. S. C.
Registered: Feb. 20th, 1806.

---

(682)

(Page)
(682) EDWARD GOSSACK : to : DEED OF WARRANTY JACOB HARTMAN :

Date: Feb. 18th, 1806.
Consideration: $416.
Amt. of land: 75 acres.
Location: Sullivan County, Tennessee.
Description: A certain tract or parcel of land containing 75 acres be the same more or less said land lying and being in the county aforesaid and on Muddy Creek.
Witness: John Anderson.
Acknowledged: In open court by Edward Gossack, State of Tennessee, Sull8van County, Feb. Session, 1806. Test: Matw. Rhea, C.S.C.
Registered: Feb. 21st, 1806.

---

(683) GEORGE LITTLE : to : DEED OF WARRANTY JOHN SHELL :

Date: Feb. 24th, 1806.
Consideration: $300.00 current money of Tennessee.
Amt. of land: 100 acres.
Location: Sullivan Counyt, Tennessee.
Description: A certain tract or parcel of land lying in the county aforedaid on the Bank of Holston River on the South Side adjoining land of Jacob Fleener and Arnold Shelland is to be Surveu 100 acres.
Witnesses: Jacob Gitt, Samule Mcorkle.
Acknowledged: In open court and oredered to be registered Feb. 21, 1806. Test: Matw. Rhea, C. S. C.

---

(684) MARY MKONKEY : to : DEED OF WARRANTY WILLIAM GODDARD, SENR. :

Date: Aug. 16th, 1805.
Consideration: $120.00.
Amt. of land: 49 acres.
Location: Sullivan County, Tennessee.
Description: A certain tract or parcel of land containing 49 acres be the same more or less.
Witness: John Anderson.
Proven: In open court by John Anderson, State of Tennessee, Sullivan County August Session, 1803. Test: Matw. Rhea, C.S.C.
Registered: Feb. 21st, 1806.

---

(685) JOHN SHARP : to : DEED OF WARRANTY JOHN KING ;

Date: Nov. 8th, 1799.

Consideration: #333.33.
Amt. of land: 90 acres.
Location: Sullivan County, Tennessee.
Description: A certain tract or parcel of land situate lying and being in the county aforesaid between the River Watauga and Holston and nearly adjoining the former, containing 90 acres, be the same more or less.
Witnesses: James Gregg.
Proven: In open court by James Gregg, Sullivan County Feb. Session, 1806. Test: Matw. Rhea, C. S. C.
Registered: Feb. 21st, 1806.

---

(686) JAMES GAINES & THOMAS GAINES : to : DEED OF WARRANTY JOHN SEMCLAIRE :

Date: May 21st, 1805.
Consideration: $494.00.
Amt. of land: 247 acres.
Location: Sullivan County, Tennessee.
Description: One certain tract of land containing 247 acres lying and being in the county of Sullivan on both sides of Reedy Creek being part of a tract of land granted to Edmund Pendleton of the State of Virginia, deceased, and by Edmund Pendleton acting Executor of the last will and Testament of the sd. Edmond Pendleton deceased and John Taylor conveyed by deed to the said James Gaines and Thomas Gaines.
Witnesses: James T. Gaines, Ambrose Gaines, Joseph Newland.
Proven: In open court by James Newland Sullivan County, Feb. Session, 1806. Test: Matw. Rhea, C. S. C.
Registered: Feb. 21st, 1806.

---

(687) WALTER JAMES : to : DEED OF WARRANTY THOMAS GODDARD :

Date: Aug. 23d, 1804.
Consideration: $270.00.
Amt. of land: 34 acres.
Location: Sullivan County, Tennessee.
Description: A certain tract of land lying and being in said county containing 34 acres be the same more or less.
Acknowledged: In open court by Walter James, State of Tennessee. Sullivan County, August Session, 1804. Test: Matw. Rhea, C.S.C.
Registered: Feb. 22d, 1806.

---

(688) THOMAS ROCKHOLD, SHERIFF : to : SHERIFF'S DEED ROBERT ALISON :

Date: Feb. 11th, 1805.
Consideration: $4.50.
Suit: Execution of Pleuris Fire Facias against William Hughes on behalf of sd. Robert Alison form the Superior Court of Law and Equity of Washington District.

Sale: Exposed to Publick sale it first being advertised according to law lot of land granted to William Hughes from the State of North Carolona originially which will apppear as to propréty of William Hughes from the State of North Carolina and to satisfy said writs of Pleuris Fire Facies for and in consideration of the sum of $4.50. Sold enfair and open sale at the highest bidder the buyer which was Robert Alison the said lock or parcel of land being parcel of a grant to sd. Hughes by North Carolina appears to be the right title of said Hughes by his title.
Description: Sd. lot of land lying in Sullivan County in the District of Washinton in the fork between Holsto & Watauga River, 3 acres more or less.
Acknowledged: Sullivan County, Nov. Session, 1805, in open court by Thomas Rockhold, Sheriff. Test: Matw. Rhea, C. S. C.
Registered: Feb. 22d, 1806.

---

(689) JAMES GAINES AND THOMAS GAINES to THOMAS TITSWORTH : DEED OF WARRANTY

Date: May 24th, 1805.
Consideration: $100.00
Amt. of land: 60 acres.
Location: Sullivan County, Tennessee.
Description: A tract or parcel of land containing 60 acres be the same more or less lying and being in the county of Sullivan on the South side of Reedy Creek.
Witnesses: Ambrose Gaines, James T. Gaines.
Proven: State of Tennessee; Sullivan County, August Session, 1805, in open court by James Gaines.
Registered: Feb. 22d, 1806.

---

(690) DAVID PROTHRO & THOMAS PROTHRO to HENRY MYERS : DEED OF WARRANTY

Date: Nov. 28th, 1805.
Consideration: For a valuable condideration.
Amt. of land: 208 acres.
Location: Sullivan County, Tennessee.
Description: A certain tract or parcel of land lying and being in the county aforesaid and on the waters of Watauga, containing 208 acres.
Witnesses: John Scott, John Alison, John King.
Proven: In open court by the oath of John Scot and John Alison Sullivan County, Feb. Session, 1806. Test: Matw. Rhea, C.S.C.
Registered: Feb. 22d, 1806.

---

(691) THOMAS TITSWORTH to JACOB BARE : DEED OF WARRANTY

Date: Dec. 2d, 1805.

Consideration: $733.1/3
Amt. of land: 192 acres.
Location: Sullivan County, State of Tennessee.
Description: A certain tract of land containing by estimation 192 acres be the same more or less situate lying and being in the county and state aforesaid on the South Side of Holston River opposite to the Long Island of Holston including the plantation where said Thomas Titsworth purchased of Michael Cross.
Witness: Stephen Hicks.
Acknowledged: In open court by Thomas Titsworth, Sullivan County, February Session, 1806. Test: Matw. Rhea, C. S. C.
Registered: Feb. 24th, 1806.

---

(692) THOMAS GAINES & JAMES GAINES : to : DEED OF WARRANTY
SAMUEL MOORE :

Date: May 22d, 1805.
Consideration: $500.00.
Amt. of land: 267 acres.
Location: Sullivan County, State of Tennessee.
Description: A certain tract or parcel of land containing 267 acres lying and being in the aforesaid county and State on both sides of Reedy Creek.
Witnesses: Joseph Newland, Ambrose Gaines, James T. Gaines.
Proven: State of Tennessee, Sullivan County, Nov. Session, 1805, in open court by the oath of Ambrose Gaines.
Registered: Feb. 24th, 1806. Test: Matw. Rhea, C. S. C.

---

(693) JOHN & SARAH VANCE : to : DEED OF WARRANTY
JAMES PICKENS, SENR. :

Date: April 3d, 1805.
Consideration: $430.00.
Amt. of land: 129 acres.
Location: Sullivan County, Tennessee.
Description: A certain tract of land containing 129 acres situate, lying and being in sd. county on Kindricks Creek.
Witnesses: James Pickins, Charles Jones, John Owens.
Proven: In open court by Charles Jones, Sullivan County, Feb. Session 1806. Test: Matw. Rhea, C. S. C.
Registered: Feb. 24th, 1806.

---

(694) ZACHARIAS WEEKS : to : DEED OF WARRANTY
THOMAS CAPPS :

Date: Aug. 22d, 1804.
Consideration: $33.00.
Amt. of land: 7 acres, 3/4, and 1/2 of 1/4.
Location: SullivanCounty, Tennessee.

[illegible]
[illegible]
[illegible] State of Tennessee,
Sullivan County, August Session, 1804.
Registered: Feb. 24th, 1806. Test: Matw. Rhea, C. S. C.

---

(695) SANFORD BIRDWELL :
to : DEED OF WARRANTY
ABRAHAM WANTLING :

Date: Feb. 17th, 1806.
Consideration: $407.00.
Amt. of land: 122 acres.
Location: Sullivan County, Tennessee.
Description: A certain tract or parcel of land lying and being in the county aforesaid containing 122 acres be the same more or less.
Witnessesx John Anderson.
Acknowledged: In open court by Sanford Birdwell, Sullivan County, February Session, 1806. Test: Matw. Rhea, C. S. C.
Registered: Feb. 25th, 1806.

---

(696) WILLIAM DOWNS :
to : DEED OF WARRANTY
STEPHEN HICKS :

Date: Jan. 1st, 1798.
Consideration: $180.00.
Amt. of land: 69 acres.
Location: Sullivan County, Tennessee.
Description: A certain tract of land containinf 69 acres be the same more or less.
Witnesses; John Anderson, Walter James, Jacob Earneart.
Acknowledged: In open court by William Downs, Sullivan County, Feb. 1799. Test: Matw. Rhea, C. S. C.
Registered: Feb. 25th, 1806.

---

(697) LEONARD HART :
to : DEED OF WARRANTY
GEORGE MALONE :

Date: Nov.____, 1802.
Consideration: 86 L/
Amt. of land: 401 acres.
Location: Sullivan County, Tennessee.
Description: A certain tract or parcel of land containing 100 acres being part of a atract of land granted unto John Pitner containing 401 acres No. 530 as by the patent doth appear.
Witnesses: Walter Cunningham, John Malone.
Proven: In open court by the oath of John Malond, State of Tennessee, Sullivan County, Feb. Session, 1804. Test: Matw. Rhea. C. S. C.
Registered: Feb. 25th, 1806.

(698) JACOB DROKE : to : DEED OF WARRANTY PETER HANNAH :

Date: Dec. 21st, 1805.
Consideration: For a valuable consideration.
Amt. of land: 80 acres.
Location: Sullivan County, Tennessee.
Description: A certain tract or parcel of land containing 80 acres said land lying and being in the county and state aforesaid.
Witnesses: John Anderson, Zachariah Weeks.
Acknowledged in open court by Jacob Droke, Sullivan County, Feb. Session 1806. Test: Matw. Rhea, C. S. C.
Registered: Feb. 25th, 1806.

---

(699) WILLIAM STACY : to : DEED OF WARRANTY WALTER KING :

Date: Aug. 30th, 1804.
Consideration: $1000.00.
Amt. of land: 200 acres.
Location: Sullivan County, Tennessee.
Description: A certain tract or parcel of land containing by estimation 200 acres lying and being in Sullivan County, State of Tennessee, South side of Holston River on each side of Kendricks Creek and including the mill.
Witness: George Moorelock.
Proven: Sullivan County, Nov. Session, 1805, in open court by George Moorelock. Test: Matw. Rhea, C. S. C.
Registered: Feb. 25th, 1806.

---

(701) ALEXANDER PORTER : to : DEED OF WARRANTY WILLIAM GODDARD :

Date: Aug. 20th, 1805.
Consideration: $150.00.
Amt. of land: 150 acres.
Location: Sullivan County, Tennessee.
Description: A certain tract of land containing 150 acres by survey lying and being on the waters of Reedy Creek a south brnach of Holston River which may more fully seen by the original plot or deed accompanying this. Acknowledged in open court by Alexander Porter.
~~Witnesses: Walter Cunningham, John Malone.~~
Registered: Feb. 25th, 1806. Test: Matw. Rhea, C. S. C.

---

(702) SAMUEL SHIPLEY, ELIZABETH SHIPLEY, PARKER SHIPLEY, POLLY SHIPLEY, AQUILLA SHIPLEY : to : DEED OF WARRANTY ABRAHAM HEDRICK :

Date: Jan. 10th, 1806.
Consideration: $100.00.

Amt. of land: 74 acres.
Location: Sullivan County, Tennessee.
Description: A certain tract or parcel of land containing 74 acres lying and being in the county and state aforesaid on the Nor Nor side of Holston River including the plantation where the said Samuel Shipley now lives.
Witnesses: Martin Roller, John Jennings.
Proven: In open court by the oaths of Martin Roller and John Jenings Sullivan County, Feb. Session, 1806.
Registered: March 1st, 1806. Test: Matw. Rhea, C. S. C.

---

(703) AGATHA CAWOOD : to : DEED OF WARRANTY WILLIAM BLEVINS :

Date: Feb. 21st, 1806.
Consideration: $2000.00.
Amt. of land: 740 acres.
Location: Sullivan County, Tennessee.
Description: 740 acres of land which was willed by the late husband John Cawood, dec'd. together with all the improvements thereon.
Witnesses: Isaac Brownlow.
Acknowledged: In open court by Agatha Cawood, Sullivan County, Feb. Session, 1806.
Registered: March 12th, 1806. Test: Matw. Rhea, C. S. C.

---

(704) JOHN SHARP & WILLIAM KING : to : DEED OF WARRANTY MARTIN BOCHER :

Date: Feb. 17th, 1806.
Consideration: $950.00.
Amt. of land: 365 acres.
Location: Sullivan County, Tennessee.
Description: A certain tract or parcel of land containing 365 acres more or less said land lying and being in the county aforesaid and on Sinking Creek.
Witnesses John Anderson.
Acknowledged: In open court by John Shapp and William King, Sullivan County, Feb. Session, 1806. Test: Matw. Rhea, C. S. C.
Registered: Aug. 26th, 1806.

---

(705) PETER BRICKBILL : to : DEED OF WARRANTY MARTIN BOOHER :

Date: Dec. 27th, 1805.
Consideration: $1100.00.
Amt. of land: 127 1/2 acres.
Location: Sullivan County, State of Tennessee.

(Page)
(706) Description: One certain tract or parcel of land lying and being in the county and state aforesaid containing 127 1/2 acres lying on Sinking Creek.
Witnesses: Conrad Sharetze, John Booher, Hoseph Owen.
Acknowledged: In open court by Peter Brackbill, Sullivan County, Feb. Session, 1806. Test: Matw. Rhea, C. S. C.
Registered: April 26th, 1806.

ISAACH SHELBY : DEED OF WARRANTY
to :
CATHERINE SHELBY :

Date: Nov. 22d, 1804.
Consideration: $5000.00.
Amt. of land: 463 acres.
Location: Sullivan County, Tennessee.
Description: A certain tract or parcel of land in Sullivan County within the old patent line belonging to the said Shelby and containing 463 acres be the same more or less.
Acknowledged: State of Tennessee, Sullivan County, Nov. Session, 1804, in open court ny Isaac Shelby. Test: Matw. Rhea, C. S. C.
Registered: May 5th, 1806.

---

(708) JACOB WORK & JOSEPH WORK : DEED OF WARRANTY
to :
JENKIN WHITESIDE :

Date: Oct. 9th, 1805.
Consideration: $1000.00.
Amt. of land: 341 1/2 acres.
Location: Sullivan County, Tennessee.
Location: Sullivan County, State of Tennessee.
Description: 1 lot or piece of land containing 1/4 of an acre being a lot in the town of Blountville and known by lot No. 3 in the plan of said town which was conveyed by the commissioners of sd. town to sd. Robert Work in his life time by deed bearing date the 23d of August, 1796; 1 other lot or piece of land containing 1/4 of an acre being a lot in the sd. town of Blountville and known by Lot No. 4 in the plan of said town being the same on which John Richardson now lives which was conveyed to said Robert Work in his life time by the Commissioners of said town by deed bearing date the 25th of August, 1795; also one other tract or parcel of land containing 90 acres more or less which was conveyed by Samuel Hampton to said Robert Work in his life time by deed bearing date the 17th of December, 1793; also one other tract or parcel of land containing 192 acres which was granted to the sd. Robert Work in his lifetime by patent bearing date the 17th of November, 1797; also one other tract or parcel of land containing 59 acres more or less bounded by the other tract of land so conveyed by said Samule Hampton , land of Nathan Lewis and the sd. tract of land so granted to Robert Work in his life time which 59 acres was conveyed to Robert Work by Joseph Key bydeed bearing date the 24th of November, 1798.
Jacob Work and Joseph Work were heirs and assigns of Robert Work.

(Page)

Witnesses: Thomas Hopkins, John Scott.
Proven: In open court by the oaths fo Thomas Hopkins and John Scott State of Tennessee, Sullivan County, May Session, 1806.
Registered: May 20th, 1806. Test: Matw. Rhea, C. S. C.

---

(711) THOMAS DODD : to : DEED OF WARRANTY ANDREW MAUK :

Date: Sept. 25th, 1801.
Consideration: $ 266.00.
Amt. of land: 162 acres.
Location: Sullivan County, Tennessee.
Description: A certain tract or parcel of land containing 162 acres be the same more or less lying and being in the county and state aforesaid.
Witnesses: John Sinclair, Anthony Howel. (Hall)
Proven: State of Tennessee, Sullivan County, May Session, 1802, by the oath of Anthony Hall.
Registered: May 22d, 1806. Test: Matw. Rhea, C. S. C.

---

(101) DALLAM CASWELL : to : REVOCATION OF POWER OF ATTORNEY ALEXANDER OUTLAW :

Date: April 25th, 1806.
Revocation: By my letter of authoriy bearing date Jan. 1797, did make, constitute and appoint Alexander Outlaw my attorney for the recovery of all sums of money whatsoever due to me the sd. William Caswell as Executor to the last will and testament of Richard Caswell, deceased, and also to sell and convey lands lying in sd. State of Tennessee belonging to the said deceased by the said letter of Attorney my appear now know ye that the sd. Dallam Caswell for divers good causes and considerations have revoked, conntermand and annul and make void the said letter given or intended to be given to the sd. Outlaw.
Witnesses: Wm. Lovick, Richard W. Caswell.
Proven: State of Tennessee, Sullivan County, May Session, 1806, revocation of a power of attorney was proven in open court by the oath of Richard W. Caswell,
Recorded in office May 19th, 1806, Vol. 2, page 457.
Registered: May 22d, 1806. Test: Matw. Rhea, C. S. C.

---

(712) DALLAM CASWELL, EXECUTOR, : to : POWER OF ATTORNEY JOHN GOTTEN, ATTORNEY :

Date: April 25th, 1806.
Appointment: For divers good causes and considerations do make and appoint John Gotten my true and lawful attorney for me and in my name and for my own purpose use benefit as Executor to ask, demand Sue for and Recover and receive of and from all persons living in the State of Tennessee indebted to the sd. Richard Caswell for whom I am Executor, either by note or bond or book account. And also to sell and convey all the lands lying in the sd. State belonging to the

Estate of the sd. Richard Caswell that remains unsold which conveyance shall be as good and lawful as if I was personally presnnt at the doing of the same. And also to ask, demand, sue for and recover from James Glasgow his Executors or Administrators the full value of a certain tract of land containing 640 acres.
Description: A certain tract of land containing 640 acres entered by the aofresaid Richard Caswell in the county of Washington September 2d, 1778 at the foot of the Iron Mountain on the head of Indian Creek or place known by the name of the Lime Stone Cove which land warrant was conveyed by the sd. James Glasgow to Charles Colyer, Sept. 10th, 1792, which conveyance I hereby declare to be illegal and without any authority he the said James Glasgow derived from the will of the sd. Richard Caswell as he has stated in the conveyance of said warrant and also to askfor, demand, sue for recover and receive from Alexander Outlaw, Esq.aforesaid, all such sums of money as he may have received for me by virtue of power of attorney given him by Winston Caswell and myself as acting executors of the sd. Richard Caswell and to transact all necessary things as if I myself were present. D. Caswell.
Witnesses: Richard W. Caswell, Wm. Lovick.
Proven: Power of attorney proven in open court by the oath of Richard Caswell, State of Tennessee, Sullivan County, May Session, 1806.
Recorded in office May 19th, 1806, Vol. 2 page 450.
Executed May 22d, 1806. Registered. Test: Matw. Rhea, C. S. C.

---

(714) GEORGE CRUMLEY to JACOB CROMLEY, DANIEL CROMLEY : DEED OF WARRANTY

Date: March 1st, 1806.
Consideration: $50.00.
Amt. of land: 34 acres.
Location: Sullivan County, Tennessee.
Description: A certain tract or parcel of land lying and being in the county of Sullivan on the South side of Holston River containing 34 acres more or less.
Witnesses: Ireson Longacre, Thomas Jones, John Carrier.
Proven: State of Tennessee, Sullivan County, May Session, 1806, in open court by Ireson Longacre. Test: Matw. Rhea, C. S. C.
Registered: May 22d, 1806.

---

(715) GEORGE CROMLEY, SENR. to JACOB CROMLEY & DANIEL CROMLEY : DEED OF WARRANTY

Date: March 1st, 1806.
Consideration: $300.00.
Amt. of land: 100 acres.
Location: Sullivan County, Tennessee.
Description: A certain tract or parcel of land containing 100 acres more or less lying and being in the county of Sullivan on the South side of Holston River.

Witnesses: Ireson Longacre, Thomas Jones, John Carrier.
Proven: State of Tennessee, Sullivan County, May Session, 1806, in open court by Ireson Longacre. Test: Matw. Rhea, C. S. C.
Registered: May 22d, 1806.

---

(716) GEORGE CROMLEY, SENR., :
to : DEED OF WARRANTY
JACOB CROMLEY & DANIEL CROMLEY :

Date: March 1st, 1806.
Consideration: $300.00.
Amt. of land: 100 acres.
Location: Sullivan County, Tennessee.
Description: A certain tract or parcel of land containing 100 acres more or less lying and bing in the county of Sullivan on the South side of Holston River.
Witnesses: Ireson Longacre, Thomas Jones, John Carrier.
Proven: State of Tennessee, Sullivan County, May Session, 1806, in open court by the oath of Ireson Longacre.
Registered: May 22d, 1806. Test: Matw. Rhea, C. S. C.

---

(716) GOERGE CROMLEY, SENR., :
to : DEED OF WARRANTY
JACOB CROMLEY & DANIEL CROMLEY :

Date: March 1st, 1806.
Consideration: $200.00.
Amt. of land: 100 acres.
Location: Sullivan County, Tennessee.
Description: A certain tract or parcel of land containing 100 acres more or less lying and being in the county of Sullivan on the South side of Holston River, on Weaver Creek.
Witnesses: Ireson Longacre, Thomas Jones, John Carrier.
Proven: In open court by the oath of Ireson Longacre and John Carrier, State of Tennessee, Sullivan County, May Session, 1806.
Registered: May 22d, 1806. Test: Matw. Rhea, C. S. C.

---

(717) GEORGE CRUMLEY, SENR. :
to : DEED OF WARRANTY
JACOB CRUMLEY & DANIEL CRUMLEY :

Date: March 1st, 1806.
Consideration: $200.00.
Amt. of land: 100 acres.
Location: Sullivan County, Tennessee.
Description: A certain tract or parcel of land containing 100 acres more or less lying andbbing in the county of Sullivan on the South side of Holston River.
Witnesses: Ireson Longacre, John Carier.
Proven: State of Tennessee, Sullivan County, May Session, 1806, in open court by the oath of Ireson Longacre & John Carrier.
Registered: May 22d, 1806. Test: Matw. Rhea, C. S. C.

GEORGE CROMLEY : to : DEED OF GIFT
JACOB CROMLEY & DANIEL CROMLEY :

Date: March 1st, 1806.
Consideration: Love, good will and affection.
Amt. of land: Home site.
Location: Sullivan County, Tennessee.
Description: All singular my goods and chattles& dwelling house in the county aforesaid together with three head of horses, ten (10) head of cattle, and seven sheep also all the hogs I now have.
Witnesses: Ireson Longacre, John Carrier.
Proven: In open court by the oath of Ireson Longacre and John Carrier, State of Tennessee, Sullivan County, May Session 1806.
Registered: May 22d, 1806. Test: Matw. Rhea, C. S. C.

---

(719) JACOB WEAVER : to : DEED OF WARRANTY
JOHN CARRIER :

Date: ____ 16th, 1806.
Consideration: 132 £ , 5 s.
Amt. of land: 87 1/2 acres.
Location: Sullivan County, Tennessee.
Description: A certain tract or parcel of land containing 87 1/2 acres lying and being in the county of Sullivan on the south side of Holston River.
Witness: John Anderson.
Acknowledged: State of Tennessee, Sullivan County, May Session, 1806, in open court by John Weaver. Test: Matw. Rhea, C. S. C.
Registered: May 22d, 1806.

---

(720) SAMUEL BAUGHMAN : to : DEED OF WARRANTY
JONATHAN BAUGHMAN :

Date: May 17th, 1806.
Consideration: Natural love and affection.
Amt. of land: 181 1/2 acres of land.
Location: Sullivan County, Tennesse.
Description: All that tenement of land containing 181 1/2 acres of land be the same more or less situate lying and being in said County of Sullivan on the west side of Horse Creek beginning at Nathan Baughman's corner.
Witnesses: George Vincent, Nathan Baughman, George Molouck.
Proven: In open court by the oaths of George Morelock and Nathan Baughman, State of Tennessee, Sullivan County, May Session, 1806.
Registered: May 24th, 1806. Test: Matw. Rhea, C. S.C.

---

(722) SAMUEL BAUGHMAN : to :
JOHN BARNETT, SENR. :

Date: May 20th, 1806.

(722) Consideration: $100.00.
Amt. of land: 145 acres.
Location: Sullivan County, Tennessee.
Description: All that tract of land situate lying and being in sd. county of Sullivan containing 145 acres part of a tract of l land on Horse Creek granted to Vashal Dillingham by patent from North Carolina .
Witnesses: George Vincent, George Morelock.
Proven: State of Tennessee, Sullivan County, May Session, 1806, in open court by the oath of George Vincent, George Morelock.
Registered: May 24th, 1806. Test: Matw. Rhea, C. S. C.

---

(723) SAMUEL BAUGHMAN : to : DEED OF WARRANTY GEORGE MORELOCK :

Date: May 17th, 1806.
Consideration: Natural love and affection.
Amt. of land: 95 acres.
Location: Sullivan County, Tennessee.
Description: All that tract of land containing 95 acres be the same more or less lying and being in sd. county of Sullivan on Horse creek including all the lands and improvements where Thomas McClain now lives and joining by the lines that George Vincent surveyed for said Morelock and is part of land of a tract of land on sd. creek granted to Vactrel Dillingham by patent under the great seal of North Carolina.
Witnesses: George Vincent, Jonathan Baughman, John Bamd.
Proven: State of Tennessee, Sullivan County, May Session, 1806, in open court by the oath of John Bamd and Jonathan Baughman.
Registered: May 24th, 1806. Test: Matw. Rhea, C. S. C.

---

(724) AMBROSE GAINES : to : DEED OF WARRANTY SAMUEL EDGMAN :

Nov. 2d, 1805.
Consideration: $30.00.
Amt. of land: 30 acres.
Location: Sullivan County, Tennessee.
Description: A certain tract or parcel of land containing 30 acres be the same more or less lying and being in the county aforesaid on Reedy Creek.
Witnesses: Martin Waddle, Phillemon Bohannon.
Proven: In open court by the oath of Martin Waddle and Phillemon Bohannon, State of Tennessee, Sullivan County, Feb. session, 1800.
Registered: May 24th, 1806. Test: Matw. Rhea, C. S. C.

---

(725) JOHN STONE : to : DEED OF WARRANTY BENJAMIN HUFFMAN :

Date: March 8th, 1806.
Consideration: $500.00.

Amt. of land: 200 acres.
Location: Sullivan County, Tennessee.
Description: A certaintract or parcel of land containing 200 acres situate lying and being in sd. county and state aforesaid on Walkers fork of Horse Creek including the plantation where Abselom Rossberry now lives.
Proven: State of Tennessee, Sullivan County, May Session, 1806, in open court by the oath of Phillip Snapp & Elkanah Dulaney.
Registered: May 24th, 1806. Test: Matw. Rhea, C. S. C.

---

(727) ROBERT EASLEY, EXECUTOR, to ARIN BACON : DEED OF WARRANTY

Date: Oct. 7th, 1805.
Consideration: $210.00.
Amt. of land: 200 acres.
Location: Sullivan County, Tennessee.
Description: One tract or parcel of land containing 200 acres lying and being in Sullivan County, being the property of the late Joseph Moody for whom Robert Easley is Executor.
Witnesses: Benjamin Easley, Moses Robinson.
Acknowledged: In open court by Robert Easley, State of Tennessee, Sullivan County, May Session, 1806.
Registered: May 24th, 1806. Test: Matw. Rhea, C. S. C.

---

(728) JOHN YANCEY to WILLIAM KING : DEED OF WARRANTY

Date: March 3d, 1806.
Consideration: $200.00.
Amt. of land: 1/4 of an acre with the houses thereon.
Location: Sullivan County. Tennessee.
Description: A certain lot or larcel of land containing 1/4 of an acre in the town of Blountville the county of Sullivan aforesaid adjoining one of the public lots and designated, known and distinguished in the plan of said town by number 20 which said lot was originally conveyed by the commissioners of said town to John Shelby and by him sold to James King who sold the same to Alexander McCrabb by whom it was conveyed to the sd. John Yancey by indenture bearing date Oct. 20th, 1804.
Witnesses: David Steel, John Punch.
Proven: State of Tennessee, Sullivan County, May Session, 1806, in open court by the oath of John Punch.
Registered: May 25th, 1806. Test: Matw. Rhea, C. S. C.

---

(729) JAMES GAINES & THOMAS GAINES to SAMUEL EXGMAN : DEED OF WARRANTY

Date: May 24th, 1805.
Consideration: $600.00

(Page)

Amt. of land: 200 acres.
Location: Sullivan County, Tennessee.
Description: A certain tract or parcel of land containing 200 acres lying and being in the county of Sullivan and on both sides of Reedy Creek being part of a tract of land granted to Edmond Pendleton by paten grant bearing date the 17th of August, 1756.
Witnesses: Ambrose Gaines, James T. Gaines.
Proven: In open court by Ambrose Gaines, State of Tennessee, Sullivan County, August Session 1805.
Registered: May 25th, 1806. Test: Matw. Rhea, C. S. C.

---

(730)

GEORGE VINCENT :
to : DEED OF GIFT
JOHN VINCENT :

Date: May 20th, 1806.
Consideration: Natural love and affection.
Amt. of land: 105 acres.
Location: Sullivan County, Tennessee.
Description: All that tract of land containing 105 acres be the same more or less lying and being in sd. county of Sullivan on Horse creek including all the lands and improvements that the sd. George Vincent posesseth where Edward Lepler now lives.
Witnesses: George Morelock, Nathan Bachman, Jonathan Bachman.
Proven: In open court by the oaths of Jonathan Bachman and George Morelock, State of Tennessee, Sullivan County, May Session, 1806.
Registered: May 25th, 1806. Test: Matw. Rhea, C. S. C.

---

(733) JAMES GRAGG :
to : DEED OF WARRANTY
LUDWIG RINEHARD :

Date: July 29th, 1802.
Considertaion: $166.00.
Amt. of land: 50 acres.
Location: Sullivan County, Tennessee.
Description: A certain piece of parcel of land lying in the county of Sullivan between Holston and Watauga River being part of the survey whereon the said James Gragg now lives.
Witnesses: Thomas King, John King.
Acknowledged: In open court by James Gragg, State of Tennessee, Sullivan County, May Session, 1806.
Registered: May 25th, 1806. Test: Matw. Rhea, C. S. C.

---

(735) DAVID CAROTHERS :
to : DEED OF WARRANTY
ISAAC JONES :

Date: Nov. 18th, 1805.
Consideration: $500.00.
Amt. of land: 90 acres.
Location: Sullivan County, Tennessee.

Description: A certain tract or parcel of land lying and being in the county of Sullivan containing 90 acres be the same more or less.
Witnesses: David Yearsley, John Jenings.
Acknowledged: In open court by David Carathers, State of Tennesseee Sullivan County, Nov. Session, 1805.
Registered: May 25th, 1806. Test: Matw. Rhea, C. S. C.

---

(736) JAMES GAINES & THOMAS GAINES : to : DEED OF WARRANTY AMBROSE GAINES :

Date: May 20th, 1805.
Consideration: 96 £, 10 s.
Amt. of land: 273 acres.
Location: Sullivan County, Tennessee.
Description: A certain tract or parcel of land containing 273 acres be the same more or less lying and being in the county aforesaid on Reedy Creek including the place whereon he now lives.
Witnesses: James T. Gaines, Philemon Bachman, Joseph Newland.
Proven: In open court by Phillemon Bachman, State of Tennessee, Sullivan County, August Session, 1805.
Registered: May 26th, 1806. Test: Matw. Rhea, C. S. C.

---

(737) JONATHAN BACHMAN : to : DEED OF WARRANTY JACOB BARE :

Date: May 17th, 1806.
Consideration: $1000.00.
Amt. of land: 500 acres.
Location: Sullivan County, Tennessee.
Description: A tract or parcel of land containing 500 acres, reserving 51 acres that John Smith sold and laid off for Nathan Peoples Senr. the ballance of said tract of land conveyed to Jacob Bare including all the improvements where John Smith formerly lived on Horse Creek in said County of Sullivan.
Witnesses: George Vincent, George Morelock.
Acknowledged: In open court by Jonathan Bachman, State of Tennessee, Sullivan County, May Session, 1804.
Registered: May 26th, 1806. Test: Matw. Rhea, C. S. C.

---

(739) WALLACE WILLOUGHBY : to : DEED OF WARRANTY JACOB BOOHER :

Date: May 21st, 1805.
Consideration: $15.00.
Amt. of land: 40 poles.

Location: Sullivan County, Tennessee.
Description: A certain lot of land lying and being in the county and state aforesaid on Cinking Creek in the county and state aforesaid adjoining in the lot that the daid Booher now lives on.
Acknowledged: In open court by Wallace Willoughby State of Tennessee Sullivan County, May Session, 1805. Test:xWalinza Matw. Rhea, C.S.C.
Registered: May 27th, 1806.

STEPHEN MAJORS : to : DEED OF GIFT THOMAS MAJORS :

Date: Feb. 26th, 1806.
Considerati n: Natural love and affection whihh I have for my son and for other good causes, including $150.00 to be paid to my daughter
Amt. of land: 100 acres.
Location: Sullivan County, Tennessee.
Description: 100 acres of land where I now live on situate lying and being in thecounty and state aforesaid on the North side of Holston river, five head of horses 7 fifteen head of horn cattle, & all my stock of hogs and all the family utensils and 3 beds and the furnitute thereunto belonging and my house hold furniture & 1 negro man the name of Top & it is to be remembered that my son Thomas Majors is to pay unto my daughter Ann Hawkins the wife of Henry Hawkins, Junr. that the sum of $150.00 is to be paid in trade 12 months from the date thereof and my son Thomas Majors is to maintain me and his mother during our natural life time an a deceant like manner.
Acknowledged: In open court by Stephen Majors , State of Tennessee, Sullivan County, May Session, 1806. Test: Matw. Rhea, C. S. C.
Registered: May 27th, 1806.

---

(740) JOHN CRUM : to : DEED OF WARRANTY DAVID ROSS :

Date: July 13th, 1805.
Consideration: $177.00.
Amt. of land: 88 3/4 acres.
Location: Sullivan County, Tennessee.
Description: A certain tract or parcel of land lying and being in the county and state aforesaid on the south side of Reedy Creek, being part of a tract of land granted to Edmund Pendleton by patent grant 16th of August, 1756 & At 100 acres of which was conveyed to the sd. John Crum by James and Thomas Gaines by deed bearing ddate the 24th of May, 1804. Its well understood that this deed excepts 13 1/2 acres lott in the town of Manchester and the housesand house John Crump lives in with 5 acres adjoining all the ballance of the 100 conveyed by James and Thomas Gaines is intended to be constituted by this deed.
Witnesses: James Gaines, John Olar.
Proven: In open court by the oath of James Gaines, State of Tennessee Sullivan County, May Session, 1806. Test: Matw. Rhea, C. S. C.
Registered: May 26th, 1806.

(Page)

(742) ELISHA COLE : to : BILL OF SALE GEORGE MELONE :

Date: Dec.1st, 1801.
Consideration: $266.00, good and lawful money of Tennessee.
Description: According to just form of law in that case and provided do bargain set over and deliver unto the sd. George Malone one negro woman about 23 years old names Cate.
Witnesses: Phillip Hobback, Cate Hobback.
Proven: In open court by Phillip Hobback, State of Tennessee, Sullivan County May Session, 1806.
Registered: June 11th, 1806. Test: Matw. Rhea, C. S. C.

---

* (743) JOHN ANDERSON, ELKER. DULANEY?, JAVOB STURM, COMMISSIONERS, to WILLIAM KING : COMMISSIONERS DEED.

Date: May 22d, 1806.
Consideration: $101.00.
Amt. of land: 1/4 of an acre.
Location: Blountville, Tennessee.
Description: A certain lot of land containing 1/4 of an acrex be the same more or less said lot lying and being in the sd. town of Blountville and distinguished by lot number 21 and known by the name of the jail lot.
Witnesses: John Anderson, Elk. R. Dulaney, Jacob Sturm.
Acknowledged: In open court by John Anderson, Jacob Sturm, State of Tennessee, Sullivan County, May Session, 1806.
Registered: July 30th, 1806. Test: Matw. Rhea, C. S. C.

---

(744) ELKANAH DULANEY, JAMES GAINES, GEORGE RUTLEDGE, COMMISSIONERS, to WILLIAM KING : COMMISSIONERS DEED

Date: March 21st, 1806.
Consideration: $43.00.
Amt. of land: 2 acres.
Location: Town of Blountville.
Description: 2 certain lots or parcels of land in the town of Blountville aforesaid containing each one acre and designated and distinguished in the plan of said town as back lots Nos. 3 and 4 on the South side of town adjoining William Deary's lot No. 2 on the back street.
Signed: John Anderson, Elkanah R. Dulaney, James Gaines,
Acknowledged: In open court by John Anderson, State of Tennessee, Sullivan County, May Session, 1806. Also acknowledged by Elkanah Dulaney.
Registered: June 30th, 1806. Test: Matw. Rhea, C. S. C.

(Page)

(746) JACOB WEAVER, SENR. : to : DEED OF WARRANTY JACOB TAYLOR :

Date: May 12th, 1806.
Consideration: 5 L.
Amt. of land: 2 acres.
Location: Sullivan County, Tennessee.
Description: A certain tract or parcel of land containing 2 acres lying and being in said county of Sullivan on the south side of Holston River including part of the plantation where sd. Weaver now lives.
Witness: John Anderson.
Acknowledged: In open court by Jacob Weaver, State of Tennessee, Sullivan County, May Session, 1806.
Registered: July 24th, 1806. Test: Matw. Rhea, C. S. C.

---

(747) ALEXANDER McCRABB : to : DEED OF WARRANTY JOHN YANCEY :

Date: Oct. 20th, 1804.
Consideration: $333 1/3.
Amt. of land: 1/4 of an acrex.
Location: Town of Blountville,
Description: One certain lot of land in the town of Blountville containing 1/4 of an acre known by and designated by No. 20 which said lot was formerly granted by the Commissioners to John Shelby and by him sold to James King and by sd. King to the sd. Alexander McCrabb. Test: Matw. Rhea, C. S. C.
Registered: Aug. 5th, 1806.

---

(748) JAMES KAINE : to : DEED OF WARRANTY PATRICK WRIGHT :

Date: Feb. 21st, 1805.
Consideration: $400.00.
Amt. of land: 93 acres.
Location: Sullivan County, State of Tennessee.
Description: A certain tract or parcel of land containing 93 acres be the same more or less lying and being in sd. county and state aforesaid.
Witnesses: John Jening, Joseph Wm. Looney.
Registered: Aug. 5th, 1806. Test: Matw. Rhea, C. S. C.

---

(749) JOHN FITZGERALD : to : DEED OF WARRANTY JAMES PROFIT :

Date: Sept. 17th, 1805.
Consideration: $75.00.
Amt. of land: Supposed to be 10 acres.
Location: Sullivan County, Tennessee.
Description: A certain tract or parcel of land situate lying and being in the county of Sullivan and and State aforesaid supposed to be 10 acres be the same more or less.
Witnesses: John Billingsby, William Cox.

Proven: State of Tennessee, Sullivan County, Aug. Session, 1806, in open court by the oath of Wm. Cox.
Registered: Aug. 19th, 1806. Test: Matw. Rhea, C. S. C.

---

(750) JOHN TALLY : to : DEED OF WARRANTY JOHN BEARD :

Date: March 6th, 1806.
Consideration: $583.33.
Amt. of land: 140 acres.
Location: Sullivan County, Tennessee.
Description: A certain tract or parcel of land situate lying and b being in the county of Sullivan as by grant containing 140 acres lying on the North side of Holston River.
Witnesses: Endymion Baker, Charles Baker, Benjamin Rogers.
Proven: In open court by the oath of Charles Baker and Benjamin Rogers, State of Tennessee, Sullivan County, August Session, 1806.
Registered: Aug. 19th, 1806. Test: Matw. Rhea, C. S. C.

---

(752) STATE OF NORTH CAROLINA : RICHARD DOBBS SPAIGHT, GOV. : LAND GRANTXx to : NO. 584. HENRY HUGHES :

Date: June 27th, 1793.
Consideration: 50 shillings for every 100 acres of land.
Amt. of land: 100 acres.
Locati n: Sullivan County, North Carolina.
Description: A tract of land lying and being in our county of Sullivan on a fork of Reedy Creek.
Richard Dobbs Spaight, Gov. By Comd. J. Glasgow, Sec.
Regst: Aug. 20th, 1806.

---

(753) STATE OF NORTH CAROLINA : ALEXANDER MARTIN, GOV. : to : LAND GRANT JAMES HOLLIS : NO. 332.

Date: Nov. 10th, 1784.
Consideration: 50 shillings for every 100 acres of land.
Amt. of land: 420 acres.
Location: Sullivan County, Tennessee.
Description: A tract of land containing 420 acres lying and being in our county of Sullivan on the North fork of horse Creek that lies oposit to beach creek.
Alexander Martin, Gov. By W. William D. Sec.
Regst: August 20th, 1806.

JACOB ISLEY : to : DEED OF WARRANTY JOHN YANCEY :

Date: Aug. 19th, 1806.
Consideration: A valuable consideration.

Amt. of land: 117 acres.
Location: Sullivan County, Tennessee.
Description: A certain tract or parcel of land containing 117 acres be the same more or less said land lying and being in sd. county and on the waters of Reedy Creek.
Witnesses: John Anderson, Henry Mauk.
Acknowledged: In open court by Jacob Isley, State of Tennessee, Sullivan County, August Session, 1806.
Registered: Aug. 25th, 1806. Test: Matw. Rhea, C. S. C.

---

(755) HENRY MAUK : DEED OF WARRANTY
to
GEORGE WILYARD

Date: Aug. 16th, 1806.
Consideration: $400.00.
Amt. of land: 136 acres.
Location: Sullivan County, Tennessee.
Description: A certain tract or parcel of land lying and being in the county aforesaid containing 136 acres.
Witnesses: Thomas Morrison, John Yancey.
Acknowledged: In open court by Henry Mauk, State of Tennessee, Sullivan County, Aug. Session, 1806.
Registered: Aug. 25th, 1806. Jos. M. Rhea, D. C. for Mathew Rhea, C. S. C.

---

(756) WALLACE WILLOUGHBY : DEED OF WARRANTY
to
PETER BRIGHT BILL

Date: Uag. 18th, 1806.
Consideration: $15.00.
Amt. of land : 1/4 of an acros
Location: Sullivan County, Tennessee.
Description: A certain lot or larcel of land lying in the county and state aforesaid near the bank of Sinking Creek containing 1/4 of an ac re.
Witness: Jacob Booher.
Acknowledged: In open court by Wallace Willoughby, State of Tennessee, Sullivan County, August Session, 1806.
Registered: Aug. 25th, 1806.

---

(757) WALLACE WILLOUGHBY : DEED OF WARRANTY
to
JOHN THOMAS

Date: Aug. 18th, 1806.
Consideration: $15.00.
Amt. of land: 1/4 of an acre.
Location: Sullivan County, State of Tennessee.
Description: A certain lot or parcel of land lying in the county and

state aforesaid near the bank of Sinking Creek agreeable ot a plan of the town laid off by said Willoughby and thereby designated by No. 20 the said lot containing 1/4 of an acre.
Witness: Jacob Booher.
Acknowledged: State of Tennessee, Sullivan County, August Session, 1806, in open court by Wallace Willoughby.
Registered: Aug. 26th, 1806. Test: Matw. Rhea, C. S. C.

JAMES KING :
to : DEED OF WARRANTY
THOMAS KING :

Date: Aug. 16, 1806.
Consideration: $1169.00.
Amt. of land: 640 acres.
Location: Sullivan County, Tennessee.
Description: A certain tract or parcel of land lying and being in Sullivan County on the North side of Watauga River being a part of 640 acres of land granted to Edward King, deceased, joining a tract of land pertaining to the heirs of Nathan Gregg , lying on Kick Branch then with the various courses of the said branch to the river.
Acknowledged: State of Tennessee, Sullivan County, August Session, 1806, by James King. Test: Matw. Rhea, C. S. C.
Registered: Aug. 26th, 1806. Test: Matw. Rhea, C. S. C.

---

(759) JAMES KING :
to : DEED OF WARRANTY
JOHN KING :

Date: Aug. 16th, 1806.
Consideration: $231.00.
Amt. of land: 44 1/2 acres of land.
Location: Sullivan County, Tennessee.
Description: A certain parcel of land lying on the North side of Watauga in the county of Sullivan aforesaid being part of 640 acres of land granted to Edward King.
Acknowledged: By James King, State of Tennessee, Sullivan County, August Session, 1806. Test: Matw. Rhea, C. S. C.
Registered: August 26th, 1806.

---

(760) SUSANAH THOMPSON :
to : DEED OF WARRANTY
CHRISTIAN PEOPLAR :

Date: Aug. 15th, 1803.
Consideration: $80.00.
Amt. of land: 100 acres.
Location: ~~Sullivan County~~, Tennessee. Washington County.
Description: A certain tract or parcel of land containing 100 acres proceeding from a grant issued to the said to the said Susanah Thompson beating date Dec, 5th, 1800, lying in the county of Washington County on the waters of Reedy Creek.
Witnesses: Jas. Gaines, John Kennedy.
Registered: Aug. 27th, 1806. Test: Matw. Rhea, C. S. C.

(Page) 100

(762) THOMAS GAINES & JAMES GAINES
to
PHILLEMON BOHANNON

Date: May 24th, 1805.
Consideration: $500.00.
Amt. of land: 251 acres.
Location: Sullivan County, Tennessee.
Description: A certain tract or parcel of land containing 251 acres be the same more or less lying and being in the aforesaid county and state on both sides of Reedy Creek, being part of a tract of land granted to Edmund Pendleton by patent bearing date the 16th day of August, 1756.
Witnesses: Ambrose Gaines, James T. Gaines.
Proven: In open court at Blountville in the county of Sullivan & State of Tennessee by the oath of Ambrose Gaines, Aug. 20th, 1805, to let it be registered: Aug. 20th, 1805. Mattw. Rhea, C. S. C.

---

(763) DANIEL ALLEN : to : DEED OF WARRANTY WALTER JAMES :

Date: Oct. 10th, 1801.
Consideration: $1800.00.
Amt. of land: 277 1/4 acres.
Location: Sullivan County, Tennessee.
Description: All that plantation or tract of land whereon the sd. Daniel now lives situate lying and being in Sullivan County aforesaid containing 2271/4 acres. But for every acre that may be lacking of said complement the said Daniel is to pay or allow to the said Walter at the rate of $4.42 per acre, but should there be more land within said lands than the said 271 acres and 1/4 of an acre the said Walter is to hold the same as part of the tract hereby bargained and sold without making any allowance for the same.
Witnesses: Richard Haile, John Phillips.
Proven: In open court by the eaht of John Phillips, State of Tennessee, Sullivan County, November Session, 1801.
Registered@ Aug. 28th, 1806. Test: Matw. Rhea, C. S. C.

---

(765)
EDMUND PENDLETON, JOHN TAYLOR : to : DEED OF WARRANTY JOHN WADDLE :

Date: Feb. 8th, 1802.
Consideration: 50 L. (50L)
Location: Sullivan County, Tennessee.
Amt. of land: 152 1/2 acres.
Description: A tract or parcel of land containing 152 1/2 acres it being a part of a tract of land granted to the sd. Edmond Pendleton by patent bearing date August 16th, 1756, on Reedy Creek joining Edmund Stevenses now John Sintclaires corner.
Proven: In open court by the oath of James Gaines, State of Tennessee, Sullivan county, Feb. Sessions, 1802.
Wtinesses: James T. Gaines, John O Brine, Thomas Hopkins.
Registered: Aug. 28th, 1806. Test: Matw. Rhea, C. S. C.

STATEOF NORTH CAROLINA : LAND GRANT
SAMUEL ASHE, GOV. : NO. 744.
to
SETH PORTERFIELD

Date: Nov. 17th, 1797.
Consideration: 50 shillings for every 100 acres of land.
Amt. of land: 48 acres.
Location: Sullivan County, Tennessee.
A tract of land containing 48 acres lying and being in our county of Sullivan on the North side of Holston River.
Samuel Ashe, Gov. By his Excellys. Comd. J. Glasgow, Sec.

---

(768) DAVID PROFFET : DEED OF WARRANTY
to
JAMES PROFFET

Date: April 23d, 1801.
Consideration: Love and good will that the sd. David Proffet hath and doth bare towards his son James Proffet.
Amt. of land: Containing by estimation54 acres.
Witnesses: John Billingsby, John Proffitt.
Proven: State of Tennessee, Sullivan County, August Session, 1806, proven in open court by the oath of John Proffett. Test: Matw. Rhea, C. S. C.
Registered: Aug. 27th, 1806.

---

(769) JEREMIAH TAYLOR : DEED OF WARRANTY
to
WALTER JAMES

Date: Dec. 14th, 1805.
Consideration: $600.00.
Amt. of land: 156 acres.
Location: Sullivan County, Tennessee.
Description: A certain tract or parcel of land containing 156 acres be the same more or less lying on the waters of Kindrick Creek on the south side of Holston River between Huffman and Collier.
Witnesses: John Jennings, Joseph Cox.
Registered: Aug. 27th, 1806.
Proven: In open court by the oath of Joseph cox and John Jenings, Sullivan County, Feb. Session, 1806.

---

770) SAMUEL SHIPLEY,EXECUTOR, : DEED OF WARRANTY
to
MARSHAL GALLOWAY

Date: July 14th, 1804.
Consideration: $63 1/3.
Amt. of land: 19 acres with all improvements,
Location: Sullivan County, Tennessee.
Description: All that tract or parcel of land situate in the county aforesaid containing 19 acres. Samuel Shipley is Executor of Richard Shipley, deceased.
Witnesses: Adam Stoke, John Parker.
Proven: In open court by the oath of Adam Stoke, State of Tennessee,

Sullivan County, Nov. Session, 1804. Test: Matw. Rhea, C. S. C.
Registered: Aug. 27th,

---

(771) NATHANIEL DAVIS : to : DEED OF WARRANTY CHARLES HILTON :

Date: May 23d, 1797.
Consideration: $500.00.
Amt. of land: 200 acres.
Location: Sullivan County, Tennessee.
Description: A certain tract of land containing 200 acres be the same more or less lying and being in the county of Sullivan being the said tract of l land where the said Davis formerly lived reserving the diad Davis a certain small Island including thr original grant.
Witnesses: Richard Gammon, Joseph Taylor, Grason Gifford.
Proven: In open coutt by the oath of Richard Gammon Sullivan County, November Session, 1799. Test: Matw. Rhea, C S. C.
Registered: Aug. 27th, 1806.

---

(773) WALTER KING : to : DEED OF WARRANTY JOSEPH CORN :

Date: Aug. 24th, 1805.
Consideration: $450.00.
Amt. of land :175 acres.
Location: Sullivan County, Tennessee.
Description: A certain tract or parcel of land containing by estimation 175 acres lying and being in the county and state afforesaid on Kendrick's Creek South side of Holston River and joining Walter James line and William Allen's land being part of the 200 acres of land granted to Thomas Smith by the state of North Carolina No. 492 Nov. 7th, 1780, the othre part of the original granted land being conveyed by the said Walter King to John Allen and is now the property of William Allen the same being 25 acres mo re or less.
Witnesses: Jacob Jobe, Walter James.
Proven: In open coutt by the oath of Walter James, State of Twnnessee, Sullivan County, August Session, 1806. Test: Thos. M. Rhea, D. C. for Mattw. Rhea, C. S. C.
Registered: Aug. 28th, 1806.

---

(774) JOHN TIPTON : to : DEED OF WARRANTY WILLIAM DERY :

Date: July 22d, 1806.
Consideration: $23.625.
Amt. of land: 1 1/4 acres and 10 sq. poles.
Location: Sullivan County, Tennessee.
Description: A certain piece or lot of land situate in the county of Sullivan in the town of Blountville,

Witnesses: James Phagan, D. Yearsley, Laurence Snapp.
Proven: In open court by the oath of David Yearsley and James Phagan, State of Tennessee, Sullivan County, August Session, 1806.
Registered: Aug. 28th, 1806. Matw. Rhea, C. S. C.

---

(775) JAMES HOLLISS by his Attorney JOHN ADAIR to THOMAS BRAGG : DEED OF WARRANTY

Date: Feb. 20th, 1786.
Consideration: 130 L.
Amt. of land: 420 acres.
Location: Sullivan County, Tennessee.
Description: A certain tract or parcel of land containing 420 acres be the same more or less lying and being in sd. county of Sullivan on the North fork of Horse Creek that lies oposit to Beach Creek.
Witnesses: David Bragg, Charles Bragg, Bryce Russell.
Proven: In open court by the oaths of David Bragg and Bryce Russell, Sullivan County June Session, 1806.
Registered: Aug. 28th, 1806. Test: Matw. Rhea. C. S. C.

---

(776) HENRY HUGHES to JAMES KAIN : DEED OF WARRANTY

Date: Aug. 21, 1799.
Consideration: 40 L.
Amt. of land: 100 acres.
Location: Sullivan County, Tennessee.
Description: A certain tract or parcel of land lying and being in sd. county containing 100 acres patensed by the daid Henry Hughes dated 1793, joining Pendleton's old line, on or near Henry Roberts line, and Robert Jackson's line.
Witnesses: Samuel Pearson, Martin Waddle.
Proven: By the oaths of Samuel Pearson and Martin Waddle, Sullivan County, August Session, 1799. Test: Matw. Rhea, C. S. C.
Registered: Aug. 28th, 1800.

---

(778) WILLIAM ROYCE to THOMAS PERSEY : DEED OF WARRANTY

Date: May 10th, 1802.
Consideration: $666.66 current money.
Amt. of land: 107 acres.
Location: Sullivan County, Tennessee.
Description: A certain tract or parcel of land containing 107 acres be the sam more or less lying and being in sd. county of Sullivan on Horse Creek including the plantation where said Persey now lives containing all the land that Isaac Titsworth, Senr. granted to David Bragg, by deed of conveyance.
Witnesses: George Vincent, Ellenor Vinvent, Nancy Vincent.
Proven: In open court by the oath of George Vincent, State of Tennessee, Sullivan County, May Session, 1802. Mattw. Rhea, C. S. C.
Registered: Aug. 28th, 1806.

(Page)

(779) ANDREW GREER : to : DEED OF WARRANTY
MICHAEL MONTGOMERY :

Date: Aug. 21, 1799.
Consideration: $1000.00.
Amt. of land: 1000 acres.
Location: Middle District, on Camin Creek the waters of Elk.
Description: A certain tract or parcel of land containing by estimation 1000 acres and being in our Middle District on Cain Creek the waters of Elk about 8 or 10 miles from the mouth of said creek.
Witnesses: John Anderson, William Mcerinack.
Registered: October 4th, 1806.

---

(780) SAMUEL VANCE : to : BILL OF SALE
SAMUEL EVANS :

Date: Dec. 30th, 1805.
Consideration: $1000.00.
Sale: Samuel Vance of the county of Sullivan and State of Tennessee sold to a certain Samuel Evans three negroesnamed Poll and her two children Joshua and Edmond for the sum of $1000.00.good and lawful money.
Witnesses: D. Yearsley, Samuel Sherley.
Registered: Oct. 4th, _______.

---

(781) UNITED STATES OF AMERICA
ROBERT EASLEY : to : DEED OF WARRANTY
WILLIAM ODEL :

Date: March 10th, 1806.
Consideration: 150 £.
Amt. of land: 100 acres.
Location: Sullivan County, Tennessee.
Description: A certain tract or parcel of land containing 100 acres be the same more or less lying and being in the county of Sullivan lying on the South side of Holston River.
Witnesses: Stpehen Walling, Abraham Vandevanter, Jonthan Combs.
Registered: Nov. 11th, 1806.

---

(782) ANDREW RUSSELL : to : DEED OF WARRANTY
CHARLES BAKER :

Date: March 2d, 1799.
Consideration: $25.00.
Amt. of land: 36 acres.
Location: Sullivan Counzty, Tennessee.
Description: A part of a certain tract of land lying and being in the county of Sullivan on the North side of Holston River joining aforesaid Baker's present plantation.
Witness: Charles Hilton.

(Page)

(783) JOHN PARKER, SENIOR, : to : DEED OF WARRANTY JOHN PARKER, JUNIOR. :

Date: Sept. 26th, 1806.
Consideration: $333.33.
Amt. of land: 113 acres.
Location: Sullivan County, Tennessee.
Description: A certain tract or parcel of land containing 113 acres be the same more or less said land lying and being in the county aforesaid joining George Nicelys line and said Goddards line.
Witnesses: John Anderson, Joseph Goddard, Samuel Bowder.
Proven: State of Tennessee, Sullivan County, Nov. Session, 1802, in open court by the oath of John Anderson, Joseph Goddard & Samuel Bowdere.
Registered: Dec. 1806. Test: Joseph M. Rhea, D.C. for Matw. Rhea, C. S. C.

JOSEPH WILLSON : (784) to : DEED OF WARRANTY WILLIAM WILLSON :

Date: Jan. 17th, 1800.
Consideration: $800.00 current money of the State of Virginia,
Amt. of land: 108 acres.
Location: Sullivan County, Tennessee.
Description: A certain tract or parcel of land containing 108 acres being a part of the tract that the st sd. William Willson now livws on being part of the survey made in the name of Robert Willson, Senr & William Willson.
Witnesses: William N. Gale, Joseph Willson, Zachariah Wicks.
Proven: In open court by the oath of William N. Gale and Zachariah E Weeks.
Test: Joseph M. Rhea, D. C. bor Matw. Rhea, C. S. C.
Registered: Dec. 15th, 1806.

(786)

LEWIS SHROYER : to : DEED OF WARRANTY DAVID SHAVER :

Date: June, 1806.
Consideration: A valuable consideration.
Amt. of land: 285 acres.
Location: Sullivan County, Tennessee.
Description: A certain tract or parcel of land containing 285 acres be the same more or lesslying and being in the county aforesaid and on the waters of Reedy Creek lying at the furnace road joining the land of John Kelshaw.
Witnesses: Jas. Gaines, Henry Click, Randolph Bowen.
Proven: State of Tennessee, Sullivan County, Nov. Session, 1806, in open court by the oath of Henry Click. Joseph M. Rhea, D. C. for Matw. Rhea, C.SC.
Registered: Dec. 15th, 1806.

ABRAHAM PALLET : to : DEED OF WARRANTY WILLIAM PALLET :

Date: March 24th, 1806.

Consideration: $800.00.
Amt. of land: 100 acres.
Location: Sullivan County, Tennessee.
Description: A certain tract or parcel of land containing 100 acres lying and being in said county and state aforesaid and, beginning on Patrick Wtight's line. There is provided in a certain deed of conveyance signed by Jeremiah Taylor to Robert Pallet for the daid land respecting an over plus or defeciancy in said 100 acres. The sd. Abraham Pallet assigns his right agreeabel to said proviso mentioned in said deed. Said Abram Pallet for himdelf and his heirs and assigns doth relinquish all right and claim to the 1 1/2 acres of land allowed by Jeremiah Taylor and now used as a place of religious worship.
Witnesses: Robert Pallet, John Jennings.
Acknowledged: State of Tennessee, Sullivan County, Nov. Session, 1806, in open court by Abraham Pallet. Test: Matw. Rhea, C. S. C.
Registered: Dec. 20th, 1806.

---

(789) SAMUEL BILLINGSLEY
to
INDERMAN BACON
: DEED OF WARRANTY

Date: May 14th, 1803.
Consideration: $300.00.
Amt. of land: 100 acres.
Location: Sullivan County, Tennessee.
Description: All and every part and parcel of a certain tract of land situated lying and being in the county of Sullivan as by grant containing 100 acres lying on the North side of Holston River.
Witnesses: John Kelsay, Samuel Billingsby.
Proven: In open court by the oath of Samuel Billingsby, State of Tennessee, Sullivan County, May Session, 1803. Test: Matw. Rhea, C. S. C.
Registered: Dec. 20th, 1806.

---

(789) JAMES KAINE
to
SAMUEL RAMSEY
: DEED OF WARRANTY

Date: Nov. 20th, 1806.
Consideration: $300.00.
Amt. of land: 140 acres.
Location: Sullivan County, Tennessee.
Description: A certain tract or parcel of land containing 140 acres situate lying and being in the county of Sullivan aforesaid lying on the waters of Reedy Creek on Andrew Russell's line being the same land granted by the State of North Carolina to Alexander Ford.
Witnesses: John Kennedy, John Richardson.
Acknowledged: In open court by the oath of James Kaine, State of Tennessee Sullivan County, Nov. Session, 1806. Test: Joseph Rhea, D.C. S. C.
Registered: Dec. 27th, 1806.

STATE OF TENNESSE ?
WILLIAM BLEVINS
to
JOHN BLEVINS
: DEED OF WARRANTY

Date: Sept, 26th, 1806.

Consideration: $100.00.
Amt. of land: Acreage not stated:
Description: All and sungular the claim or claims that the said William Blevins has either through heirship or otherwise to the land formerly the property of the aforesaid William Blevins, Colonel, now deceased.
Witnesses: Thomas Rockhold, John Richardson.
Proven: In open court by the oath of Thomas Rockhold and John Richardson, State of Tennessee, Sullivan County, Nov. Session, 1806.
Registered: Dec. 26th, 1806. Test: Matw. Rhea, C. S. C.

---

(792) STATE OF NORTH CAROLINA :
ALEXANDER MARTIN, GOVERNOR, :
to : LAND GRANT
JOHN WHEALER : NO. 149.

Date: Oct. 24th, 1782.
Consideration: 50 shillings for ever 100 acres of land,
Amt. of land: 99 acres.
Location: Washington County, Tennessee.
Description: A tract of land containing 99 acres lying and being in our c county of Washington on the clear fork of Horse Creek beginning at a birch tree on John Crawford's line.
Witnesses: Alex. Martin, Gov. By his Excellys. Comd. J. Glasgow, Sec.
Recorded in the Secretary's office Dec. 27th, 1803. Regst.

**---

(793) WALTER BLEVINS :
to : BILL OF SALE
EDMOND MORALL :

Date: Sept. 15th, 1806.
Consideration: $400.00.
Description: Walter Blevins have bargained and sold and delivered unto Edmond Morall one negro boy named Georg for in consideration of the sum of $400.00.
Witnesses: Nathan Morrall, John Blevins, Thomas Morrell.
State of Tennessee, Sullivan County:
Bill of sale proven in open court by the oath of John Blevins, Thomas Morrell, Nathan Morrall.
Registered: Feb. 16th, 1807. Test: Joseph Rhea, DC. S. C.

---

(794) WILLIAM COOPER :
to : DEED OF WARRANTY
WALTER KING :

Date: May 5th, 1798.
Consideration: $1000.00.
Amt. of land: By estimation 300 acres.
Location: Sullivan County, State of Tennessee.
Description: A certain tract or parcel of land by estimation 300 acres including 2 original grants, Nos. 53 in the name of Patrick Thompson and the other No. 82 in the name of JamesWaldrope sithate lying and being in the state and county aforesaid South side of Holston River on Jarretts branch and agreeable to the lines and courses of the old original grant.
Wtinesses: Nicholas Messer, Richard Hail.

Proven: In open court by the oath of Richard Hail, State of Tennessee, Sullivan County, August Session, 1806. Test: Matw. Rhea, C. S. C.
Registered: Feb. 16th, _____.

---

(795) WILLIAM GRIMSLEY : to : DEED OF WARRANTY ALEXANDER HAIL :

Date: Feb. 19th, 1806.
Consideration: $27.84.
Amt. of land: 8 acres& 100 poles.
Location: Sullivan County, Tennessee.
Description: A certain tract or parcel of land lying and being in our county of Sullivan on the waters of Sinking Creek being part of the tract whereon now the said Grimsley now lives.
Witnesses: Jacob Sleughter, John Tayton, Benjamin Vanpraile.
Proven: In open court by 1 subscribed, State of Tennessee, Sullivan County, Feb. Sessioh, 1803.
Registered: Feb. 16th, _______.

---

(796) JACOB ISLEY & DANIEL ROLLER : to : DEED OF WARRANTY JAMES KAINE :

Date: Feb. 19th, 1806.
Consideration: $600.00.
Amt.of land: 142 1/2 acres.
Location: Sullivan County, Tennessee.
Description: A certain tract or parcel of land lying and being in the county of Sullivan on both sides of Fall creek.
Witnesses: John Jenings, Thomas Marion.
Acknowledged: In open court by Jacob Isley and David Roller, State of Tennessee, Sullivan County Feb. Sessioh, 1806.
Registered: Feb. 16th, 1807. Test: Matw. Rhea, C. S. C.

---

(797) RICHARD SMITH : to : DEED OF WARRANTY WILLIAM GODDARD :

Date: Feb. 20th, 1804.
Consideration: $200.00.
Amt. of land: 92 acres.
Location: Sullivan County, Tennessee.
Description: Two tracts or parcels of land lying and being o n the waters of Reedy Creek in the county aforesaid ans containing together 92 acres, one tract containing 44 acres which was conveyed by Joseph Cook to James Cook . Anotherr tract containing 48 acres which was conveyed by Robert Whitnal to James Cook beginning at a poplar on Thomas Tobert's line which two parcels of land were conveyed to the said Richard Smith by said James Cook by deed dated Sept. 21, 1799.
Witnesses: Thomas Rockhold, John Anderson.
Acknowledged: State of Tennessee, Sullivan County, acknowledged in open court by Richard Smith. Test: Matw. Rhea, C. S. C.
Registered: Feb. 16th, 1807.

(Page)

(798) ROGER BROWNING : DEED OF WARRANTY
to
WALTER KING

Date: March 2d, 1801.
Consideration: $400.00.
Amt. of land: Estimation 175 acres.
Location: Sullivan County, State of Tennessee.
Description: A certain tract or parcel of land containing by estimation 175 acres be the same more or less situate lying and being in the county and state aforesaid on the south side of Holston River and on Kendrick's Creek-.
Witnesses: Richard Hail, Decury McCrocury.
Proven: Proven: In open court by the oath of Richard Hail, State of Tennessee, Sullivan County, Aug. Session, 1806. Test: Matw. Rhea, C. S. C.
Registered: Feb. 16th, 1807.

(799) JOHN PARKER : DEED OF WARRANTY
to
THOMAS MCCALLEY

Date: Aug. 21, 1805.
Consideration: $250.00.
Amt. of land: 92 acres.
Location: Sullivan County, Tennessee.
Description: Two tracts of land lying in the county of Sullivan the waters of Reedy Creek 92 acres in ooen tract and one tract containing 44 acres which was conveyed from Joseph Cook to James Cook and joining Joseph Whitnals land and Robert Whitnal to James Cook, & joining Tobery's line which was Robert Snapp's.
Acknowledged: In open court by John Parker ..., State of Tennessee, Sullivan County, August Session, 1805. Matw. Rhea, C. S. C.
Registered: Feb. 16th.

(801) WILLIAM GODDARD : DEED OF WARRANTY
to
JOHN PARKER

Date: Nov. 19th, 1804.
Consideration: $200. 00.
Amt. of land: 92 acres.
Location: Sullivan County, Tennessee.
Description: Two tracts or parcels of land situate lying and being on the waters of Reedy Creek in the county aforesaid and containing together 92 acres one containing 44 acres which was conveyed to Joseph Cook by James Cook joining Robert Whitnal's line and the other tract containing 48 acres conveyed by Robert Whitnal to James Cook corner of Tobery's line which said 2 parcels of land was conveyed to the said William Goddard to the sd. Richard Smith Febl 20th, 1804.
Acknowledged: In open court by William Goddard, State of Tennessee, Sullivan County, November Session, 1804.
Registered: Feb. 17th, .

****

(802) JONATHAN PHILLIPS : DEED OF WARRANTY
to
WILLIAM CHILDRESS

Date: Feb. 12th, 1782.

(Page)
(803) STATE OF VIRGINIA :
* JAMES MONROE, GOVERNOR : LAND GRANT
to :
DAVID LOW :

Terms of grant: By virtue of a Treasury Warrant No. 1210940 Isued the 12th of February, 1782, there is granted by the Commonwealth of Virginia to David Low the following land.
Date: Nov. 4th, 1800.
Consideration: Treasury Warrant aforesaid.
Amt. of land: 50 acres.
Location: Washington, County.
Description: A certain tract or parcel of land containing 50 acres by survey bearing date April 5th, 1797, lying and being in the county of Washintpn on the waters of Reedy Creek and in the Rich Valley joining Stephens line.
David Low hath title to the within 50 acres. Signed: James Monroe.
Registered: Match 7th, 1807. Book 47 page 267.

STATE OF VIRGINIA :
(804) JAMES MONROE : LAND GRANT
* to :
DAVID LOWE :

Terms of grant: By virtue of a traseury Warrant No. 10940 Isued Feb. 12th, 1782, there is granted by the Commonwealth of Virginia to David Lowe the following land.
Date: Nov. 4th, 1800.
Amt. of land: 50 acres.
Location: Washington County.
Description: A certain tract or parcel of land containing 50 acres by survey bearing date August 16th, 1797, lying and being in the county of Washington on the North Fork of Reedy Creek a north branch of Holston River.
Xtixxxx David Low hath title to the within 50 acres.
Registered: In Book 47 Page 269.

WALLACE WILLOUGHBY :
to : DEED OF WARRANTY
JACOB BOOHER :

Date: Feb. 14th, 1807.
Consideration: $62.50.
Amt. of land: 1 acre, 112 poles, be the same more or less.
Location: Town of Greenfield.
Description: A certain lot or piece of land being now in said Booher's actual possession in the town of Greenfield containing 1 acrex and 112 poles be the same more or less.
Acknowledged: In open court by Wallace Willoughby, State of Tennessee, Sullivan County, Feb. Session, 1807. Test: Matw. Rhea, C. S. C.
Registered: March 7th, 1807.

---

(805) GEORGE RUTLEDGE :
to : DEED OF WARRANTY
JAMES RHEA :
Date: Feb. 17th, 1807.

Consideratinn: $100.00.
Amt. of land: 1/4 of an acre.
Location: Sullivan County, Tennessee.
Description: A certain tract or parcel of land containing 97 acres be the same more or less lying and being in the county and state aforesaid joining John Stewarts on Jarratts branch.
Witnesses: Peter Jackson, William Talley, Isaac Whealor.
Proven: In open court by the oath of Peter Jackson, Sullivan County, Feb. Session, 1798. Test: Matw. Rhea. C. S. C.
Registered: March 4th, 1807.

---

(807) JOSEPH YOUNG : DEED OF WARRANTY
to
JOHN SHARP

Date: Sept. 11th, 1806.
Consideration: $1000.00.
Amt. of land: 132 acres.
Location: Sullivan County, Tennessee.
Description: A certain tract or parcel of land situate lying and being in the county and state of Tennessee, containing 132 acres more or less.
Witnesses: Thos. McChesney, David King, John Vance.
Proven: State of Tennessee, Sullivan County, Feb. Session, 1807, in open court by the oath of Thomas McChesney and David King.
Registered: March 16th, 1807. Test: Matw. Rhea, C. S. C.

---

(809) HENRY MAGERT : DEED OF WARRANTY
to
SAMUEL MOORE

Date: Feb. 17th, 1807.
Consideration: $400.00.
Amt. of land: 140 acres.
Locatinn: Sullivan County, State of Tennessee.
Description: A certain tract or parcel of land containing 140 acres be the same more or less lying and being in the county and state aforesaid on the south side of Reedy Creek including the plantation whereon Henry Maggert now lives beginning at two large sugar trees on Pendletons old patent line a corner of John Sinclairs joining the land granted to John Pitman and Malone's corner and Cunninghams corner.
Witnesses: John Punch, John Buckles.
Acknowledged: In open court by Henry Magert, State of Tennessee, Sullivan County Feb. Session, 1807. Test: Matw. Rhea, C. S. C.
Registered: March 17th, 1807.

---

(810) LEONARD HART : DEED OF WARRANTY
to
JOHN SMITH

Date: Jan. 1st, 1807.
Consideration: $700.00.
Amt. of land: By estimation 150 acres.
Location: Sullivan County, Tennessee.

(Page)

(810) DESCRIPTION : A certain tract or parcel of land whereon the said Leonard now lives lying in the county of Sullivan on the south side of Holston River above the mouth of Beaver Creek, joining the land granted to John Pittman and Malone corner and Cunninghmas corner.
Acknowledged: In open court by ~~Leonard~~ Hart, State of Tennessee, Sullivan County, Feb. Session, 1807. Test: Matw. Rhea, C. S. C.
Registered: March 16th, 1807.

(811)

THOMAS BRIGHT :
to : DEED OF WARRANTY
DAVID LOWE :

Date: Feb. 16th, 1807.
Consideration: $100.00.
Amt. of land: 43 acres.
Location: Sullivan County, Tennessee.
Description: A certain tract or parcel of land containing 43 acres more or less saif land lying and being in the county aforesaid and on the North Fork of Ready Creek.
Witness: John Anderson.
Acknowledged: In open court by Thomas Bright, State of Tennessee, Sullivan County Feb. Session, 1807. Test: Matw. Rhea, C. S. C.
Registered: March 17th, 1807.

---

(813) ANDREW RILEY :
to : DEED OF WARRANTY
WILLIAM SCOTT :

Date: Feb.19th, 1807.
Consideration: $540.00.
Amt. of land: 200 acres.
Location: Sullivan County, Tennessee.
Description: A certain tract or parcel of land containing 200 acres situate lying and being in the county and state aforesaid crossing fork of Indian Creek.
Acknowledged: In open court by Andrew Riley, Sullivan County, Feb. Session, 1807. Test: Matw. Rhea, C S. C.
Registered: March 17th, 1807.

---

(814) JOHN ALLISON :
to : DEED OF WARRANTY
FINLEY ALLISON :

Date: Feb. 16th, 1807.
Consideration: $416.00.
Amt. of land: 200 acres.
Location: Sullivan County, State of Tennessee.
Description: A certain tract or parcel of land situate lying and being in the county and state aforedaid on the North side of Watauga River containing 200 acres more or less granted to John Allison, deceased, whereon the said John Allison lived at the time of his decease.
Witnesses: Joseph Torbet, Thomas King,
Acknowledhed: State of Tennessee, Sullivan County, Feb. Session, 1807, in open court by John Alison, Test: Matw. Rhea, C. S. C.
Registered: March 17th, 1807.

(Page)

(815) JAMES LAUGHLIN :
to : DEED OF WARRANTY
JAMES LAUGHLIN :

Date: Feb. 14th, 1807.
Consideration: $1000.00.
Amt. of land: 139 acres.
Location: Sullivan County, State of Tennessee.
Description: A certain tract or parcel of land situate lying and being in the county and state aforesaid containing 139 acres be the same more or less and on the bank of Holston River.
Witnesses: Wm. Owens, John Laughlin.
Proven: State of Tennessee, Sullivan County, Feb. Session, 1807, in open court by the oath of William Owen and John Laughlin. Test: Matw. Rhea, C.SC.
Registered: March 18th, 1807.

---

(816) WILLIAM ALLEN :
to : DEED OF WARRANTY
CHARLES ALLEN :

Date: Oct. 16th, 1806.
Consideration: $33.33.
Amt. of land: 25 acres.
Location: Sullivan County, State of Tennessee.
Description: A certain tract or parcel of land containing 25 acres be the same more or less ;ying and being in the county and state aforesaid on the south side of Holston River along Charles Allen's line.
Witnesses: John Mauk, Mathew Rhea.
Proven: In opnn court by John Mauk and Mathew Rhea, State of Tennessee, Sullivan County, Feb. Session, 1807. Test: Matw. Rhea, C. S. C.
Registered: March 19th, 1807.

---

(817)
TIMOTHY ACUFF :
to : DEED OF WARRANTY
ISAAC ACUFF :

Date: Feb. 20th, 1807.
Consideration: The good will, love and esteem I have for my grandson, Isaac Acuff!
Amt. of land: 130 acres.
Location: Sullivan County, Tennessee.
Description: 130 acres of land adjoining the lands of Jacob Hartman and Nathaniel Munsey and including the plantation whereon the sd. Timothy Acuff lives together with a wagon and gears and all the farming utensails and appurtenances now belonging to the said plantation.
Witnesses: John Jenings, Jacob Hartman, Nathaniel Munsey.
Proven: In open court by the oath of John Jenings and Nathaniel Munsey Sullivan County, February Session, 1807. Test: Matw. Rhea, C. S. C.
Registered: March 19th, 1807.

---

(818) WILLIAM ALLEN :
to : DEED OF WARRANTY
CHARLES ALLEN :

Date: Oct. 17th, 1806.

Consideration: 300 _____.
Amt. of land: 48 acres.
Location: Sullivan County, Tennessee.
Description: A parcel of land part of a tract of land originally granted Henry Coucher from State of North Carolina b earing date 1782N. 51 beginning at a Spanish oak on the river and containing 48 acres more or less.
Witnesses: John Mauk, Mathew Rhea, C. S. C. Test: Matw. Rhea, C. S. C.
Registered: March 19th, 1807.

---

(819) SAMUEL MCDONALD : to : DEED OF WARRANTY JOHN HARR :

Date: Feb. 17th, 1807.
Consideration: $330.00.
Amt. of land: 66 acres.
Location: Sullivan County, Tennessee.
Description: A certain tract or parcel of land containing 66 acres be the same more or less said land lying and being in said county and on the waters of Reedy Creek beginning at Richard Smith's corner.
Witnesses: John Punch, Martin Harkleroad, John Foust.
Acknowledged: State of Tennessee, Sullivan County , Feb. Session, 1807, in open court by Samuel McDonald. Test: Matw. Rhea, C. S. C.
Registered: March 20th, 1807.

---

(821) NICHOLAS WOLFE : to : DEED OF WARRANTY WILLIAM THOMAS :

Date: Nov. 13th, 1806.
Consideration: $100.00.
Amt. of land: 40 acres.
Location: Sullivan County, Tennessee.
Description: All that tract or parcel of land Situate, lying and being in the county of Sullivan aforesaid on the North side of Holston River, begining on James Hollis Line and joining John Shoemaker's line containing 40 acres and it is a part of a tract of land granted by a patent by the State of North Carolina.
Witnesses: George Moody, Mary Pope, Asahail Johnson.
Proven: In open court by the oath of George Moody and Mary Pope, State of Tennessee, Suhlivan County, Feb. Session, 1807. Test: Matw. Rhea, C.S.C.
Registered: March 20th, 1807.

---

(822) JOHN SHUTZ : SURVEY

Date: Oct. 29th, 1779.
Consideration: Not mentioned.
Location: Sullivan County, the Territory So. the River Ohio on the waters of Shels Creek, the amount of la d being 400 acres.
Surveyed: July 14th, 1791. George Vincent, C. S.C
Registered: March 30th, 1807.

(826) WILLIAM AGEE : DEED OF WARRANTY
to
MICHAEL AGEE

Date: Dec. 30th, 1806.
Consideration: $200.00.
Amt. of land: 50 acres.
Location: Sullivan County, State of Tennessee.
Description: A certain tract or parcel of land supposed to contain 50 acres be the same mo e or less lying and being in the county and state aofresaid.
Wintesses: Ambrose Gaines, John Forgeson.
Proven: In open court by the oath of Ambrose Gaines and John Forgeson Sullivan County, State of Tennessee, Feb. Session, 1807.
Registered: May 4th, 1807. Test: Matw. Rhea, C. S. C.

****

(827) STATE OF NORTH CAROLINA : LAND GRANT
to
CHRISTIAN SHARITS : NO. 1039.

Date: Not stated.
Consideration: 50 shillings for every 100 acres of land.
Amt. of land: 299 acres.
Location: Washington County, North Carolina.
Description: A tract of land containing 299 acres lying and being in our county of Washington includingof an improvement and
Note: This deed is incomplete, page 828 of this deed book being almost entirely blank .

****

(829) JOHN ADAMS : DEED OF WARRANTY
to
MICHAEL ADAMS

Date: Dec. 29th, 1797.
Consideration: 200 £ lawful money of Virginia.
Amt. of land: 292 acres.
Location: Sullivan County, Territory of the U. S. A. South of the River Ohio.
Description: A certain tract or parcel of land lying and being in the county of Sullivan and territory aforesaid including the plantation where the said Michael Adams now lives and joining John Snodgrass line.
Witnesses: John Jenings, Jacob Cole.
Proven: By the oath of John Jenings, Sullivan County, Dec. Session, 1793.
Registered: May 25th, 1807. Test: Matw. Rhea, C. S. C.

---

(830) STATE OF VIRGINIA
JAMES MONROE, GOVERNOR
of the COMMONWEALTH OF VIRGINIA : LAND GRANT
to
JOHN RHEA
Terms:
Treasury Warrant No. 14,474 Issued the 26th day of September, 1782.
Amt. of land: 300 acres.
Location: Washington County, North Virginia.
Description: A certain tract or parcel of land containing 300 acres by survey

bearing date Aug. 15th, 1797, lying and being in the county of Washigton on the waters of Reedy Creek a North branch of Holston River and joining a line of James Campbell's line.
Witnesses: John Rhea, William Price, Re. L. Off. (Reg. of Land Office)
Recorded and Exd. Book No.43, Page 541.
Registered: May 27th, 1807. John Rhea hath title to the within.

(831) JAMES PHAGAN, SHERIFF, : to : SHERIFF'S DEED. JOHN RHEA :

Date: May 22d, 1807.
Consideration: $665.00. (665.00)
Suit: Valentine Pauley obtained judgment in the Superior court of law in and for the District of Washington and State of Tennessee against James Gaines at the Sept. term, 1803, for the sum of about $2063. 33 1/3 to satisfy balance of unpaid judgment being the sum of $492.16 remianing unsatisfied.
Land: Lying on Reedy Creek where David Cheilress lived part called Valentie Parley's lot, 2 tracts of land adjoining last mentioned lot the tract where Philemon Bucanan lives.
Said sale was postponed at the direction of the plaintiff for 6 months, and a writ of execution of Venditione Expones was isued form the said Superior Court of law returnable to the September term of the same Court in the year 1806, on behalf of the sd. Valentine Pauley, commanding the sd. Sheriff to sell land belonging to James Gaines so leveyed on and to make the sd. balance of $492.16, and he sold the tract known by the name of Pauley's lot 310 acres also the lot adjoining Pauley's lot 310 acres to sd. John Rhea for the sum of $665.00, said land lying and being in Sullivan County on both sides of Reedy Creek adjoining Pendleton's paten line.
Witnesses: Geo. Duffield, W. R. Cole, Matw. Rhea,
Acknowledged: In open court by James Phagan, State of Tennessee, Sullivan County, May Session, 1807.
Registered: May 27th, 1807. Test: Matw. Rhea, C. S. C.

www.ingramcontent.com/pod-product-compliance
Lightning Source LLC
Chambersburg PA
CBHW082352270326
41935CB00013B/1598
9780788489181